Bartłomiej Belcarz, Robert Gretzyngier, Tomasz J. Kopański,
Wojtek Matusiak, Marek Rogusz, Wojciech Zmyślony

Colour profiles by
Robert Grudzień, Robert Gretzyngier, Karolina Hołda,
Artur Juszczak, Zbigniew Kolacha, Teodor L. Moroșanu,
Andrzej M. Olejniczak, Thierry Vallet

Polish Fighter Colours

1939 – 1947 vol. 2

STRATUS

Published in Poland in 2021
by STRATUS
Żeromskiego 4
27-600 Sandomierz, Poland
e-mail: office@mmpbooks.biz
for
MMP Books
e-mail: rogerw@mmpbooks.biz

© 2021 MMP Books
http://www.mmpbooks.biz

All rights reserved. Apart from any fair dealing for the purpose of private study, research, criticism or review, as permitted under the Copyright, Design and Patents Act, 1988, no part of this publication may be reproduced, stored in a retrieval system, or transmitted in any form or by any means, electronic, electrical, chemical, mechanical, optical, photocopying, recording or otherwise, without prior written permission. All enquiries should be addressed to the publisher.

ISBN
978-83-65281-78-4

Editor in chief
Roger Wallsgrove

Editorial Team
Bartłomiej Belcarz
Robert Pęczkowski
Artur Juszczak

Text and research
Bartłomiej Belcarz
Robert Gretzyngier
Tomasz J. Kopański
Wojtek Matusiak
Marek Rogusz
Wojciech Zmyślony

Colour profiles
Robert Gretzyngier
Robert Grudzień
Karolina Hołda
Artur Juszczak
Zbigniew Kolacha
Teodor L. Moroşanu
Andrzej Olejniczak
Thierry Vallet

Translation
Wojtek Matusiak

Proofreading
Roger Wallsgrove

DTP
Bartłomiej Belcarz

Printed by
Wydawnictwo Diecezjalne
i Drukarnia w Sandomierzu
www.wds.pl

PRINTED IN POLAND

Photo credits and acknowledgements:

Arct family, Peter R. Arnold, Pierre Ben, Bartłomiej Belcarz, Bartłomiej Błaszkowski, Adam Borowczyk, Steve Brooking, Jim Brzozkiewicz, Daniel Buszyński, Phil Butler, Tony Buttler, Peter Celis, Aleksandr Chistyakov, the late Krzysztof Chołoniewski, Patrick Cornes, the late Michał Cwynar, the late Jerzy B. Cynk, Jerzy Czownicki, Wojtek Deluga, John Dibbs, Marek Duryasz, Filipek family, Seweryn Fleischer, Colin Ford, Gabszewicz family, Andrzej Glass, the late Jerzy Główczewski, the late Czesław Główczyński, Ryszard Górecki collection, Kazimierz Górski, Franciszek Grabowski, Robert Gretzyngier, Tony Holmes, Wacław Hołyś, Zdeněk Hurt, Adam Jackowski, Adam Jarski, Michał Jaroszyński-Wolfram, Mick Jennings, the late Jerzy Jędrzejewski, Greg Karais, Grzegorz Klimasiński, Zbigniew Kolacha, Tomasz J. Kopański, Tadeusz Królikiewicz, Russ Kyler via Piotr Wiśniewski, Malcolm Laird, Paweł Leszczuk, Zbigniew Legierski, Wojciech Łuczak, Jean Charles Macé, Mach family, Steve MacLean, Wojtek Matusiak, Piotr Matwiej, the late Jerzy Mencel, Andrzej Michalski, Piotr Michalski, the late Henryk Mietelski, the late Marian Mikołajczuk, Miszkowicz family via Małgorzata Jagieniak, the late Andrzej Morgała, Lechosław Musiałkowski, Michael Parrot, Pawlik family via Krzysztof Kubala, Aleksander Pietrzak family, Henryk Pietrzak family, Jiří Rajlich, Peter Randall, Wilhelm Ratuszyński, Rock Roszak, Jerzy Różański collection, Józef Różański family via Dariusz Węgliński, Różycki family, Ruczka family via Bartłomiej Belcarz, Kazimierz Rutenberg, Olga Ryżko-Łoniewska, Mariusz Rzeszutek, Wojciech Sankowski, the late Mieczysław Sawicki, the late Tadeusz Sawicz, Allan Thomason, the late Stanisław Sadowski, Paweł Sembrat, Christopher Shores, Piotr Sikora, Graham Skillen, Grzegorz Sojda, the late Ludwik Steinke, Nick Stroud, Mieszko Syski, Szymankiewicz family, Grzegorz Śliżewski, Ian Thirsk, Andy Thomas, Chris Thomas, Piotr Trąbiński, Paweł Tuliński, the late Stanisław Wandzilak, Waś family, Simon Watson, Więckowicz family, Piotr Wiśniewski, Wanda and Ana Witkowski via Cathy Young, Wojciech Woźniakowski, Waldemar Wójcik, Józef Zieliński, Wojciech Zmyślony.

Institutions:

23 Baza Lotnictwa Taktycznego, 307 Squadron Project – Exeter, Muzeum Lotnictwa Polskiego – Cracow, Muzeum Wojska Polskiego – Warsaw, Royal Air Force Museum – Hendon, The Polish Institute & Sikorski Museum – London.

Title page:

Sgts Jan Żurakowski (foreground, not to be confused with the famous test pilot Janusz Żurakowski), Stanisław Muszyński (behind him) and Witold Gajewski (right) pose in 1945 on a No. 308 Sqn Spitfire XVI (presumably TB613/ZF-H) in occupied Germany. Typically for Polish fighters during the later part of the war, the aircraft displays the Polish national marking on the nose and the squadron badge near the windscreen.

Table of contents

Supermarine Spitfire IX

Polish Squadrons

The Mk IX was the second most widely used Spitfire version in the Polish Air Force. It was first introduced in Polish squadrons in the summer of 1942 and continued to be used by PAF units until mid-1946.

From 1942 until the end of the war it was the principal front-line fighter type of the RAF and allied units. Between late 1942 and mid-1944 it was used by the 1st Polish Wing, while the squadrons of the 2nd and 3rd Polish Wings were still equipped with the Mk V. In mid-1944 also No. 303 Sqn of the 3rd Polish Wing re-equipped with the Mk IX, and towards the end of the year first Spitfire IXs were delivered to No. 318 Sqn.

The first variant of the Spitfire IX used by Polish squadrons was known officially as the F.IX (its wing design was similar to that in the Mk VC and it is today commonly, but incorrectly, known as the "Mk IXC").

From mid-/late 1943 onwards an improved variant was delivered to PAF units, powered by a modified Merlin engine optimised for use at lower altitudes. Its official designation was LF.IX, but it was initially known under the improvised names of "Mk IXB" or "Mk IXL" (the former sometimes leads modern authors to an incorrect assumption that some Spitfire IXs were fitted with wings of similar design to those in the Mk VB, which was not the case).

In 1944–1945 a small number of Spitfire HF.IXs (with high-altitude optimised engines) were delivered to Polish squadrons.

The most unusual Spitfire of the Polish AF: MK520 was the personal aircraft of W/Cdr Marian Duryasz, Polish Liaison Officer to HQ 2nd TAF/BAFO. As far as can be ascertained this aeroplane was not really on the inventory of either the RAF of the Polish AF at the time, having been struck off charge in 1944. The Polish pilot acquired it in 1945 in a, more or less, private deal. It was in natural metal finish (most probably the only such Spitfire flying in Polish colours), with the personal code MB-D (the initials of W/Cdr Duryasz and his wife Barbara), the Polish AF chequered square on the nose and W/Cdr pennant near the cockpit.

Spitfire F.IXs of the 1st Polish Wing taxi at Northolt in the spring of 1943, led by EN526, the personal mount of Northolt Wing Leader W/Cdr Wojciech Kołaczkowski. EN526 was maintained by No. 306 Sqn, but Kołaczkowski had it coded RF-K: the usual code of his earlier Spitfires in No. 303 Sqn (although that unit was not part of the Northolt Wing at the time). Even the 'Kościuszko badge' of No. 303 Sqn was applied beneath the windscreen. EN526 was later used by the next Wing Leader at Northolt, W/Cdr Gabszewicz (see p. 311).

While leading the wing, Gabszewicz also used his old squadron markings on his personal aircraft. LF.IX NH342, used by G/Cpt Gabszewicz from June until mid-October 1944, was one of these SZ-G-coded Spitfires. Similar to his other Spitfires, it also featured his 'Boxing Dog' personal emblem. On this aeroplane the triangular badge of No. 316 Sqn was applied below the windscreen.

NH342 was succeeded by LF.IX NH214/SZ-G in October 1944. On this Spitfire the 'Boxing Dog' was applied on the cowling and No. 316 Sqn badge on the fuselage spine. It also displayed the name 'City of Warsaw' and the G/Cpt pennant near the windscreen.

In the first half of 1945 the 1st Polish Wing replaced its Mk IXs with Mk XVIs. No. 303 was the last purely fighter squadron of the Polish AF to use Spitfire IXs on operations (until March 1945), while No. 318, a fighter-reconnaissance squadron employed in the Italian theatre of operations, used Mk IXs (both with and without cameras) until the summer of 1946.

Altogether, squadrons of the Polish Air Force used about 190 Spitfire F.IXs, about 300 LF.IXs and no more than 5 HF.IXs.

No. 302 Squadron 'City of Poznań'

The unit converted to Spitfire IXs in September 1943, when it arrived at Northolt and took over the F.IXs used previously by No. 316 Sqn. It thus rejoined the 1st Polish Wing, now labelled as No. 131 (Polish) Wing in the 2nd TAF structure, which remained at Northolt until the end of March 1944.

No. 302 Squadron Spitfire F.IXs lined up at Northolt in late September 1943, soon after the unit re-equipped from Mk Vs. WX-H is believed to be BR601 (a Spitfire still surviving today), even though documents fail to confirm positively that the aircraft was ever used by the unit. All Mk IXs of No. 302 Sqn displayed the codes in this layout, with 'WX' near the cockpit and the aircraft letter between the roundel and the tail.

F/Lt Bolesław Gładych commanded the 'B' Flight of No. 302 Sqn at the time of re-equipment and until January 1944. At that time the unit's F.IXs featured the squadron badge near the windscreen, as shown here.

P/O Stanisław Nawarski in Spitfire LF.IX ML309/WX-F formates with a B-17 of the 92nd BG 325th BS in the first days of June 1944. It seems the Spitfire was flown only once in No. 302 Sqn markings before application of the D-Day bands.

A close-up of F/Sgt Stanisław Celak in the cockpit of MH712 reveals an interesting item applied on the side: the Polish stencil 'WYCIERAĆ OBUWIE' ('WIPE YOUR FOOT-WEAR') near the cockpit door. This inscription was seen on many Spitfires of No. 131 Wing after it deployed to muddy/dusty forward airfields.*

In the first days of April 1944 the entire wing moved to Deanland and before the end of the month it was based at Chailey, where it would remain until the Normandy landings. From then on No. 302 Squadron (with the entire wing) was employed more and more on ground-attack duties, both by dive-bombing and strafing. In May 1944 No. 302, with the other squadrons of No. 131 Wing, exchanged the Spitfire F.IXs for the improved LF.IX variant. The wing's (and thus No. 302 Sqn's) subsequent airfields were located at Appledram (late June to mid-July) and Ford (second half of July 1944) in the south of England. In the first days of August the wing moved to Plumetot in liberated France (B.10 in Allied code). It then returned briefly to England for a pre-scheduled gunnery training. No. 302 Sqn's subsequent airfields on the Continent were Lille-Vendeville (B.51) from mid-September, Antwerp-Deurne (B.70) from early October, and Ghent-St Denijs Westrem (B.61) from mid-October. The next move, to Grimbergen (B.60) coincided with the squadron's conversion onto the Spitfire XVI.

By the spring of 1944 the unit badges were banned on 2nd TAF fighters and No. 302 discontinued the application of its emblem. Personal markings continued to be applied, though, as shown on LF.IX MH712/WX-D adorned with the image of an attractive girl seated on a 500 lb bomb, with the name 'Pat'. The pilot on the Spitfire is W/O Henryk Dygała. This photo was taken a few months after the Normandy landings, by which time the black-and-white invasion markings were reduced to just the lower surfaces of the aircraft.

No. 303 Squadron 'City of Warsaw'

The most famous Polish squadron in Britain first received Mk IXs at the beginning of June 1943, when it took over ex-No. 315 Sqn aircraft at Northolt. The unit continued to fly Spitfire IXs with the 1st Polish Wing (No. 131 Wing) until November 1943 when it left for a period of rest, leaving the Mk IXs behind for No. 308 Squadron and reverting to the now obsolete Mk Vs.

In mid-July 1944 No. 303 Sqn, now based Merston, started to receive Mk IXs again. These were mostly worn-out F.IXs, with a sprinkling of LF.IXs and HF.IXs as loss replacements. In the second week of August 1944 the squadron moved to Westhampnett, and in late September 1944 to RAF Coltishall where it remained until spring 1945. Although allocated to the Air Defence of Great Britain, the squadron flew escort and patrol missions over the continent, engaged heavily in 'Big Ben' operations against the German V2 rocket launch pads. During that period the squadron used a varied mix of F.IXs, LF.IXs and HF.IXs, plus a few Spitfire Vs as hacks and a single LF.XVI. In April 1945 No. 303 Sqn moved to RAF Andrews Field and converted to North American Mustang IVs.

S/Ldr Zygmunt Bieńkowski commanded No. 303 Sqn at the time of its re-equipment with Spitfire IXs in June 1943. He is shown in the cockpit of his personal F.IX MA304/RF-H with the 'Kościuszko badge' and squadron code letters 'RF' in their standard positions.

Spitfire F.IX MA222/RF-A displays the typical layout of codes on the starboard side of No. 303 Sqn Spitfires in 1943.

MA304/RF-H at Northolt in late June 1943. The arrangement of codes and markings followed the general pattern of all Mk IXs used by the 1st Polish Wing.

MH910/RF-G taking off in the summer of 1944. The layout of codes and markings on the port side of No. 303 Sqn Spitfire IXs remained unchanged when the unit re-equipped with Mk IXs for the second time, in 1944. Note the residual invasion bands on the bottom of the fuselage.

Unlike those of the 2nd TAF, the UK-based fighter squadrons retained the Sky spinner and rear fuselage band markings in 1945. This photo of F.IX MA528/RF-E was taken at Coltishall in late January 1945.

When No. 303 Sqn re-equipped with Mk IXs for the second time, in 1944, the layout of codes on the starboard side of the aircraft was reversed, as shown in this photo of F.IXs MH674/RF-A and MA420/RF-N.

No. 306 Squadron 'City of Toruń'

No. 306 was the first Polish squadron to re-equip with the Mk IX, when it reached operational capability on the new Spitfires at the end of September 1942. In October it was the first Polish unit to engage German aircraft while flying the Mk IX. On 31 December 1942 No. 306 Sqn Spitfire IX pilots claimed what was officially credited as the 500th and 501st German aircraft destroyed by Polish fighters in Britain during the war.

After half a year of flying the latest Spitfire variant, at the end of the second week of March 1943, No. 306 Sqn handed its Mk IXs over to No. 316 Squadron and left Northolt, reverting to Mk Vs.

S/Ldr Kazimierz Rutkowski commanded No. 306 Sqn when it re-equipped with Spitfire IXs in September 1942 as the first Polish unit. This photo was most probably taken on 2 November 1942, after his 100th sweep over France. He is seated in the cockpit of F.IX BS463/UZ-G, which displays the squadron badge and code letters in their standard positions.

Spitfire F.IX BS459/UZ-T photographed at RAF Northolt in late 1942. The factory-fresh camouflage and the layout of markings on the starboard side are shown to advantage. By that time the arrangement of codes and emblems on Northolt-based Spitfires of the 1st Polish Wing had been standardised in this form: the Polish AF chequered square on the nose, squadron badge below the windscreen and squadron code letters near the cockpit, on either side of the fuselage.

No. 308 Squadron 'City of Cracow'

This was the last Polish fighter squadron to convert onto the Mk IX when it arrived at Northolt on 11 November 1943 to replace No. 303 Sqn. It thus joined the 1st Polish Wing/No. 131 Wing and would remain part of it until the end of its existence. In early April 1944 the entire wing moved to Deanland and at the end of the month to Chailey. In May No. 308 replaced the Spitfire F.IXs with LF.IXs. In late June the unit moved to Appledram and in mid-July 1944 to Ford, in the south of England. In the first days of August the entire wing moved to Plumetot (B.10) in liberated France. In the first days of September 1944 Nos. 308 and 317 Squadrons moved again, to Fresnoy Folny/Londiniere (B.31), and a few days later to Lille-Vendeville (B.51). In early October the wing moved to Antwerp-Deurne (B.70), and a week later to Ghent-St Denijs Westrem (B.61). In early January 1945 No. 308 Sqn (with the entire wing) moved to Grimbergen (B.60), and in the second week of March to Gilze-Rijen (B.77) in Holland. It was there that No. 308 Squadron re-equipped with Mk XVIs in mid-March.

Spitfire F.IX MH880/ZF-V photographed at RAF Northolt, presumably in early 1944, with another machine, coded ZF-R (probably MA740) in the background. No. 308 was the last Polish fighter squadron to re-equip with Mk IXs. MH880 was delivered to the unit in late December 1943. Note the squadron badge applied below the windscreen, in typical fashion of the 1st Polish Wing at the time.

Spitfire LF.IX ML316/ZF-T in full invasion markings provides backdrop for preparations to celebrate No. 308 Sqn Day on 24 June 1944 at Chailey. By that time squadron badges had been obliterated, or not applied at all, on Polish Spitfires of the 2nd TAF squadrons.

No. 315 Squadron 'Dęblin'

No. 315 Squadron replaced its Mk Vs with Mk IXs in November 1942, as the second Polish unit to do so. It continued to operate from Northolt with the 1st Polish Wing until the beginning of June 1943, when it left Northolt for a period of rest, handing its Mk IXs to No. 303 Sqn.

Right: *Spitfire F.IX coded PK-P, believed to be BR624, in a souvenir photo of an anonymous airman and two soldiers. 'PKP' has been the acronym for the Polish National Rail and, predictably, No. 315 Sqn personnel were known as 'railwaymen' throughout the Polish Air Force. Note that the squadron badge had not been applied, yet, near the cockpit.*

Left: *P/O Michał Cwynar in the cockpit of Spitfire F.IX BS513/PK-Z, with the badge of No. 315 Sqn shown in its usual position.*

Below: *Brand new F.IX BS515/PK-F at Northolt in the autumn of 1942. Initially, the Polish marking on the nose of No. 315 Sqn Spitfire IXs was not accompanied by the 'POLAND' stencil below. Note that the squadron badge is yet to be applied below the windscreen.*

No. 316 Squadron 'City of Warsaw'

In mid-March 1943 No. 316 Sqn replaced No. 306 at Northolt, taking over its Mk IXs. It remained with the 1st Polish Wing there until late September, when it departed for a period of rest, leaving its aircraft behind for No. 302 Sqn.

Above: *Close-up of the unit code and badge on an F.IX of No. 316 Sqn. This was the only unit of the 1st Polish Wing at the time that did not apply the squadron badge under the windscreen.*

Above, right: *P/O Andrzej Próchnicki by the side of Spitfire F.IX AB508/SZ-D. This was one of the early Mk IXs converted from Mk VC airframes. Note the clear marks of overpainting previous codes: AB508 had earlier been used by No. 611 Squadron, coded FY-R (on 6 December 1942 F/Lt William Crawford-Compton scored an FW 190 probably destroyed in it).*

Below: *Spitfire F.IX BS463/SZ-G with No. 316 Squadron badge and code letters in their standard positions. The Spitfire had earlier been used by No. 306 Sqn (compare photo on p. 287) and when it was transferred to No. 316, only the unit code was reapplied, while the aircraft letter was retained in its original size, much larger than the 'SZ'. Note the stencil breaks in the squadron code letters. These were retouched on most aircraft.*

A Spitfire F.IX photographed inside a hangar at Northolt during the mass to celebrate No. 317 Squadron Day on 16 March 1944. Note that the code is JH-Y on the fuselage, but N on the bottom cowling. After F.IX BS445/JH-Y was damaged in an accident on 26 February 1944 the lower cowling panel was cannibalised from another damaged machine, BS508/JH-N, to repair it. By the time this photo was taken, No. 317 Sqn Spitfires no longer displayed the unit badge under the windscreens (in line with the 2nd TAF policy of the period).

No. 317 Squadron 'City of Wilno'

No. 317 Sqn was the first Polish unit to take delivery of Spitfire IXs when it received a few of these aircraft in August 1942. However, the squadron soon left Northolt for a period of rest, before it could convert onto the new version.

In late September 1943 the unit returned to Northolt and replaced its Spitfire Vs with the latest LF.IXs. It flew this variant until 27 January 1944 when these were handed over to the Norwegian No. 332 Squadron, in exchange for the latter's F.IXs. In April, together with the rest of the wing, No. 317 Sqn moved to Deanland and then to Chailey. In May 1944 the wing re-equipped with Spitfire LF.IXs. In late June the three squadrons moved to Appledram and in mid-July to Ford. In early August the wing moved to Plumetot (B.10) in liberated France. In early September No. 317 Squadron moved to Fresnoy Folny/Londiniere (B.31) and a few days later to Lille-Vendeville (B.51). In October the wing arrived in Belgium, first at Antwerp-Deurne (B.70) and then at Ghent-St Denijs Westrem (B.61). In January 1945 the three Polish squadrons moved to Grimbergen (B.60) near Brussels and in March to Gilze-Rijen (B.77) in Holland. In the first half of April the wing entered Germany, with a base at Nordhorn (B.101). In late April it moved to Varrelbusch (B.113) where it saw the end of the war. During May No. 317 Sqn re-equipped with Mk XVIs.

No. 317 Sqn LF.IXs at Plumetot (B.10) airfield in France in August 1944: JH-V in the foreground is probably MK316, with MK963/JH-S behind it and MK413/JH-U further to the left. The aeroplanes display partial invasion markings on lower surfaces of the fuselage and wings. Note 500 lb bombs on under-fuselage carriers.

Spitfire LF.IX coded JH-Q in early 1945. By that time the propeller spinner had been repainted black, and the Sky fuselage band overpainted with camouflage. The latter process resulted in overpainting the serial number, which was probably MK403, a Spitfire earlier used by No. 302 Sqn as WX-Q. Note clear traces of overpainted previous code beneath the JH.

No. 318 Squadron 'City of Gdańsk'

No. 318 Sqn operated in Italy from the spring 1944 as a tactical recce unit with secondary ground attack role, equipped with Spitfire Vs. Mk IXs first entered service with No. 318 Sqn very briefly in the second half of September 1944, when the unit's base at Cassandro became unserviceable due to heavy rains. A group of No. 318 pilots were detached to Iesi and flew a few Mk IXs made available by No. 4 Air Despatch and Reception Unit. By the end of the month the detachment rejoined the squadron and its Mk Vs at Rimini. In the second half of November No. 318 Sqn started true conversion onto Mk IXs at Bellaria. In the first days of December 1944 the squadron moved to Forli where it would stay until the end of April 1945. By the end of 1944 it had nine Mk IXs of all three principal variants: F.IX, LF.IX and HF.IX. The squadron continued its conversion to Mk IXs virtually until the end of the war, the last Mk V operational sortie being recorded in late April 1945. In early May the unit moved to La Russia, a few days later to Treviso and in mid-May to Tissano. Even after the war had officially ended, No. 318 Sqn continued to fly operational missions until 20 May (reconnoitring the Soviet Army movements in Austria). In mid-August 1945 the unit moved to Lavariano, but in late January 1946 it returned to Tissano and in the second week of March to Treviso. It flew from there until mid-August 1946, when it gave up its aircraft and left by train for Britain.

No. 318 Sqn 'A' Flight Spitfires at Forli during the winter of 1944/1945 were a mix of Mk Vs and Mk IXs. Nearest camera is F.IX MA706 LW-A, followed by Mk VC ES136 FK-T (personal aircraft of S/Ldr, later W/Cdr, Zbigniew Moszyński), Mk VB ER123 LW-F, a Mk IX (possibly MJ426 LW-E), and Mk VC LW-B (probably JG937). Although by that time all these Spitfires were supposed to be finished in the Day Fighter scheme on upper surfaces, the actual hues of (nominally) 'Ocean Grey' and 'Dark Green' were probably quite varied, judging by their different appearance in black and white.

Spitfire LF.IX TA864 LW-L in the factory applied Day Fighter scheme. Note the trace of the Sky band around the rear fuselage that had been overpainted in a single tone (including bottom surface). The layout of codes with 'LW' applied between the roundel and the tail, was typical on the starboard side of No. 318 Sqn Spitfires.

Above: No. 318 Sqn markings on the port side of the fuselage consisted of the code letters 'LW' (applied near the cockpit on this side as standard) and the informal squadron emblem depicting three playing cards: 3 of hearts, ace of spades and 8 of diamonds (symbolising the squadron number), applied below the windscreen (this side only).

Below: Spitfire FR.IX MA423/LW-F, with an oblique camera fitted in the fuselage (with the port for the lens located on the roundel). The Polish AF chequered square on No. 318 Sqn Spitfires was smaller than that in other squadrons. Note how the 'POLAND' stencil was broader than it. F/O Jan Grodziński is standing on the left.

Polish Combat Team In Africa

Early 1943 saw the formation of a Polish unit called officially the Polish Combat Team. Polish documents usually refer to it as the African Team or the Polish Fighting Team, and it has been commonly known under the informal name of 'Skalski's Circus'. About a dozen Polish pilots formed a semi-independent flight attached to No. 145 Sqn RAF. Initially equipped with Spitfire Vs, it converted to Mk IXs in late March 1943, becoming the first unit in Africa equipped solely with the version (RAF squadrons in the theatre, equipped with the Mk Vs, were initially only allocated a section of the new variant Spitfires).

F.IX EN267/ZX-5 photographed at a North African airfield, with the nose of EN300/ ZX-9 in the foreground (the peculiar shaped dark stain is a give-away) and an unidentified Mk IX further away.

Spitfire F.IX EN300/ZX-9 of the Polish Combat Team in similar scenery, with W/O Marcin Machowiak in the cockpit. The aircraft was given a coat of the Desert scheme (Dark Earth and Middle Stone) over its factory-applied Day Fighter camouflage. The propeller spinner was resprayed in red (which has spilled onto blade roots). The bottom surfaces are probably in Azure Blue. The colour of the codes is not known, but it was probably a medium blue similar to that seen in the colour photo of EN459/ZX-1 (see p. 176 of vol. 1). The letters 'ZX' were applied between the tail and the roundel on this side of the Spitfires, and near the cockpit on the other side. It is likely that the Spitfire had the Polish AF chequered square applied forward of the cockpit on the other side of the fuselage, plus one or two white swastika victory markings.

Due to the mobile nature of operations on the ground, the flight changed airfields several times, whenever the front line advanced significantly. Initially it was based at Bu Grara, in the second week of April it moved to La Fauconnerie, a few days later to Goubrine, at the end of the first week of May to Hergla, and two weeks later to Ben Gardane.

Once the African campaign was over the flight was disbanded in June and most pilots returned to Britain, although three stayed on in the Mediterranean, assuming command of RAF units.

Poles in RAF and Allied Fighter Squadrons

Although (as explained in vol. 1) the exiled Polish Air Force during WWII was not part of the RAF, Polish pilots (and other servicemen) were occasionally posted on exchange to RAF units. This was much less frequent in the later part of WWII, though, and according to available documents only one Pole flew Spitfire IXs in combat with an RAF unit in the West European theatre: F/Lt Michał Kolubiński with No. 66 Sqn in 1944.

It was different in the Mediterranean. In mid-1943 three Polish pilots, Władysław Drecki, Eugeniusz Horbaczewski and Stanisław Skalski, flew with Nos. 43, 145, 152 and 601 Squadrons RAF, each equipped with a mix of Mk V, VIII and IX aircraft at the time. Skalski and Horbaczewski

A Spitfire IX raises a cloud of dust as it taxies on a Normandy landing ground immediately following the allied invasion. The aircraft code, J, is applied beneath the propeller spinner, and the machine is believed to be from No. 66 Sqn, which makes it LF.IX MK569/LZ-J. F/Lt Kolubiński flew it on 4 July 1944 when he was credited with a Messerschmitt 109 shared destroyed: the last enemy aircraft claimed by a Polish pilot flying with an RAF unit. Note that the black and white striping had already peeled completely off the leading edge.

Spitfire IX coded LZ-K of No. 66 Sqn, displaying the invasion striping on under surface only, as used from July until late 1944. This is probably LF.IX PL325, flown repeatedly by F/Lt Kolubiński in July, August and September 1944.

JL132/WU-X was an early LF.IX used by No. 225 Squadron RAF in Italy. In late June 1944 it was flown by F/Lt Lew Kuryłowicz, attached to that unit from No. 318 Sqn. The colouring of the aircraft is puzzling. The 'fighter band' around the rear fuselage suggests standard Day Fighter scheme, but the camouflage pattern is 'B' (when JL132 was built all Spitfires were leaving factories in the 'A' pattern). The Spitfire was originally delivered to the Mediterranean in late 1943, when different colour schemes were used there, so it was probably refinished in Dark Green and Ocean Grey (or similar hues) about mid-1944. The bottom colour could be either Azure Blue or Medium Sea Grey. The small letters 'J P' flanking the aircraft code letter may refer to the initials of F/Lt J. Pratt of No. 225 Sqn. Note the night-flying anti-glare shield fitted on the side of the fuselage ahead of the windscreen.

Two Spitfire LF.IXs of No. 601 Squadron RAF taking off for a ground attack mission, each armed with a 500 lb bomb on the centreline carrier (note the distinctively different tail units of the bombs). Both Spitfires were flown by Polish pilots attached to that unit: F/Lt Zdzisław Uchwat in mid-/late July and F/Lt Jerzy Hamankiewicz in early/mid-August. MJ532/UF-G appears to be in standard Day Fighter scheme. Its fuselage band in Sky has been re-camouflaged (a small piece of it can be seen where the last two digits of the serial number had been masked off) and the spinner was repainted red (a recognition marking of the Mediterranean theatre). The squadron badge, a winged sword in red, is applied in the white circle above the fin flash. MJ250/UF-Q (regularly flown at the time by flight commander F/Lt Desmond Ibbotson) appears to have been among the first Spitfires used operationally in natural metal finish. It had most certainly left the factory in standard camouflage, which was then removed in service and the fabric-covered tail surfaces were painted Aluminium. Note the distinctively different shade of the armour cover over the fuselage fuel tank ahead of the windscreen, almost certainly due to it being a different alloy. This aircraft, too, has the Squadron badge in red on a white disc on the fin, and the propeller spinner in red.

HF.IX TA804/7B-H of No. 595 Sqn in the line-up of Spitfires prepared for the Battle of Britain flypast in September 1945. G/Cpt Douglas Bader is in the cockpit of his personal HF.IX RK917/DB in the foreground. Both the camouflage of RK917 and its fuselage roundel seem to be in non-standard hues, unlike those on TA804 which appears to be in perfectly typical Day Fighter scheme with all the prescribed markings. P/O Szczepan Mierzejewski flew TA804/7B-H with No. 595 Sqn on several occasions in 1945.

subsequently commanded Nos. 601 and 43, respectively, and Drecki was a flight commander in No. 152 Sqn (see vol. 1). A year later a number of Polish pilots from No. 318 Sqn were temporarily attached to RAF and Commonwealth fighter and fighter-reconnaissance squadrons in Italy. Those who went to Nos. 225 and 601 Sqns flew Mk IXs.

Non-operational Units

Apart from operational units, at the end of the war and afterwards Polish AF pilots also flew Spitfire IXs in training and auxiliary squadrons.

Polish pilots performed test flights in these aircraft at various experimental establishments, production plants and maintenance units.

High ranking officers occasionally used such aircraft of various RAF communications units.

Polish pilots ferried Spitfire IXs between RAF and allied units, both in Britain and across Africa (in fact ferry pilots, some of them female, were the first Poles to fly the variant!). They ferried the Spitfires both with RAF units and with the Air Transport Auxiliary (a quasi-military organisation made up of pilots who were not liable to air force service due to their age, health condition or sex).

Spitfires of No. 5 Refresher Flying Unit at Perugia during the winter of 1944/1945. The unit's Spitfires were identified by a single code letter A followed by a number. Polish pilots posted to No. 318 Squadron in Italy underwent short refresher courses at No. 5 RFU. P/O Kazimierz Karlikowski logged several flights in A-9 and A-12 in March 1945. In this photo MA7../A-9 seems to be in a standard 'A' pattern Day Fighter camouflage, while MA545/A-12 displays a non-standard camouflage pattern that loosely resembles the 'B' pattern, which means it had earlier been finished in the Desert scheme and was repainted in the Mediterranean.

F.IX BR592 may well have been the very first Mk IX ever flown by a Polish pilot. It was ferried on 12 June 1942 by 1st/Off Anna Leska, ATA, from Eastleigh to No. 33 MU at Lyneham. It was in factory-fresh condition with standard RAF camouflage and markings.

Spitfire LF.IX MK994/N of the Fighter Command Communications Squadron photographed at Hethel or Coltishall in May 1946 when W/Cdr Stefan Janus (from the Polish Liaison Office at the HQ No. 11 Group) flew it from Northolt to inspect Polish fighter squadrons. The camouflage and markings of the aircraft seem quite standard. Note that the Spitfire's cannon had been removed and there is a rounded plug in the inboard cannon mount tube.

Spitfire HF.IX RK889 in factory fresh condition ('EDMONTON II' was a presentation name). On 6 October 1944 1st/Off Stefania Wojtulanis of No. 6 Ferry Pilots Pool ATA ferried it from the Castle Bromwich Aeroplane Factory to Sherburn, on its way to No. 45 Maintenance Unit at Kinloss. It then went to No. 3501 Servicing Unit and on 13 February 1945 F/Lt Józef Mierzejewski (a fighter pilot who was 'resting' with No. 1 Delivery Flight at the time) ferried it from Middle Wallop to Odiham (in connection with the unit's move). In 1948 the Spitfire was delivered to Denmark, where it subsequently served under a new serial no. 41-420 until written off in an accident in October 1954.

Supermarine Spitfire F.IX BS456/UZ-Ż, No. 306 Squadron, Northolt, September 1942–March 1943. Upper surface camouflage colours: Ocean Grey and Dark Green ('A' pattern); under surface colour: Medium Sea Grey. Standard British national markings. No. 306 Sqn badge below the windscreen, facing forward on both sides of the fuselage. Polish national marking on both sides of forward fuselage, with 'POLAND' stencil underneath. Aircraft letter applied in black below the propeller spinner. The aircraft letter Z was applied as Ż (a generic Polish character: a 'z' with a dot above), the initial of F/Lt Józef Żulikowski, the regular pilot of this aircraft.

BS456 was an early Supermarine-built Spitfire F.IX, delivered brand new to No. 306 Sqn in September 1942. It was coded UZ-Ż rather than UZ-Z, as the personal marking of F/Lt Józef Żulikowski, who chose this Spitfire as his personal mount. Otherwise the Spitfire displayed standard markings and codes.

A closer look at the Spitfire with P/O Józef Jeka in the cockpit and the squadron badge below the windscreen. This photo also shows that on this Spitfire the yellow stripe along the wing leading edge (a quick recognition marking for head-on identification) ended near the gun port, well outboard of the cannon.

A different view from the same photographic session, this time with P/O Jeka by the propeller (note his initials on his Mae West). The position of the squadron badge and of the squadron code is shown.

The head-on view of BS456 UZ-Ż shows the aircraft letter 'Ż' applied under the spinner. It was standard for No. 306 Sqn to apply this code there in black. Note that each wing was fitted with just one 0.303 in. Colt-Browning machine gun, a standard fit on Spitfire F.IXs at Northolt at the time. For this reason only the inboard gun port was covered with the red-coloured fabric patch that was replaced each time the gun was fired. The outboard gun port on each wing was patched over permanently and overpainted with the yellow stripe.

Supermarine Spitfire F.IX BS410/PK-E, No. 315 Squadron, Northolt, November 1942–April 1943. Upper surface camouflage colours: Ocean Grey and Dark Green ('A' pattern); under surface colour: Medium Sea Grey. Standard British national markings. No. 315 Sqn badge below the windscreen, facing forward on both sides of the fuselage. Polish national marking on both sides of forward fuselage. Aircraft letter applied in red below the propeller spinner.

Left: Capt. Francis 'Gabby' Gabreski hugging the propeller of a Spitfire F.IX marked with the letter 'E' on the bottom of the cowling and the Polish AF chequered square marking on the side. When 'Gabby' arrived in Britain in 1942, he volunteered to fly on operations with a Polish AF squadron before moving to a USAAF unit. He flew his first combat sortie over Europe on 21 January 1943, using BS410 PK-E.

Left: No. 315 Sqn badge as applied on the starboard side, on the skin panel from Spitfire BS410 recovered in December 2005 at its crash site in France (it crashed there in May 1943). Until this panel was found, most authors and artists depicted the triangular outline of the badge as red or yellow, but it seems to have been silvery grey. © Peter R. Arnold

Above: More recovered parts of the Spitfire: a starboard skin panel and battery compartment cover showing the position and shape of the serial number. © Peter R. Arnold

Left: Capt. Gabreski in the cockpit of, presumably, the same Spitfire on the same occasion. Note the shape and position of the squadron code letters and of the squadron badge.

Supermarine Spitfire F.IX EN527/SZ-A 'Ewunia', No. 316 Squadron, Northolt, March–August 1943. Upper surface camouflage colours: unspecified grey (lighter than the regulation Ocean Grey) and Dark Green ('A' pattern); under surface colour: Medium Sea Grey. Standard British national markings. No. 316 Sqn badge aft of the cockpit, facing forward on both sides of the fuselage. Polish national marking on both sides of forward fuselage, with 'POLAND' stencil underneath. Aircraft letter applied in black below the propeller spinner. 'Ewunia' ('Little Eva') personal name applied under the windscreen, probably on the port side only.

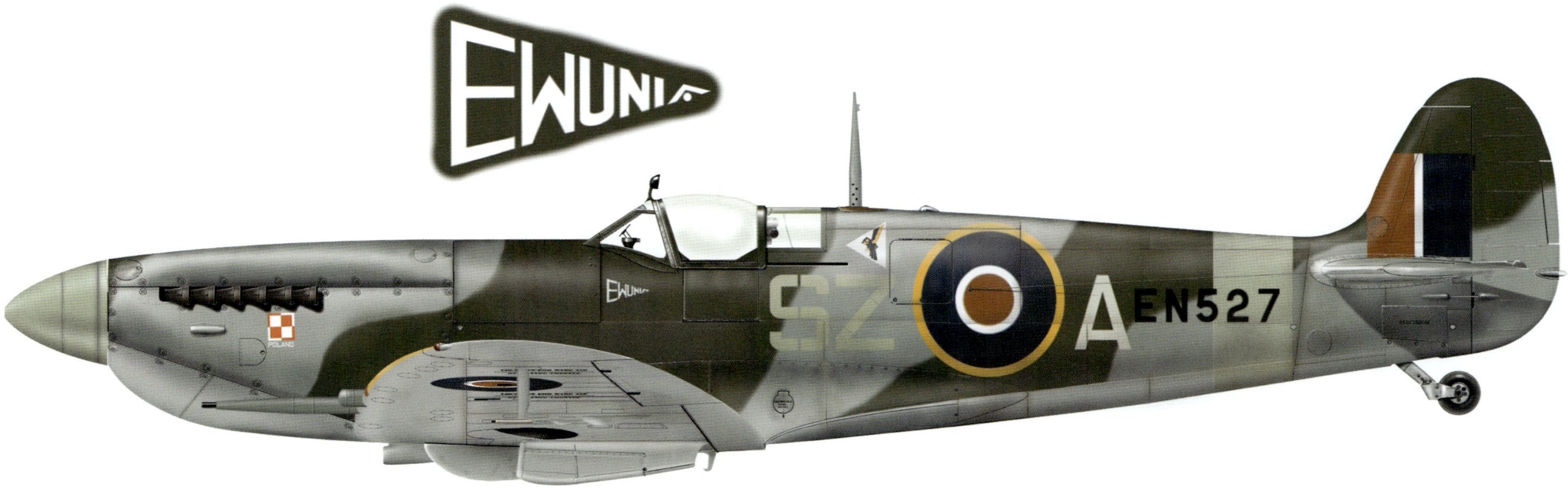

Spitfire F.IX EN527 photographed at Northolt during late spring or summer of 1943. This Spitfire had been built as a Mk VC airframe by Supermarine and converted to a Merlin 63-powered F.IX by Rolls-Royce. Mk IXs completed by Rolls-Royce had a slightly different camouflage pattern and it seems that non-standard hue of grey was used on upper surfaces in place of Ocean Grey on some of these aircraft. Also the characters of the serial number on the rear fuselage were spaced more widely than on Supermarine-built aircraft.

F/O Ludomir Ciastuła by the nose of EN527. Note the non-standard camouflage pattern on the port side of the cowling, applied on some Spitfire IXs completed by Rolls-Royce. The aircraft code letter was applied in black in this position.

S/Ldr Marian Trzebiński leaves his personal Spitfire at Northolt. The name 'Ewunia' ('Little Eva') was a personal marking also seen on his earlier personal Spitfires. Note the distinctive breaks in the stencilled code. It seems that this photo was taken soon after the original rectangular rear-view mirror was replaced with the new, round version: the rear windscreen framing is unpainted and the mirror fairing seems to be in the factory-applied black finish.

Supermarine Spitfire F.IX EN355/ZX-0, Polish Combat Team, Africa, April 1943. Upper surface camouflage colours: Dark Earth and Middle Stone ('A' pattern); under surface colour: probably Azure. Standard British national markings. Possibly Polish national marking on the port side of fuselage forward of the windscreen. Codes probably black.

A Spitfire F.IX at a desert airfield, with the code digit 4 visible on the fuselage and below the propeller. Although no unit code or other markings are visible, this is most probably ZX-4 of the Polish Combat Team. Two Spitfires used this code: first EN313, in which F/Lt Wacław Król was credited with three enemy fighters destroyed, and then EN257. Whichever this one is, it is finished in the Desert scheme sprayed rather carelessly over the original camouflage.

Spitfire F.IX EN355 ZX-0 in which F/O Mieczysław Wyszkowski was downed on 18 April 1943 (the only loss of the Polish Combat Team). The aircraft digit, zero, was circle-shaped. The codes look distinctively darker than the roundel, it seems they were applied in black. Note the shadow of the photographer, looking like a non-standard camouflage patch.

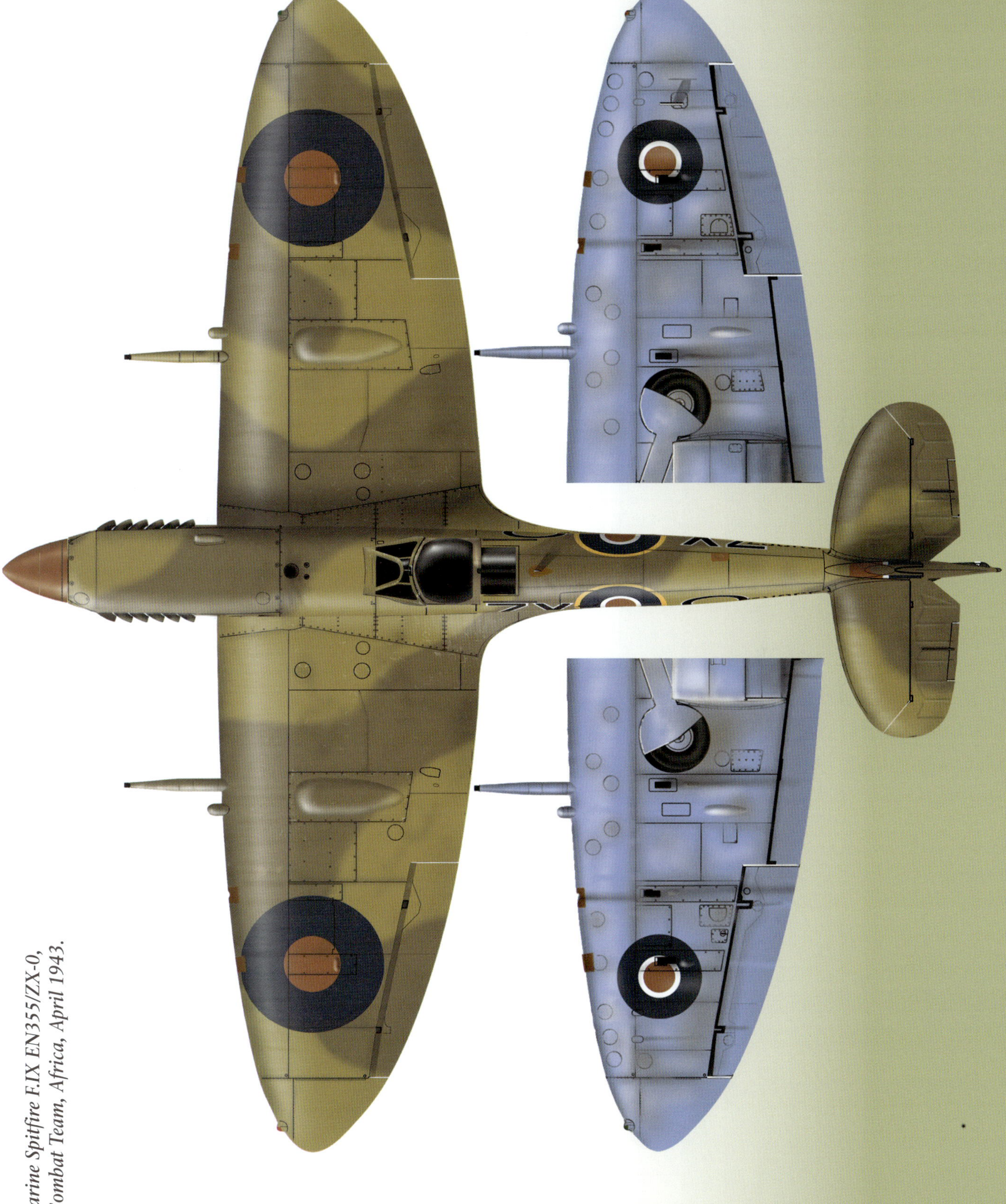

Supermarine Spitfire F.IX EN355/ZX-0, Polish Combat Team, Africa, April 1943.

Supermarine Spitfire F.IX EN315/ZX-6, Polish Combat Team, Africa, April–May 1943. Colour scheme unknown (unlikely to be the standard Desert scheme), shown hypothetically as the Temperate Sea scheme of Extra Dark Sea Grey and Dark Slate Grey ('A' pattern) on upper surfaces (the prescribed scheme for Malta Spitfires) with Sky under surfaces. Standard British national markings. Polish national marking on the port side of fuselage forward of the windscreen. Victory markings (white swastikas) below the windscreen. Codes probably medium blue (like on most PCT Spitfires). Aircraft digit (6) applied in white below the propeller spinner.

Spitfires of the Polish Combat Team and No. 145 Squadron RAF at an airfield in North Africa in the spring of 1943, with EN315/ZX-6 in the foreground. Standing at far right is G/Cpt Mateusz Iżycki, the Polish Liaison Officer at the HQ RAF Middle East, who visited the Polish Combat Team in the last days of April. This sequence of photos has long puzzled researchers by the seemingly single-tone upper surface finish on EN315 as compared to the two-tone camouflage pattern easily distinguishable on next Spitfires in the line. Many authors assume incorrectly that all Spitfire fighters in the Mediterranean were finished in the desert camouflage scheme of Middle Stone and Dark Earth with Azure Blue under surfaces. Although this was the prescribed scheme for operations over desert areas, some Spitfires operating in the theatre (and particularly those on Malta) were finished in other colour schemes. Notably, in late January 1943 RAF high commanders in the theatre asked for Spitfire IXs originally earmarked for Malta to be diverted to North Africa, so some 'Skalski's Circus' Spitfire IXs may well have been painted in the Maltese scheme. In view of the findings of Brian Cauchi and the late Edgar Brooks, Spitfires used on Malta at the time were supposed to be finished in the Temperate Sea scheme of Extra Dark Sea Grey and Dark Slate Grey. On aircraft with this upper surface scheme the under surfaces may have been repainted Sky or left in the factory-applied Medium Sea Grey.

Above and below: *Other photos in the same sequence taken at a North African airfield in the spring of 1943, with EN315/ZX-6 in the foreground. The Polish AF chequered square was applied forward of the cockpit. The white swastikas below the windscreen symbolised 'kills' credited to various pilots while flying this aircraft, rather than any specific pilot's personal score. Aircraft digit 6 in white can be made out on the bottom of the engine cowling immediately aft of the propeller spinner. Note how the outer 20 mm cannon stub has been plugged flat in EN315.*

Right: *F/Lt Kazimierz Sporny in the cockpit of EN315. The sixth swastika was added after W/O Mieczysław Popek scored the Spitfire's last victory, a Macchi 202 destroyed, on 28 April 1943.*

Supermarine Spitfire F.IX BS451/RF-M 'Joan', No. 303 Squadron, Northolt, June–November 1943. Upper surface camouflage colours: Ocean Grey and Dark Green ('A' pattern); under surface colour: Medium Sea Grey. Standard British national markings. No. 303 Sqn badge below the windscreen, on both sides of the fuselage. Polish national marking on both sides of forward fuselage, with 'POLAND' stencil underneath. Serial number applied in small size characters at the top of the rear fuselage band. Aircraft letter in Sky below the propeller spinner. 'Joan' personal name applied under the windscreen on the port side only.

Right: F/Lt Michał Antoni Kolubiński posing on the Spitfire. On 24 June 1943 this pilot flew the Spitfire when he claimed a Focke-Wulf 190 damaged during 'Ramrod 102'. The name 'Joan' is very prominent on the side of the fuselage, while the aircraft letter in Sky can just be made out below the propeller spinner.

A starboard view of the Spitfire at Northolt, showing clearly the camouflage pattern and the layout of codes and markings.

Left: The Spitfire shown to visiting Brasilian AF officers at Northolt in early November 1943. The raised tail of the aircraft and the exposed ammunition feed mechanism visible above the wing surface suggest the photograph was taken during cannon harmonisation. The F/Sgt on the wing is talking to RAF Northolt Station Commander, G/Cpt Frederick Rosier (visible directly above gun port). G/Cpt Tadeusz Rolski, commanding No. 18 (Polish) Wing of the 2nd TAF can be seen behind Rosier's shoulder. By that time this photo was taken two machine guns had been fitted in each wing of Northolt-based Mk IXs. On this aeroplane the yellow stripe on the leading edge extended to about mid-way between the cannon and the inboard gun. The serial number on this Spitfire was applied in 2 in. characters at the top of the Sky band.

Supermarine Spitfire F.IX EN526/SZ-G, of Northolt Wing Leader, W/Cdr A. Gabszewicz, June–September 1943. Upper surface camouflage colours: unspecified grey (lighter than the regulation Ocean Grey) and Dark Green ('A' pattern); under surface colour: Medium Sea Grey. Standard British national markings. No. 316 Sqn badge aft of the cockpit, facing forward on both sides of the fuselage. Polish national marking on both sides of forward fuselage, with 'POLAND' stencil underneath. Wing Commander pennant below the windscreen (positioned unusually low) and 'Boxing Dog' personal emblem of W/Cdr Aleksander Gabszewicz forward of the windscreen, both on port side only. Aircraft letter applied in black below the propeller spinner.

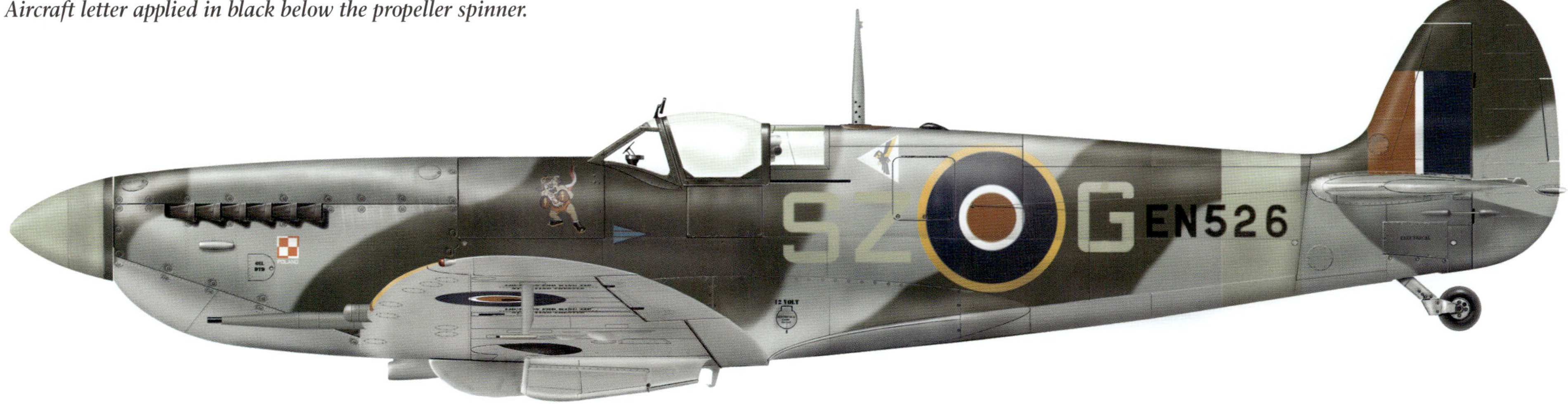

W/Cdr Aleksander Gabszewicz on the wing of his personal Spitfire. This was the first personal aircraft of this pilot to be adorned with the emblem of a boxing dog wearing Polish national team colours. This aeroplane carried the emblem forward of the windscreen. The Wing Commander pennant was located unusually low below the windscreen. It must have been applied there during the time when this Spitfire was flown by the previous Northolt Wing Leader, W/Cdr Kołaczkowski, when No. 303 Sqn badge was applied immediately below the windscreen and above the pennant. This photo was taken in mid-1943 when the Spitfire only had one machine gun in each wing. Note that the yellow stripe on the leading edge extended to just outboard of the cannon.

A group of mechanics (including Sgt Paweł Kulesza in pale coat) posing with Spitfire F.IX EN526/SZ-G in the summer of 1943. Gabszewicz's personal emblem can be seen forward of the cockpit. Note the unusually pale appearance of the upper surface colour supposed to be Ocean Grey.

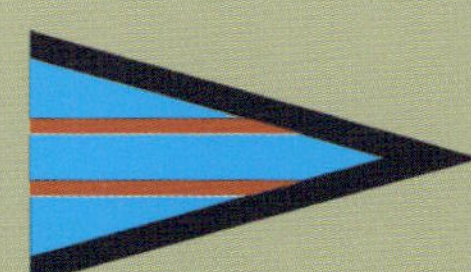

Another photo of mechanics (including Sgt Paweł Kulesza second right) and Spitfire F.IX EN526/SZ-G at Northolt in the summer of 1943. With exception of the personal emblem and W/Cdr pennant, the Spitfire displayed perfectly standard markings of No. 316 Squadron, including the SZ codes and badge on the fuselage aft the cockpit. This was another Rolls-Royce assembled Mk IX, with the letters/digits of the serial applied with wider spaces between them than was standard on Spitfires completed at other assembly plants.

Supermarine Spitfire LF.IX MH727/JH-T, No. 317 Squadron, Northolt, September 1943–January 1944. Upper surface camouflage colours: Ocean Grey and Dark Green ('A' pattern); under surface colour: Medium Sea Grey. Standard British national markings. No. 317 Sqn badge below the windscreen, facing forward on both sides of the fuselage. Polish national marking on both sides of forward fuselage. Aircraft letter probably applied in black below the propeller spinner.

Brand new Spitfire LF.IX MH727 at Northolt in the autumn of 1943. Note the shiny finish. The aircraft displays a full set of regulation markings, including No. 317 Squadron badge under the windscreen

Supermarine Spitfire F.IX MH353/WX-K, No. 302 Squadron, Northolt, early 1944. Upper surface camouflage colours: Ocean Grey and Dark Green ('A' pattern); under surface colour: Medium Sea Grey. Standard British national markings. No. 302 Squadron badge below the windscreen. Polish national marking on both sides of forward fuselage. Individual emblems: the name 'Susan' below the windscreen, a cartoon of a turtle fighting a snail forward of it, and a white-red band around each cannon fairing. Prominent traces of overpainting the previous codes and badge of No. 316 Sqn.

Above: Spitfire F.IX MH353 WX-K at Northolt in late 1943. Oddly, the aircraft letter 'K' was applied on a patch of new paint as if on an overpainted previous code, but available documents suggest the Spitfire had been coded SZ-K in No. 316 Sqn (its first unit) and retained the same aircraft letter in No. 302 Sqn.

Right: MH353 WX-K photographed at Halesworth on 25 February 1944, when F/Lt Witold Łanowski visited his USAAF friends there. Note that by that time No. 302 Sqn badge had been applied near the cockpit. This photo shows that the personal emblem, which showed a turtle fighting a snail, was captioned, somewhat mysteriously, 'WALKA BYKA Z PAROWOZEM' ('A FIGHT BETWEEN A BULL AND A STEAM ENGINE'). Its connection (if any) with the name 'Susan' is obscure. Note the white-red band around each cannon fairing.

Supermarine Spitfire LF.IX MK924/WX-A 'Freda C.', No. 302 Squadron, Chailey, June 1944. Upper surface camouflage colours: Ocean Grey and Dark Green ('A' pattern); under surface colour: Medium Sea Grey. Standard British national markings. No squadron badge. Polish national marking on both sides of forward fuselage. Full invasion markings in form of white and black bands on the fuselage and wings. Codes partly obliterated by these bands. Individual name (its meaning unclear) below the windscreen and ground attack mission markings in form of bomb silhouettes (probably yellow) on forward fuselage.

F/Sgt Michał Murayda in the cockpit of his Spitfire MK924/WX-A with full invasion markings. Most of the serial number and half of the codes were obliterated by D-Day striping. The aircraft letter was re-applied on the black stripe aft of the roundel. It was also applied carelessly (probably chalked) on the roundel, both on the red centre and at the top of the blue ring. The aircraft was only used by No. 302 Sqn until 11 June, but the black paint on cannon fairings in the foreground is peeling already, within a week of their application!

Supermarine Spitfire LF.IX MK924/WX-A 'Freda C', No. 302 Squadron, Chailey, June 1944.

Supermarine Spitfire LF.IX MK984/ZF-R, No. 308 Squadron, St Denijs Westrem, autumn 1944. Upper surface camouflage colours: Ocean Grey and Dark Green ('A' pattern); under surface colour: Medium Sea Grey. Standard British national markings. No squadron badge. Polish national marking on both sides of forward fuselage. Partial invasion markings in form of white and black bands on the lower half of the fuselage. Individual name 'Lala' ('Doll') forward of the windscreen on both sides of the fuselage. Ground attack mission markings in form of bomb silhouettes (probably yellow) on the port side of forward fuselage.

Above: *S/Ldr Witold Retinger photographed with his personal Spitfire about the time of his departure from No. 308 Squadron in late November 1944. This was the definitive number of bomb symbols painted on the cowling, which remained unaltered after he left the unit (they probably signified all ground attack missions he had flown, not just those in MK984, of which there were only 18).*

Left: *S/Ldr Retinger and his ground crew by his personal Spitfire, presumably photographed on the same occasion. By the end of November 1944 the invasion bands had been reduced to just the lower half of the fuselage.*

Right: *S/Ldr Witold Retinger in the cockpit of his Spitfire, with the style of the name 'Lala' shown to advantage.*

Above: *Starboard view of the Spitfire. The name 'Lala' was also applied on this side of the fuselage (discernible in the shadow of the fitter standing on the wing), but bomb symbols were not. The invasion bands had been removed completely from the wing and only retained on lower fuselage.*

Supermarine Spitfire F.IX MH702/LW-B, No. 318 Squadron, Italy, March–April 1945. Upper surface camouflage colours: Ocean Grey and Dark Green ('A' pattern); under surface colour: Medium Sea Grey. Standard British national markings. Possibly the informal squadron badge was applied near the windscreen on the port side only. Polish national marking on both sides of forward fuselage.

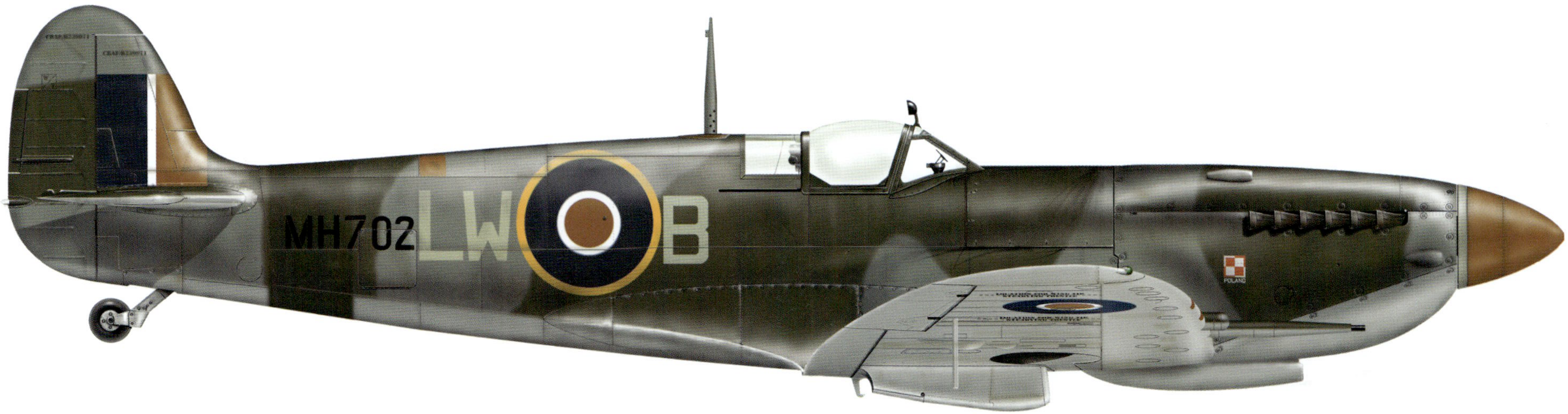

Spitfire F.IX MH702 in flight on 2 April 1945. The photo is slightly out of focus, which renders the white ring of the roundel unusually broad. The propeller spinner was probably red, with the backplate left in the factory-applied Sky.

F/O Mieczysław Sawicki, who crash-landed in MH702/LW-B in enemy territory in April 1945, photographed by the wreckage of the Spitfire after Allied troops captured the location of his crash-landing.

Supermarine Spitfire LF.IX MK910/JH-C, No. 317 Squadron, Varrelbusch (Germany), May 1945. Upper surface camouflage colours: Ocean Grey and Dark Green ('A' pattern); under surface colour: Medium Sea Grey. Standard British national markings. No squadron badge. Probably Polish national marking on both sides of forward fuselage.

Spitfire LF.IX MK910 JH-C following the accident of F/Lt Roman Nartowicz on 25 May 1945 at R.27 Großsachsenheim (Untermberg) near Stuttgart (upon conversion onto Mk XVIs No. 317 Sqn pilots delivered their Spitfire LF.IXs to French squadrons of No. 339 Wing RAF based there, note a No. 326 Sqn Spitfire coded 8J-Y in the background). Note how the Sky band was overpainted on the fuselage and the serial number re-applied there. Typically for No. 317 Sqn Spitfires at the time, the aircraft letter is smaller and paler than squadron letters. The size and position of the wing roundel is noteworthy. The small (fuselage size) new roundel in four colours was applied at the very tip of the wing, outboard of the overpainted large two-tone one.

Supermarine Spitfire LF.IX MK910/JH-C,
No. 317 Squadron, Varrelbusch (Germany), May 1945.

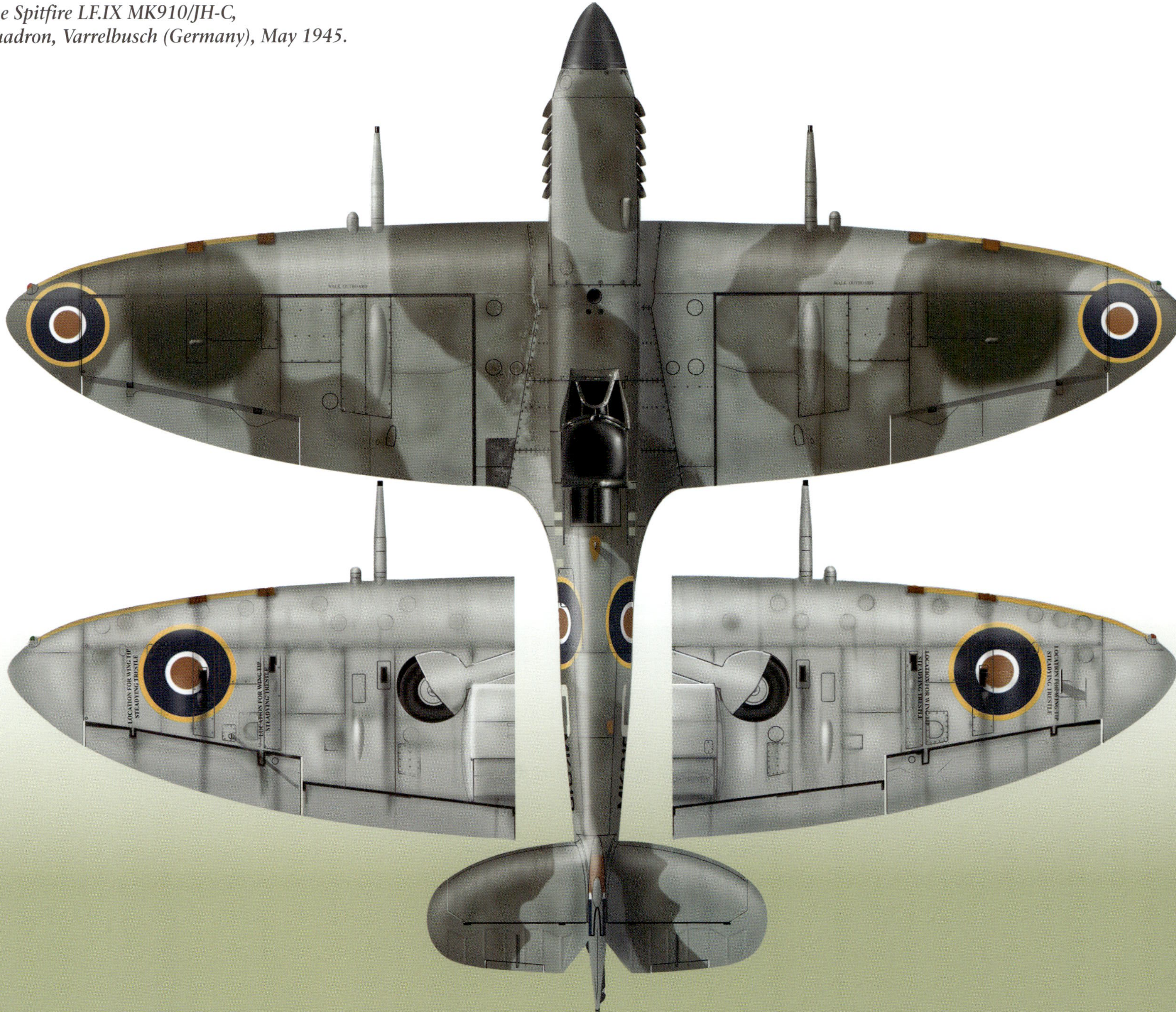

Supermarine Spitfire XVI

Polish Squadrons

The Spitfire XVI was, essentially, a Mk IX with a Merlin engine built in the USA under licence. In engineering terms there was less difference between a Mk IX and a Mk XVI manufactured at the same time than between early and late Mk IXs.

The three squadrons of No. 131 Wing re-equipped with Spitfire XVIs in the first half of 1945, and then continued to use them until their disbandment in late 1946.

In early 1945 re-equipment of No. 303 Sqn with Spitfire XVIs was also considered. The squadron received a single Mk XVI in mid-February, but eventually none followed and the unit re-equipped with Mustang IVs in April.

Altogether, squadrons of the Polish Air Force used about 125 Spitfire XVIs, of which about 20 were in the late variant with a cut-down rear fuselage and tear-drop canopy.

Few Polish wing commanders used their own initials as personalised codes on their Spitfires. W/Cdr Wacław Król was among the few, his Spitfire XVI TD238 displaying the letters WK-L (his initials plus the initial of his fiancée's first name). Otherwise the aircraft was in standard camouflage and markings. As far as can be ascertained, it did not carry the Wing Commander's pennant emblem.

An anonymous soldier of the Polish Army poses on Spitfire XVI TE206/JH-A, which displays a Group Captain's pennant on the fuselage, but has standard No. 317 Sqn markings (compare photo on p. 319). This must have been the machine of G/Cpt Stefan Witorzeńć, OC No. 131 Wing, the only officer holding this rank in the wing at the time. The broken yellow line around the cockpit hood and door was a regulation 'rescue marking', meant to help passers-by locate and open the cockpit from outside in case of an emergency landing.

No. 302 Squadron 'City of Poznań'

The squadron converted to Mk XVIs in January 1945 at Grimbergen (B.60) in Belgium. In the second week of March the entire No. 131 Wing moved to Gilze-Rijen (B.77) in Holland. By mid-April No. 302 (with the wing) had moved to Nordhorn (B.101), and by late April to Varrelbusch (B.113), both in Germany. In August the squadron code letters were changed from 'WX' to 'QH'. In mid-September 1945 the wing, including No. 302, moved to Ahlhorn (B.111) in Germany. It was based there until October 1946, when it moved to RAF Hethel, near Norwich, where it disbanded at the end of 1946.

F/Sgt Jerzy Gruszka in the cockpit of a Spitfire XVI. No. 302 Sqn badge applied after the end of the war differed in design from that used on Mk Vs and IXs in 1943 (compare photo on p. 247 of vol. 1). One pattern of the badge was applied on either side of the fuselage (the 'crow' faced rearwards on the other side).

No. 302 Sqn Spitfire XVIs at Varrelbusch in Germany in mid-June 1945: TB921 WX-D (right, parked), TB834 WX-I (left, taxiing), SM409 WX-K (taxiing behind TB921) and TD240 WX-V (centre, parked in the distance). The standard position of code letters on each side of the fuselage is shown clearly. Note that only TD240 (the squadron commander's aircraft) in the distance is adorned with the squadron emblem below the windscreen (compare photo on p. 326, taken on the same occasion). Unit badges were gradually re-introduced on Spitfires of No. 131 Wing after VE-Day, but at the time of this photo they had not been applied on all aircraft

Sgt Józef Różański posing with a Spitfire XVI. Such ornamental form of the aircraft letter below the propeller was seen on some (all?) Mk XVIs of No. 302 Sqn in the post-war period. The background shield was probably red or yellow and the letter was blue or grey.

Cpl Józef Klachacz posing with Spitfire XVI TB276/QH-J in 1946 (the aircraft is supported on jacks, undergoing maintenance – note the absence of the sliding hood under the canvas cover). No. 302 Sqn code letters were changed to 'QH' in August 1945.

Spitfire XVI TB890/ZF-M at Croydon in the summer of 1945. The aircraft has all the standard markings of the period, including the upper wing roundels similar in size and form to those on the fuselage. At the time the squadron badge had not been applied yet below the windscreen.

No. 308 Squadron 'City of Cracow'

No. 308 Squadron re-equipped with Mk XVIs in mid-March 1945 at Gilze-Rijen (B.77). By mid-April it had moved (with the entire No. 131 Wing) to Nordhorn (B.101) in Germany. In the last days of April the squadron temporarily deployed to UK for a routine tour of gunnery training. It then rejoined the wing at Varrelbusch (B.113) after VE-Day. In mid-September 1945 No. 308 moved to Ahlhorn (B.111), as did the entire wing. In October 1946 the squadron moved to RAF Hethel, where it disbanded at the end of 1946.

Spitfire XVI TB480/ZF-B with pilot Sgt Ludwik Kuczyński (right) and fitter LAC Sylwester Patoka (seated on the wing). When No. 308 Sqn badge was applied on Spitfire XVIs after the end of the war, it was just black and yellow and the arrow pointed backwards on both sides of the fuselage (compare the 1943–1944 variant of the badge on p. 251 of vol. 1). The style of the stencilled Polish AF chequered square and 'POLAND' below as seen here was typical in No. 131 Wing during 1944–1946.

No. 317 Squadron 'City of Wilno'

No. 317 Sqn re-equipped with Mk XVIs during May 1945 at Varrelbusch (B.113) in Germany. In mid-September 1945 No. 131 Wing (including No. 317), moved to Ahlhorn (B.111). In October 1946 the unit returned to UK, and at the end of 1946 it was disbanded at RAF Hethel.

Mk XVI TE206/JH-A of G/Cpt Stefan Witorzeńć (compare another photo of the aircraft, on p. 316) was nominally operated by No. 317 Sqn and featured all identification markings of the unit, including the squadron badge below the windscreen. During 1945–1946 the badge was applied in identical form on either side of the fuselage, so the 'condor' faced rearwards on this side (notably, during 1941–1943 the badge was facing forward on each side, see photo on p. 254 of vol. 1).

Spitfire XVI JH-S, probably TB635, taxiing in Germany in the summer of 1945. Unlike with Nos. 302 and 308 Sqns, No. 317's initial set of Mk XVIs were all second-hand aircraft that had seen service with other units. This explains the patches of different colour underneath 'JH' and 'S', where previous markings had been obliterated. The squadron badge had not yet been applied.

Poles in RAF and allied fighter squadrons

According to available documents only one Pole flew Spitfire XVIs in combat with the RAF: F/Lt Zbigniew Wróblewski with No. 602 Sqn in the first half of 1945.

No. 602 Sqn Spitfire XVI LO-J with W/O S. Sollitt (left) and F/Sgt C. Zuber (both RAF) in early 1945. F/Lt Zbigniew Wróblewski flew a number of Spitfires in the SM2... serial range with the unit, but it is not certain if this was one of those.

Non-operational Units

Apart from operational units, Polish AF pilots also flew Spitfire XVIs in auxiliary squadrons, test-flew them at various experimental establishments, production plants and maintenance units, and ferried them between RAF and allied units, both in RAF ferry units and the ATA.

Spitfire XVI RW388/U4-U photographed at Farnborough in the second half of 1945 with a full set of RAF Fighter Command quick-recognition markings, including the Sky fuselage band and propeller spinner. Despite that, the Spitfire was not a fighter any more, its gunsight and armament removed and the stubs faired over. It was operated by No. 667 Squadron as a target tug for gunnery training. At the time the unit had a number of Polish pilots. F/Lt Zbigniew Kalinowski suffered a landing accident in RW388 in occupied Germany on 30 November 1945.

Spitfire XVI TB757 during rocket firing trials at the Aeroplane and Armament Experimental Establishment at Boscombe Down in June 1945. S/Ldr Janusz Żurakowski test flew it on several occasions during that period. Like all series production fighters sent for trials at the AAEE, the Spitfire was in standard Fighter Command camouflage and markings.

Supermarine Spitfire XVI TB632/ZF-R, No. 308 Squadron, Varrelbusch (Germany), July–August 1945. Upper surface camouflage colours: Ocean Grey and Dark Green ('A' pattern); under surface colour: Medium Sea Grey. Standard British national markings. No. 308 Sqn badge below the windscreen, facing forward on both sides of the fuselage. Polish national marking on both sides of forward fuselage, with 'POLAND' stencil underneath. Aircraft letter possibly applied in Sky below the propeller spinner. Broken yellow line around the cockpit hood ('rescue marking'). Ground attack mission markings in form of bomb silhouettes (probably yellow) on the port side of the fuselage.

Spitfire XVI TB632/ZF-R taxiing at Varrelbusch in mid-June 1945. Note the large-size roundels on top of the wings (obtained by adding narrow yellow and white rings to the previous 'B' markings). TB632 was one of few aircraft in No. 131 Wing to have these large 'C1' roundels.

Spitfire XVI TD238/SZ-K of No. 131 Wing Leader, W/Cdr T. Sawicz, Varrelbusch (Germany), April–July 1945. Upper surface camouflage colours: Ocean Grey and Dark Green ('A' pattern); under surface colour: Medium Sea Grey. Standard British national markings. Polish national marking on both sides of forward fuselage.

TD238/SZ-K, the personal aeroplane of W/Cdr Tadeusz Sawicz, at Varrelbusch in Germany in mid-June 1945. W/Cdr Tadeusz Sawicz had his Spitfires coded SZ-K (which dated back to his time with No. 316 Sqn in 1941–1942) rather than his initials. At the time No. 316 Sqn was a Mustang squadron in Britain.

ASpitfire XVI TD238/SZ-K at No. 131 Wing airfield after the war. Upper surface 'C1' roundels in No. 131 Wing were mostly seen in the 36 in. size, as on this aeroplane.

Spitfire XVI TD242/ZF-E, No. 308 Squadron, Varrelbusch (Germany), July–August 1945. Upper surface camouflage colours: Ocean Grey and Dark Green ('A' pattern); under surface colour: Medium Sea Grey. Standard British national markings. No. 308 Sqn badge below the windscreen, facing forward on both sides of the fuselage. Polish national marking on both sides of forward fuselage, with 'POLAND' stencil underneath. Aircraft letter possibly applied in Sky below the propeller spinner. Broken yellow line around the cockpit hood ('rescue marking').

Above: *Spitfire XVI TD242/ZF-E photographed in Germany after the end of the war, displaying the standard layout of markings. The late Mk XVI variant with low rear fuselage and all-round vision canopy was favoured by higher ranking pilots and TD242 was no exception, being usually flown by the 'A' Flight commander – initially F/Lt Zbigniew Kobierzycki and then F/Lt Edward Jaworski. The black badge of No. 308 Squadron is often difficult to spot. Note the trace of the overpainted Sky band around the rear fuselage.*

Right: *Sgt Zygmunt Malinowski by Spitfire XVI TD242/ZF-E. Note the squadron badge under the windscreen and the broken yellow line around the cockpit hood. The yellow 'line' around the cockpit door is very widely spaced, with just three yellow dots per side!*

Spitfire XVI TB889/JH-T, No. 317 Squadron, Varrelbusch (Germany), May–August 1945. Upper surface camouflage colours: Ocean Grey and Dark Green ('A' pattern); under surface colour: Medium Sea Grey. Standard British national markings. No. 317 Sqn badge below the windscreen, facing forward on both sides of the fuselage. Polish national marking on both sides of forward fuselage, with 'POLAND' stencil underneath. Aircraft letter possibly applied in black below the propeller spinner. Broken yellow line around the cockpit hood and door ('rescue marking').

Spitfire XVI TB889/JH-T in 1945. The small size 'C1' roundel can be seen on top of the wing, applied on fresh camouflage where the old 'B' roundel had been overpainted. Note traces of an obliterated earlier code under the aircraft letter T (the Spitfire had already seen service with Nos. 74 and 340 Sqns). It is interesting that No. 317 Sqn badge has been applied under the cockpit but the Polish AF chequered square on the engine cowling has not (the side cowling panel might be a replacement item). The Spitfire was coded JH-T until mid-September, being usually flown by the 'B' Flight commander F/Lt Bronisław Mach.

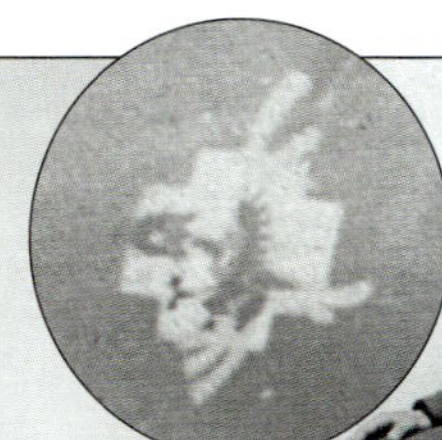

Sgt Włodzimierz Roszak (a veteran of Polish resistance, visiting friends in the Polish wing) posing on the Spitfire, with No. 317 Squadron badge under the windscreen shown to advantage.

Sgt Krzysztof Pawlik with Spitfire XVI TB889 (after it had been re-coded JH-Y). The Polish national insignia can be seen on the engine cowling.

Spitfire XVI TD240/WX-V, No. 302 Squadron, Varrelbusch (Germany), June–July 1945. Upper surface camouflage colours: Ocean Grey and Dark Green ('A' pattern); under surface colour: Medium Sea Grey. Standard British national markings. No. 302 Sqn badge below the windscreen, on both sides of the fuselage. Polish national marking on both sides of forward fuselage, with 'POLAND' stencil underneath. 'Boxing dog' (personal emblem of G/Cpt Aleksander Gabszewicz) retained from the time when the Spitfire was used by the OC No. 131 Wing.

Spitfire XVI TD240/WX-V had earlier been the personal mount of G/Cpt Aleksander Gabszewicz, OC No. 131 Wing, bearing his personalised code of SZ-G and 'boxing dog' cartoon. After G/Cpt Gabszewicz left No. 131 Wing, in mid-June 1945 TD240 became the personal mount of S/Ldr Bolesław Kaczmarek, commanding No. 302 Sqn. It was duly re-coded WX-V and No. 302 Sqn badge was applied under the windscreen in place of the G/Cpt pennant, but the 'boxing dog' emblem was retained.

Detailed view of G/Cpt Gabszewicz's personal motif on TD240. It adorned all Spitfire IXs and XVIs allocated for his personal use between 1943 and 1945, its form slightly different on each of these aeroplanes. The emblem, inspired by a popular cartoon, was designed by Sgt Wojciech Milewski, ground crew member of No. 316 Sqn and then No. 131 Wing. Milewski was also a talented sportsman and represented the Polish Air Force in international boxing competitions. Tragically, he was killed in late April 1945 in an encounter of No. 131 Wing ground troops with marauding Germans.

Spitfire XVI TB990/QH-K, No. 302 Squadron, Ahlhorn (Germany)-Hethel (UK), August 1945–December 1946. Upper surface camouflage colours: Ocean Grey and Dark Green ('A' pattern); under surface colour: Medium Sea Grey. Standard British national markings. No. 302 Sqn badge below the windscreen, on both sides of the fuselage. Polish national marking on both sides of forward fuselage, with 'POLAND' stencil underneath. Serial number applied in large characters at the under surface of both wings, but obliterated on the fuselage. Broken yellow line around the cockpit hood and door ('rescue marking').

Spitfire XVI TB990/QH-K, the personal mount of S/Ldr Jerzy Szymankiewicz, commanding No. 302 Sqn, photographed at Ahlhorn. No. 302 Sqn badge can be seen on one of the poles seen beyond the wingtip of the Spitfire, where the outdoor dance floor has been decorated for festivities, probably during Squadron Day celebrations (28 July 1946). The 'Q' in squadron codes was applied incorrectly on both sides of the fuselage (this error was seen on a number of Spitfires, as the letter 'Q' is not used in Polish). It seems the serial number on this aircraft has been obliterated, but available documents show that TB990 was the only Spitfire ever coded QH-K.

Two ground crew members of No. 303 Sqn pose with TB990/QH-K (LAC Zbigniew Więckowicz is seated on the tailplane), probably at RAF Hethel in late 1946. Delivered to No. 302 Sqn at the end of May 1945, TB990 was initially coded WX-M and the rectangular patch where the M had been overpainted can be seen clearly beneath the K code letter.

Other Spitfire/Seafire variants

Polish squadrons that fought alongside the RAF used five basic variants of the Spitfire. Mks I, II and V were described in the previous volume, while Mks IX and XVI are covered in the preceding chapters of this volume. However, Polish pilots posted to non-Polish units flew virtually every other series-produced variant of the Spitfire and Seafire, and they also test-flew some prototypes and experimental variants. This is a vast subject, and only a relatively brief overview can be offered here. All these aircraft were painted in regulation RAF/FAA camouflages and markings.

Spitfire F.VI was the first high-altitude variant of the Spitfire fitted with a pressurised cockpit. BR579 was delivered from No. 33 MU at Lyneham to No. 124 Squadron at Gravesend on 19 July 1942 by Sgt Stanisław Słowikowski, at the time serving with No. 1 Aircraft Delivery Flight RAF based at Croydon. This photograph depicts the Spitfire in No. 124 Sqn service in standard Day Fighter camouflage scheme with the usual Fighter Command markings. It is likely that during Sgt Słowikowski's ferry flight the aircraft was already adorned with the 'ON' unit code and only the aircraft letter was added upon delivery.

Spitfire F.VII was the ultimate pressurised fighter version optimised for high-altitude operations. MD124 was flown by S/Ldr Janusz Żurakowski at the AAEE between April and June 1945 on temperature measurement flights and other air tests. The Spitfire was finished in the High Altitude Fighter scheme of Medium Sea Grey on all upper surfaces and PRU Blue on under surfaces, with red-and-blue fuselage roundel and fin flash.

Poles in RAF and Allied Fighter Squadrons

A number of Spitfire versions were flown by Polish AF pilots with non-Polish squadrons.

F/O Julian Żuromski flew the pressurised Mk VI with No. 66 Squadron RAF in June 1943.

The Mk VIII was mostly used by overseas RAF and Commonwealth squadrons, and it was in these that Polish pilots used them on operations. As mentioned before, in mid-1943 three Polish pilots were posted to RAF units in the Mediterranean, eventually to take command of a flight or squadron. Between July and October 1943 they flew Spitfire VIIIs with Nos. 43 (S/Ldr Horbaczewski), 145 (F/Lt Drecki) and 601 (S/Ldr Skalski and F/Lt Drecki) Squadrons. Then in 1944 a number of pilots of No. 318 Sqn were attached to non-Polish units in the area. They flew Mk VIIIs with Nos. 92, 145, 241, 417 Squadrons.

Surprisingly, some of the Polish pilots attached in 1944 to No. 601 Sqn RAF (equipped with Spitfire IXs at the time) also flew operational sorties in Seafire IIs of No. 807 Sqn FAA when the FAA unit was transferred ashore and its aircraft pooled with the Spitfires for joint operations.

Two Griffon-engined Spitfire variants were also flown operationally by Polish AF pilots.

F/Os Jerzy Polak and Jerzy Solak both served with No. 41 Sqn on Mk XIIs. The latter was the sole Polish AF pilot credited with victories scored on Griffon-engined Spitfires. Some Mk XIIs were also flown by Polish pilots in second-line squadrons (including No. 595) on target-towing duties.

Polish pilots flew Spitfire FR.XIVs on operations with fighter-reconnaissance units of the 2nd TAF: Nos. 2, 16 and 268 Squadrons (the latter two were in fact one unit: No. 268 Sqn was renumbered No. 16 in September 1945).

Spitfire VIII JG204 was test flown by F/Lt Zbigniew Kobierzycki with Vickers in October 1943. The aircraft was finished in the Desert scheme of Dark Earth and Middle Stone on upper surfaces and presumably Azure underneath.

Mk VIII MT571 following a crash landing in India on 6 November 1945 during a ferry flight by W/O Kazimierz Jarnutowski of No. 36 Staging Post. The Spitfire was in the Temperate Land scheme of Dark Earth and Dark Green on upper surfaces. The under surfaces were probably in Sky. The British national markings were in line with the late-wartime standard in that theatre: the small-size roundels featured pale blue in place of red, as did the fin flash. There were also additional quick recognition bands in white on the wings and fin.

Spitfire XII EN224 was test flown by F/L Zbigniew Oleński at the RAE Farnborough in January 1943. The aircraft was in the standard Fighter Command finish: Dark Green and Ocean Grey on top, Medium Sea Grey underneath, with Sky spinner and rear-fuselage band. At the time of writing this Spitfire has been in the final stages of restoration to airworthiness, the sole Mk XII to fly in the foreseeable future.

The sole Spitfire VIII Trainer was in a rather unusual finish when it was tested at the AAEE by S/Ldr Żurakowski in March 1947. The aeroplane was painted bright yellow overall (this photo was taken using a colour filter that rendered warm hues unnaturally dark) with black propeller. Its only identification (rather the RAF serial number MT818) was the civil registration (notably, the Spitfire is still airworthy today, registered again as G-AIDN).

Non-operational Flying

Polish pilots performed test flights of various Spitfires at experimental establishments, production plants and maintenance units.

F/Lt Zbigniew Kobierzycki was a Vickers test pilot between September and December 1943, flying trials on a number of prototype and production Spitfires.

Spitfire XII MB858/EB-D of No. 41 Sqn, shown in the background here, was flown on operations with that unit by F/O Jerzy Solak in September 1943. MB882 (the last production Mk XII) had been test-flown by F/Lt Kobierzycki with Vickers in October 1943, before it was delivered to the RAF. The aircraft were in the standard Fighter Command colour scheme.

Pilots of the exiled Polish Air Force worked at both the Royal Aircraft Establishment at Farnborough and the Aeroplane and Armament Experimental Establishment at Boscombe Down. Probably the most famous among them was S/Ldr Janusz Żurakowski, who completed a course at the Empire Test Pilots School between March and December 1944 and then test flew a variety of aircraft types at the AAEE between January 1945 and June 1947. Throughout that period he was a Polish Air Force officer (he subsequently worked with distinction as a test pilot for many more years, but that is beyond the scope of this book, as he was no longer in Polish service). Fortunately, his flying log books were preserved and copies made available to researchers, allowing detailed study of his test-flying. While with the AAEE he flew various examples of the Spitfire VII, IX, XIV, XVI, 18, 21, 22, 24, Seafire III, XV, XVII fighters and the sole Spitfire VIII Trainer (he also test flew unarmed PR Spitfires during that time). Other notable Polish pilots at the AAEE included F/Lts Jan Pełka and Józef Regulski who test flew late Griffon-engined Seafires, such as the Mk 46, among others.

A number of other notable Polish pilots flew with the RAE at Farnborough throughout the war, including S/Ldrs Roland Kalpas and Zbigniew Oleński, and F/Lts Tadeusz Ciastuła and Kazimierz Kazimierczuk. They test flew a variety of Spitfire and Seafire variants, including the pressure-cockpit Spitfire VI and VII (in prototype and production form), the Griffon-engined Spitfire XII, XIV and 21, and the Seafire II and III.

Spitfire XIV RB146 was test flown at the AAEE by at least two Polish pilots. The flying log book of S/Ldr Janusz Żurakowski has five test flight entries for the aircraft between March 1945 and January 1946. F/Lt Antoni Majcherczyk suffered an engine failure while test flying the Spitfire on 8 October 1945, but managed to make a normal landing. This is another example of a RAF fighter tested at the AAEE in standard Fighter Command colours and markings.

Polish pilots ferried most variants of the Spitfire and Seafire, both in Britain and overseas. They ferried these aircraft both with RAF units and with the Air Transport Auxiliary. Available data show that the following fighter variants of the Spitfire/Seafire family (other than those discussed in previous chapters) were ferried by Polish Air Force pilots between 1940 and 1947: Spitfire VI, VII, VIII, XII, XIV, 18, 21, 22, Seafire I, II, III, XV, XVII.

The first production Spitfire 21, LA187, was finished in the High Altitude Fighter scheme and featured the pointed wing tips that were subsequently not fitted in the standard production aircraft. S/Ldr Żurakowski flew it no fewer than fifteen times on various trials between April and July 1945.

Spitfire XVIII(18) NH872 was test flown at the AAEE by S/Ldr Żurakowski in August 1945, after it was fitted with the enlarged rudder, as shown here.

Spitfire 21 LA262 probably looked like in this photo (less code letters, of course) when it was delivered by air to No. 33 MU at Lyneham on 4 May 1945 by Jerzy Drzewiecki of No. 2 Ferry Pool ATA. This photo was taken in No. 1 Sqn RAF, which received the Spitfire from No. 33 MU. Production Mk 21s were finished in standard Fighter Command camouflage and markings. The application of serial number in small size just above the fin flash on all three Mk 21s shown here is noteworthy (note also that the last Spitfire in the line-up is an example of the previous variant used by the unit: LF.IX MK515/JX-N).

A rare colour photo of Seafire IIC MB244/6Q of No. 899 Squadron FAA aboard HMS Indomitable *in the spring of 1943. The aircraft was originally delivered, factory-fresh, to No. 15 MU at Wroughton by 1st/Off Anna Leska of 15 Ferry Pool ATA in November 1942. It was delivered from that unit to No. 899 Sqn a month later. Presumably the only alteration to its finish during that period was the application of the code, 6Q, in red. The Seafire was in standard Temperate Sea camouflage on upper surfaces: Extra Dark Sea Grey and Dark Slate Grey, with the under surfaces in Sky.*

Seafire III NN333 in Temperate Sea camouflage with Sky under surface, without any markings except the roundels and fin flash. F/Lt Zbigniew Kobierzycki test flew the aircraft at Worthy Down on 23 October 1943 before it was delivered to the Royal Navy. Five months later, on 18 March 1944, 1st/Off Anna Leska ferried the Seafire from Lyneham to Henstridge.

Spitfire 22 PK408 was tested extensively by S/Ldr Żurakowski between February and June 1947. During that time he flew it on 32 occasions, at least 23 of these involving various bomb trials.

Supermarine Spitfire VIII JF447/UF-7, No. 601 Squadron RAF, Lentini West (Sicily), August 1943. Upper surface camouflage colours: Dark Earth and Middle Stone ('A' pattern); under surface colour: probably Azure. Standard British national markings. No. 601 Sqn badge in a white disc above the fin flash (its typical position at the time). Codes probably in Sky with a narrow black outline.

Spitfire VIII JF447/UF-7 was occasionally flown on operations in August 1943 by S/Ldr Stanisław Skalski, commanding No. 601 Sqn at the time. The Desert scheme camouflage was factory-applied on early Mk VIIIs (note the neat division between the upper and bottom surface colours on the nose, slightly below the panel line). The extended, pointed wing tips were standard on all early Mk VIIIs. The 'Winged Sword' emblem of No. 601 Sqn (referring to the coat of arms of London), was red on a white disc. It is noteworthy that the serial number was applied with gloss paint.

Seafire XV NS490, Aeroplane and Armament Experimental Establishment, Boscombe Down, January–March 1945. Upper surface camouflage colours: Extra Dark Sea Grey and Dark Slate Grey ('A' pattern); under surface colour: probably yellow. Standard British national markings. Prototype marking (capital P in a ring, in yellow) on both sides of the fuselage.

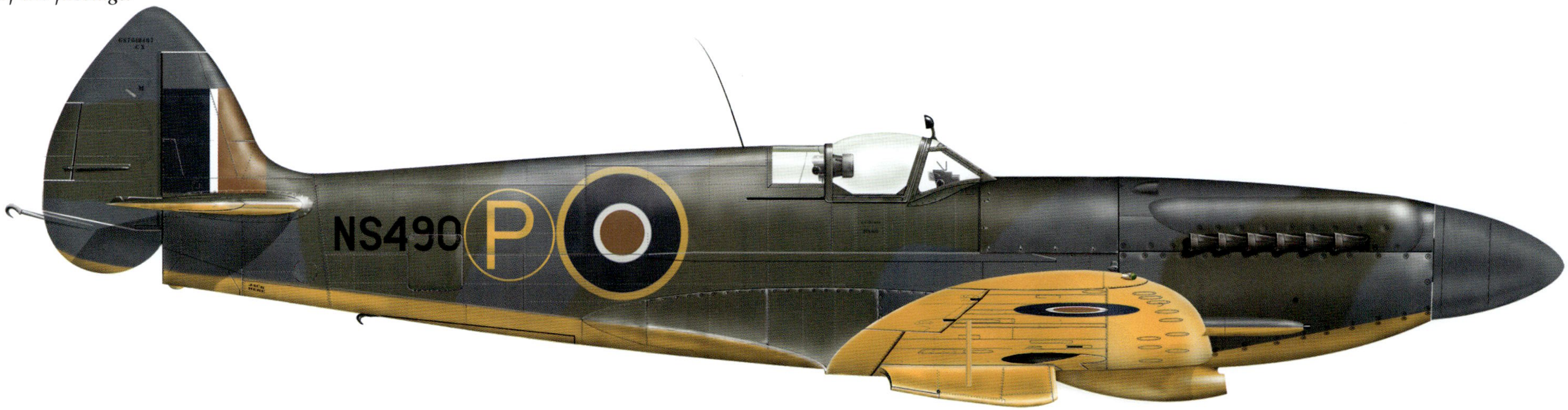

Seafire NS490 was one of the relatively few Supermarine fighters built during WWII as experimental prototypes (most test aircraft were series production airframes assigned for development work). For this reason it was most probably finished in the prototype scheme, with the undersides painted yellow. The upper surfaces were presumably finished in the Temperate Sea scheme of Extra Dark Sea Grey and Dark Slate Grey (which usually gives very little contrast, if any, in black and white photos). When S/Ldr Janusz Żurakowski flew it between January and March 1945, NS490 was used for testing related to the newly designed arrestor hook for carrier landings, fitted in the bottom of the rudder, known as the 'sting-hook'. Żurakowski's flights did not involve landings with the hook extended, but tested various aspects of the aircraft's handling with the new device fitted.

Supermarine Spitfire FR.XIV RM795/T, No. 2 Squadron RAF, Gilze-Rijen (Holland), January–February 1945. Upper surface camouflage colours: Ocean Grey and Dark Green ('A' pattern); under surface colour: Medium Sea Grey. Standard British national markings.

RM795/T was flown occasionally by F/Lt Antoni Krąkowski, a Polish pilot of No. 2 Sqn in early 1945. In line with the 2nd TAF policy at the time, the propeller spinner (previously in Sky) had been repainted black and the rear fuselage band in Sky was overpainted with camouflage colours. It seems the upper camouflage on the rear fuselage extended unusually low. Unlike pure fighter squadrons, the fighter-reconaissance units of the 2nd TAF were not allocated letter codes at the time, and their aircraft displayed just the single aircraft letter.

The other side of the Spitfire, photographed a few months later, after it was re-allocated to No. 430 Squadron RCAF. It still retained the same aircraft letter, although a vertical stripe in a pale colour was added forward of the tail unit. This photo confirms that the camouflage on the rear fuselage extended markedly lower than was usual on Spitfires. It also shows the oblique camera port in the side of the fuselage, going through the roundel.

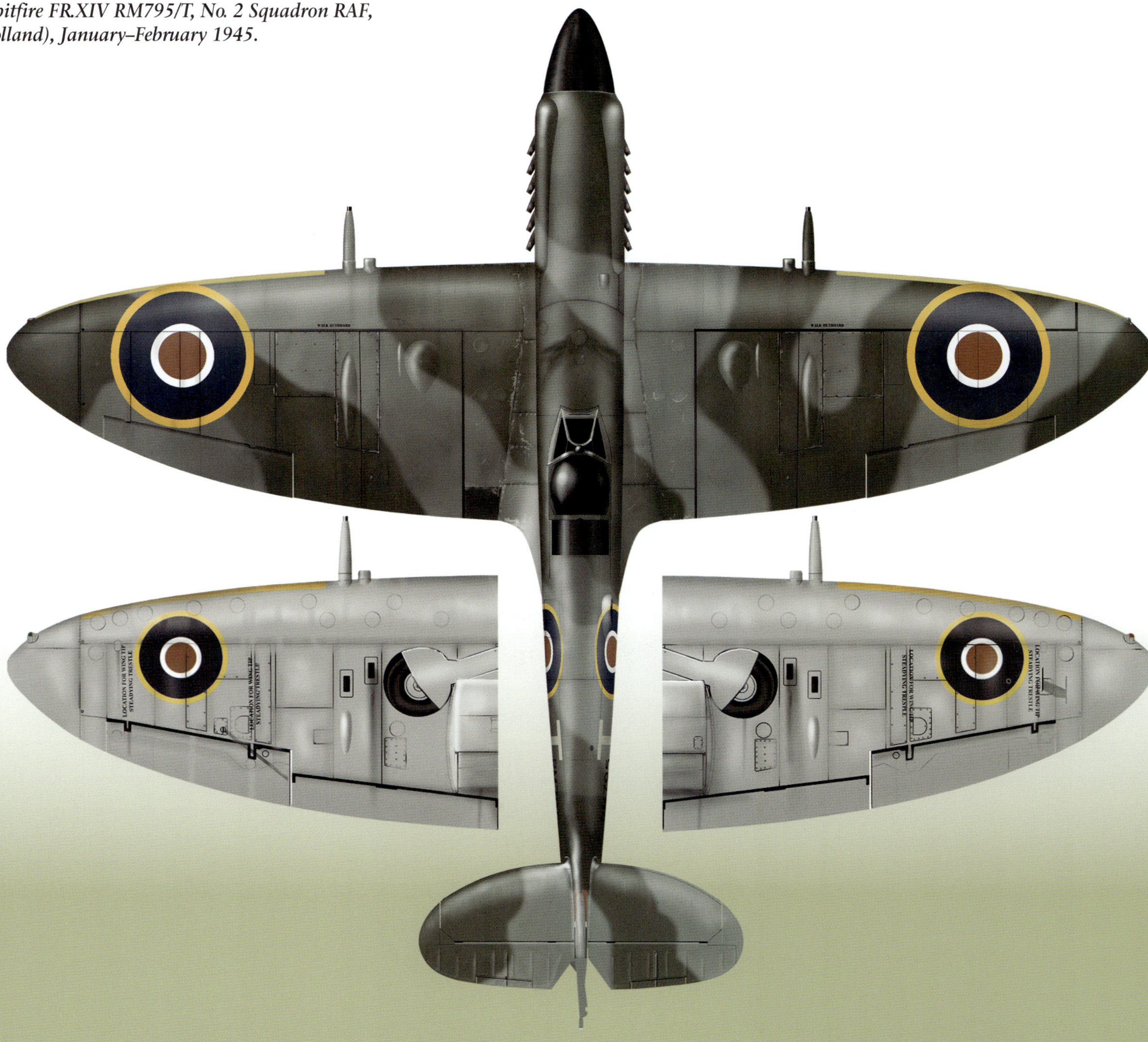

Supermarine Spitfire FR.XIV RM795/T, No. 2 Squadron RAF,
Gilze-Rijen (Holland), January–February 1945.

North American Mustang I

Polish Squadrons

The Mustang I (the XP-51 in the USAAF) was the only Allison-engined variant of the type used by the Polish Air Force. No. 309 Squadron flew these aircraft in 1942–1943 on fighter-reconnaissance duties, and then briefly in late 1944 when converting from Hurricanes to Mustang IIIs.

In 1944–1945 other Polish fighter squadrons equipped with Merlin-engined variants of the Mustang used some Mk Is for conversion training on the type and as hacks.

Altogether about 50 Mustang Is were used by No. 309 Squadron between June 1942 and December 1944 plus about six more by Polish Mustang III/IV squadrons in 1944 and 1945. Unlike all subsequent variants of the type, Mustang Is were purchased by Britain directly from the makers in the USA, so they never had any USAAF serial numbers.

Three Mustang Is of No. 309 Squadron in flight. All three are in (nominal) Day Fighter scheme of Dark Green and Ocean Grey on upper surfaces, although the contrast between the two camouflage colours on the aircraft coded 'O' (possibly AG389) is markedly lower than that on 'D' (possibly AG435) and 'L' (possibly AG423). In 1942 Army Co-Operation Command stopped applying squadron codes on aircraft of its units, and No. 309 Squadron Mustangs displayed just the aircraft letter during 1942–1943 (as opposed to its Lysanders, which had used 'AR' code during 1940–1942). The camouflage pattern on all three aircraft matches the standard RAF 'A' scheme, as seen on British-built fighters. All Mustang Is were delivered to the RAF in the Temperate Land scheme of Dark Green and Dark Earth, and the latter was oversprayed with Ocean Grey (or a similar colour) in Britain. The Fighter Command quick recognition markings in Sky: the band around the rear fuselage and the propeller spinner, were also applied after delivery. Note the variation in the fuselage roundel position: rather forward and high on 'O', similarly forward but much lower on 'L' and much further aft on 'D'. The code letter aft of the cockpit and the Polish AF marking on the nose were applied in similar positions on each of the Mustangs.

No. 309 Squadron 'Czerwieńska Province'

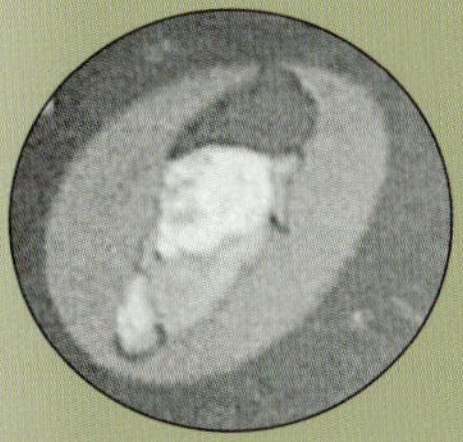

No. 309 Squadron started conversion to Mustang Is in the spring of 1942 while based at RAF Dunino (since its forming in 1940 it had been an army co-operation unit equipped with Westland Lysanders). The first two Mustangs were delivered at the beginning of June. Initially only the 'B' Flight re-equipped with these fighter-reconnaissance aircraft, while the rest of the squadron retained the now obsolete Lysanders. In July 1942 the Mustang-equipped 'B' Flight moved to Dalcross.

F/O Wincenty Miniszewski on a No. 309 Sqn Mustang which shows four 'V' mission markings below the Polish insignia. For some reason the Mustang-equipped 'B' Flight became known as the 'Dwarves' in the squadron and the personal marking on this aeroplane was probably linked with the nickname.

F/O Janusz Lewkowicz with Mustang I AG648/E. Note that the fuselage roundel on this aeroplane was even further aft, nearly touching the Sky band. The dark colour of the spinner and almost indistinguishable colour division lines on upper surfaces might indicate that at the time of the photo AG648 was still in Temperate Land. In the early period Mustangs of No. 309 Sqn were marked with the Polish AF chequered square without adding the word 'POLAND'. Lewkowicz (who had a degree in aircraft design) calculated that the Mustang could fly to Norway and back with enough fuel reserve to complete an operational mission, but his report failed to get through the British bureaucratic machine. On 27 September 1942, when he was supposed to fly a 'weather test', he completed a sortie across the North Sea, attacking opportunity targets near Stavanger in Norway and returning safely. This earned him a reprimand for unauthorised action but prompted the RAF to undertake Mustang missions across the North Sea in due course.

At the end of 1942 the Mustang flight of No. 309 Sqn was declared operational and moved to RAF Gatwick, coming under control of No. 35 Wing RAF. Their first operational sortie was flown on 5 December, this being the first ever operational mission of No. 309 Squadron. At the end of December 1942 the 'B' Flight rejoined the rest of the squadron at RAF Findo Gask. This airfield proved unsuitable for the Mustangs, however, so these moved to RAF Kirknewton.

In the spring of 1943 it was decided to reform No. 309 Sqn as an all-Mustang unit: the 'C' Flight was disbanded while the 'A' Flight replaced its Lysanders with the North American type. This involved substantial reorganisation, with all of the Lysander observers and some pilots posted to other units, while pilots experienced in flying high speed single-seat fighters were posted in.

In June 1943 No. 309 Squadron moved to RAF Snailwell and commenced tactical reconnaissance missions over Holland. Towards the end of 1943 the Mustang's Allison engines were becoming more and more troublesome, suffering from frequent failures. Despite efforts of Allison and RAF engineers these problems could not be cured satisfactorily and in February 1944 the unit started conversion onto Hawker Hurricanes (see vol. 1).

Right: F/Lt Tadeusz Żeligowski enters one of the last Mustang Is of No. 309 Squadron in late 1944. Note that at the time, following the unit's transfer to Fighter Command, a new squadron code was applied on the aircraft: 'WC'.

Above: Engine mechanics at work. At some point the word 'POLAND' started to be added to the Polish insignia. It was applied above it, probably to avoid overpainting the mission markings. In this case the 'V' symbols were much narrower.

During 1944–1945 several Mustang Is were used as trainers and hacks by Polish fighter squadrons equipped with Merlin-engined Mustangs. These were coded with digits ('6' being the highest one known from documents) and no squadron codes, as they were probably pooled at wing level. This is AM126/5 at Andrews Field, taxiing among No. 306 Sqn Mustang IIIs. The aircraft is in Day Fighter camouflage ('C' pattern).

Before No. 309 commenced operations on Mustang Is, a number of its pilots were attached to No. 26 Sqn RAF to gain experience on the type. On 13 August 1942 P/O Roman Jarema flew offensive recce to Abbeville-Drucat area in AG535/RM-E. This photo was taken in March 1943, by which time the 'RM' unit code had been obliterated. Not long afterwards the Mustang was seriously damaged in an accident. Following repairs and a period of storage at 20 MU, on 7 October 1943 1st/Off Anna Leska, a Polish ATA girl, ferried this Mustang from Aston Down to No. 4 Sqn RAF at Funtington, and then on to Odiham, as the unit was just moving between these two RAF stations.

In mid-September 1944 at RAF Drem No. 309 Squadron commenced a reverse change, replacing its Hurricanes with Mustang Is, but in early October 1944 the unit was notified that it would soon become a purely fighter one, equipped with Mustang IIIs. A few fighter-type operations were flown on Mk Is in late October and in November 1944, however.

Other Units

During spring and summer 1942 a number of Polish pilots from No. 309 Sqn were attached to No. 26 Sqn to gain experience on Mustang Is. A number of Mustang Is were flown in trials by Polish test pilots with the Royal Aircraft Establishment at Farnborough and the Aeroplane and Armament Experimental Establishment at Boscombe Down. Mustang Is were also flown by Polish pilots during training at No. 41 OTU, and by Polish ferry pilots.

Mustang I AM130 was tested by the RAE at Farnborough and the AAEE at Boscombe Down in 1943. F/Lt Zbigniew Oleński flew performance trials in it at Farnborough on 7 July 1943. Subsequently, on 6 August 1943 at the AAEE F/O Antoni Majcherczyk suffered an engine failure during a test flight of this aircraft and was forced to crash-land it. The pilot was uninjured, but the aircraft was badly damaged and eventually struck off charge. The Mustang was finished in Temperate Land scheme on upper surfaces (including a Dark Earth propeller spinner), with prototype yellow under surfaces (rendered unusually dark in this photo due to use of orthochromatic film and/or colour filter). It was presumably also marked with the 'P in ring' prototype marking on the fuselage. Note that the nose gun was removed and the port faired over. The '/G' that followed the serial number meant that the aircraft included sensitive equipment and therefore required special security while on the ground.

North American Mustang I AM213/D, No. 309 Squadron, August 1942–May 1943. Upper surface camouflage colours: Ocean Grey and Dark Green ('A' pattern); under surface colour: Medium Sea Grey. Standard British national markings. Polish national marking on both sides of forward fuselage, with 'POLAND' stencil above.

Mustang I AM213/D. Note the style of the code letter D and the position of the roundel, very far aft on the fuselage. When the squadron used Mustangs in 1942–1943 it was part of Army Co-Operation Command and then of the 2nd TAF and therefore, typically for a fighter-reconnaissance unit in that period, its aircraft carried no squadron code, just the aircraft letter.

North American Mustang I AP170/WC-M, No. 309 Squadron, October 1944. Upper surface camouflage colours: Ocean Grey and Dark Green ('B' pattern); under surface colour: Medium Sea Grey. Standard British national markings. Polish national marking on both sides of forward fuselage, with 'POLAND' stencil above.

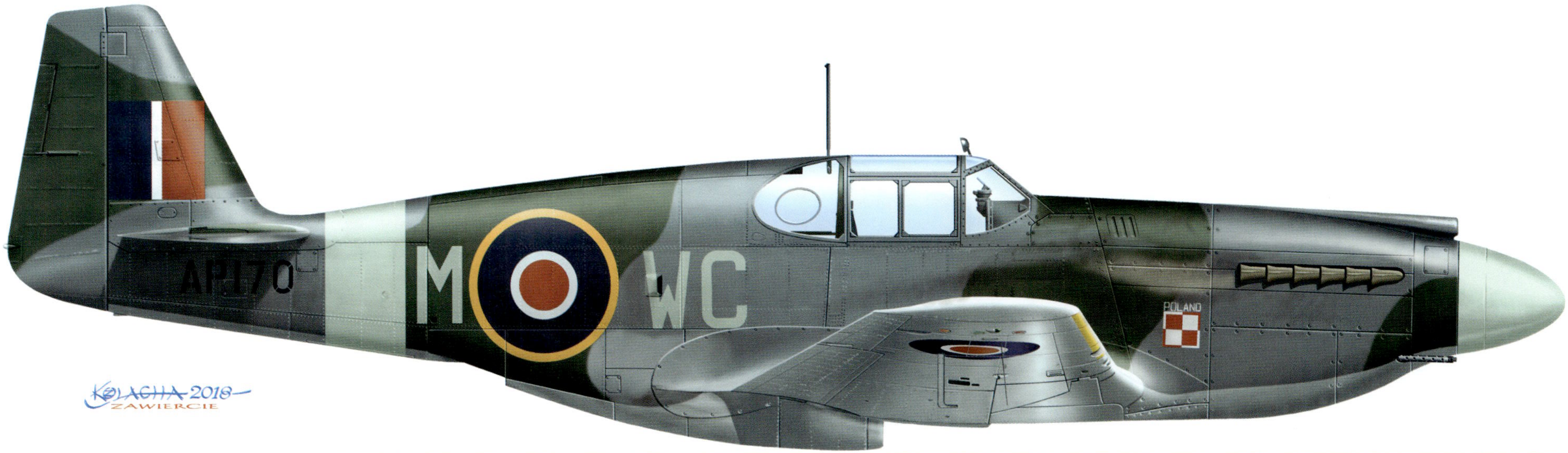

Three pilots of No. 309 Squadron, left to right: F/Os Mieczysław Befinger, Jan Mozołowski and Stanisław Zajchowski, by the side of Mustang I AP170/WC-M. When Mustang Is' were re-introduced in the squadron in late 1944, they were adorned with the unit code (WC), typically for Fighter Command. Note that the fuselage roundel is positioned much further forward, leaving enough space for the aircraft letter aft of it.

North American Mustang III

Polish Squadrons

The 2nd Polish Wing, known as No. 133 Wing in the 2nd TAF, replaced its Spitfire Vs with Mustang IIIs (P-51B and P-51C aircraft delivered to the RAF under Lend-Lease, via USAAF inventory), while still at Heston, at the end of March 1944. Upon its move to an advanced ground at Coolham, conversion training continued. At the new airfield the Wing, previously made up of just two Polish squadrons, Nos. 306 and 315, was joined by No. 129 Squadron RAF. At the same time No. 316 Sqn, technically reporting to the 3rd Polish Wing, also converted to Mustang IIIs, its main role being to accept newly trained pilots straight out of operational training units and prepare them for service with No. 133 Wing.

In late 1944 No. 316 replaced No. 315 Sqn in the wing, and then No. 309 joined it, replacing No. 129 Sqn RAF. Thus No. 133 Wing finally became an all-Polish one. At the beginning of 1945 Nos. 315 and 316 exchanged places once more. From then on Nos. 306, 309 and 315 Sqns continued to operate as one wing until the disbandment of Polish units at the end of 1946 (at the beginning of August No. 133 Wing was disbanded, and from then on the three squadrons were known simply as the Coltishall Wing). From April 1945 No. 316 Squadron, together with No. 303 Sqn on Mustang IVs, formed the 3rd Polish Wing.

Altogether, the four Polish squadrons (Nos. 306, 309, 315 and 316) used over 400 Mustang IIIs between early 1944 and the end of 1946.

Brand new Mustang IIIs delivered to the RAF (including those used by Polish AF squadrons) were finished in one of three distinctively different camouflage patterns. The 'A' pattern, as shown here on SZ-M of No. 316 Sqn (possibly HB882) in mid-1944, was the standard RAF 'A' scheme as applied to British-built fighters. It was the only one of the three schemes in which the cockpit was surrounded by Dark Green on both sides. In black and white photos Dark Green shows as a darker colour than Ocean Grey, regardless of the type of negative and/or filters used. The Mustang in this photo displays the quick recognition markings applied to avoid confusion with the Messerschmitt 109: broad white bands across the wing root and the horizontal tail surfaces plus white nose including the spinner.

This aircraft, FB185/UZ-U, is shown soon after delivery to No. 306 Squadron in April 1944 (it was soon written off, after a take-off accident of F/O Marian Wędzik on 20 May). This Mustang was finished in the 'B' scheme which used the same pattern as the 'A' scheme, but with the colours transposed (Dark Green replacing Ocean Grey and vice versa). The white Mustang quick recognition markings can also be seen here. Initially the latter also included a similar white band applied horizontally across the fin and rudder above the fin flash, and traces of this band can be discerned on this aeroplane. This marking was abandoned in late March 1944, before any Polish unit re-equipped with the type.

The 'C' pattern, as shown here on KH507/UZ-Ż of No. 306 and KH485/ PK-R of No. 315 Sqn, was somewhat similar to the 'B' pattern, but colour division lines on the fuselage and wings were generally more diagonal and less winding. The pattern on the vertical tail was quite different. Both photos were taken in April 1945 – note that KH507/UZ-Ż still featured the white nose quick recognition marking while KH485/PK-R lacked it. UZ-Ż was the personal mount of S/Ldr Józef Żulikowski, who had the aircraft letter changed into his initial by adding a dot above it (compare his personal Spitfire F.IX BS456 UZ-Ż on pp. 298–299).

The variety of 'standard' schemes often led to 'mixed' patterns when Mustang IIIs were repainted, partly or completely, in squadron service. This No. 306 Squadron aircraft coded UZ-U (serial number unknown), photographed in October 1944, combines the 'A' scheme on the fuselage with the 'B' pattern on the vertical tail. Note the badly worn condition of the aircraft and the final form of the invasion bands, applied to the bottom fuselage only. In this view the white Mustang recognition marking on the nose is shown to advantage.

Yet another UZ-U, photographed after the war (note the red spinner tip squadron marking). Although its camouflage pattern might look similar to the 'B' or 'C' scheme at first, it was in fact quite different, particularly on the tail. Note also that (even allowing for the orthochromatic rendition of colours) the blue rings of the roundels (and particularly that on the wing) look very faded (as opposed to the blue stripe of the fin flash). Such extensive fading of the blue in upper wing roundels was not unusual.

Another example of a non-standard scheme probably resulting from squadron-level repainting: No. 309 Sqn Mustang III coded WC-W (possibly FB385). The finish of the aircraft looks very worn, with paint peeling off particularly badly on the fin and around the propeller.

By mid-1945 more and more Mustang IIIs had had their camouflage removed and were being flown in natural metal finish. This No. 309 Sqn scene in the summer 1945 includes two camouflaged and two NFM Mustangs, with FZ184/WC-C in the foreground.

Most wing-level commanders of Polish Mustang units used their initials as personalised code letters. This is Mustang III HB866/JZ of W/Cdr Jan Zumbach with his personal score and the Wing Commander's pennant applied below the cockpit.

Unlike his colleagues, W/Cdr Tadeusz Sawicz never used his initials on his Spitfires nor Mustangs. Instead, he used SZ-K as his personal code, these being his 'lucky' letters from the time when he was a flight commander with No. 316 Sqn back in 1941–1942 (see p. 323). Incidentally, when he commanded the 3rd Polish Wing after the war, No. 316 Sqn was part of it. Nevertheless, the 'WingCo's SZ-K differed in its appearance from the aircraft of the squadron, not only by the Wing Commander's pennant below the windscreen, but also by the absence of the red-white striping on the nose. Notably, this particular SZ-K was HB886, previously used by G/Cpt Nowierski with the code letters TN (see pp. 362–363).

No. 306 Squadron 'City of Toruń'

The squadron converted from Spitfire Vs to Mustang IIIs in March/April 1944 as part of No. 133 Wing. The re-equipment commenced at RAF Heston, when the unit received its first two Mustangs on 26 March. On 1 April it moved to Coolham ALG, where the re-equipment was completed and the first operation on Mustangs was flown on 29 April. Throughout May and June the unit was mostly engaged in fighter sweeps and ground attack operations in preparation for, and then in support of the allied landing in Normandy. On 22 June the squadron moved to Holmesley South and five days later to RAF Ford. The same pattern of operations continued until 9 July when the squadron (and the entire No. 133 Wing) moved to Brenzett ALG.

This movement was connected with re-allocation of the wing to air defence duties against 'Divers', this being the code-name for the German V1 'buzz bombs'. No. 306 Sqn continued to fly anti-V1 patrols until early September 1944. Afterwards the squadron returned to offensive operations, mainly consisting in escort missions for heavy bombers attacking targets on the Continent. Between 17 and 22 September 1944 the wing, including No. 306 Squadron, flew patrols over the battlefield area of the operation 'Market-Garden' airborne landings.

FZ144/UZ-F was one of very few Mustang IIIs used by Polish Squadrons with the original early 'birdcage' canopies. It is shown here preparing for a ground attack mission over Normandy in June 1944. Note the very roughly applied D-Day bands, with the paint badly peeling off.

The two non-regulation markings of No. 306 Sqn as applied on Mustangs after the end of hostilities: the traditional 'Toruń Duck' squadron emblem and the forward portion of the propeller spinner finished in red. S/Ldr Józef Jeka is posing in front of FZ128/UZ-A at Coltishall. Note a small part of the last digit of the underwing serial visible on the main wheel cover.

On 11 October 1944 the squadron, and the entire wing, moved to RAF Andrews Field. From then until the end of the war the main effort was to escort heavy bombers during daylight raids into Germany. The *Luftwaffe* continued to be encountered in these missions as at the time the majority of the German air force was concentrated to defend the home territory of the Reich from air attacks. Apart from direct bomber escort missions, Polish Mustangs also flew sweeps over German territory, hunting for any German aircraft, attacking airfields and other targets of opportunity.

In March 1945 the squadron briefly resumed anti-V1 patrols, but these were discontinued in the second half of the month. The squadron, and the entire No. 133 Wing, continued to be based at Andrews Field until mid-1945.

On 10 August it moved, along with the rest of the wing, to RAF Coltishall, where it was then based until disbandment in December 1946.

P/O Zygmunt Kawnik with FX920/UZ-Z. Both the squadron badge near the cockpit and the Polish national marking on the nose were applied on white background on this aircraft. Somewhat oddly for a NMF machine, the word 'POLAND' below the chequered square was applied in white rather than red. Note that on this Mustang the under-wing serial was applied in a different position, and parts of two digits (92) can be seen on the undercarriage cover.

No. 309 Squadron 'Czerwieńska Province'

No. 309 Sqn received its first Mustang IIIs in late October at RAF Drem and in November it moved to RAF Peterhead, where it completed the conversion from Mustang Is. In early December it moved again, this time to RAF Andrews Field, where it joined No. 133 Wing. Its subsequent operations and moves were similar to those of No. 306.

In March and April 1945 there were occasional encounters with German jets and the squadron had the distinction of downing some Me 262s. From 10 August 1945 until disbandment in December 1946 the squadron was based at RAF Coltishall.

Above: *S/Ldr Henryk Pietrzak with his personal Mustang III FB380 WC-A, displaying the later 'broad' code style (compare KH574/WC-A of S/Ldr Głowacki with the early-style codes, on p. 364). On camouflaged aircraft the squadron badge was applied in the 'pale' version...*

... while the 'dark' version was used on NMF aircraft,such as FX876/WC-D here. Unlike any other Polish Mustang squadron, No. 309 applied this badge on the port side only.

W/O Antoni Murkowski photographed in the cockpit of his personal Mustang III, most probably FB385 WC-W. The pilot's score of Luftwaffe *manned aircraft and V1s was applied on the side of the fuselage next to the squadron badge.*

No. 315 Squadron 'Dęblin'

Like No. 306, No. 315 Squadron re-equipped with Mustang IIIs in March/April 1944. It received its first four Mustangs on 28 March at RAF Heston. On 1 April it moved, with the entire No. 133 Wing, to Coolham ALG, where the re-equipment was completed. The first operation on Mustangs was flown on 26 April. With the entire wing, the squadron was engaged in fighter sweeps and ground attack operations in preparation for the allied landing in France and then in support of the invading forces on the Normandy beachhead. On 22 June the squadron moved to Holmesley South ALG and on the 26th later to RAF Ford.

On 9 July the squadron moved to Brenzett ALG and from there it undertook anti-'Diver' patrols until early September 1944. There were, however, occasional offensive operations as well, and two of these were particularly noteworthy. On 30 July 1944 No. 315 Sqn flew its first operation across the North Sea to Norway and in the resulting combat six Mustangs were credited with

No. 315 Sqn Mustang III FB353/PK-H during a mission across the North Sea. The scoreboard and mission log below the cockpit are in the style of No. 316 Sqn, because the Mustang was one of a number transferred from the latter unit in October 1944. For some reason the new owners have obliterated No. 316 Sqn badge, but not the ops symbols.

NMF Mustang III FB161/ PK-J suffered an engine failure during a practice sortie on 23 July 1945 and F/O Jerzy Lenartowicz had to belly-land it. The squadron badge can just be made out near the cockpit.

F/O Andrzej Czerwiński posing on a Mustang III with another pilot's impressive log of ground attack missions on the nose and scoreboard of black crosses near the cockpit. This may be FB230/PK-U, usually flown by F/O Kazimierz Wünsche. The 'Fighting Cockerel' badge of No. 315 Squadron was applied on both sides of the fuselage, always pointing forward.

eight German fighters destroyed. The squadron's greatest success was achieved on 18 August over France. Twelve Mustangs intercepted sixty Focke-Wulfs near Beauvais, scoring 16 German fighters destroyed for the loss of one Mustang. The loss was particularly painful, however, for the squadron lost its very popular commander, S/Ldr Eugeniusz Horbaczewski.

The anti-'Diver' patrols ended in the second week of September and the squadron resumed offensive operations. Between 17 and 26 September 1944 No. 315 Squadron flew patrols over the battlefield area of the operation 'Market-Garden'.

On 10 October 1944 the squadron moved to RAF Andrews Field. Two weeks later it exchanged places and aircraft with No. 316 Squadron at Coltishall, the latter unit replacing it in No. 133 Wing. At the beginning of November it moved to RAF Peterhead, and from there it flew patrol and escort operations to Norway.

In mid-January 1945 No. 315 Squadron moved back south, to rejoin No. 133 Wing at RAF Andrews Field. From then until the end of the war its main effort was to escort daylight bomber raids of Germany and fly sweeps over German territory. Along with the other squadrons of the wing, the squadron briefly resumed anti-V1 patrols in the first half of March 1945. The squadron remained at Andrews Field until 10 August, when it moved, with the rest of the wing, to RAF Coltishall. It was then based there until disbandment in December 1946.

Three Mustangs, led by FB376 PK-H in natural metal finish, taxi at Coltishall after the war. All three aircraft display the squadron badge near the cockpit, and also the additional informal recognition marking of the unit introduced in the post-war period: the forward section of the propeller spinner painted black. On the Mustang in foreground (probably coded PK-C) the grey on the upper surfaces looks very pale. It is not clear if this was due to the use of a non-regulation colour paint or just bad fading of the standard Ocean Grey.

S/Ldr Bohdan Arct in the cockpit of his personal Mustang III FB374/SZ-A. The scoreboard used various colours to denote confirmed, probables and damaged. The 'Fighting Owl' emblem of the squadron, applied on both sides of the fuselage, always pointing forward, dated back to the pre-war 113 Eskadra, *which had originally been formed as a night fighter unit.*

FB357/SZ-E photographed in late 1944 displays No. 316 Sqn code letters but the badge of No. 315 Sqn below the windscreen. Nos. 315 and 316 exchanged their aircraft in October 1944. The 'Fighting Cockerel' emblem was retained by the new operators on some Mustangs.

No. 316 'City of Warsaw'

No. 316 Squadron re-equipped with Mustang IIIs in April 1944 at RAF Woodvale. On 29 April it moved to RAF Coltishall and that day it flew its first operation on Mustangs. Its operational flying in May and June included mostly patrols and escorts over the North Sea and Dutch coast.

From the first day of July the squadron started flying anti-V1 patrols, as the first Polish unit. While the unit was still based at Coltishall, RAF West Malling was used as a forward station for these sorties. To facilitate operations the entire unit moved to West Malling on 5 July, and then to RAF Friston on the 11th.

As the V1 threat diminished, the squadron moved back to RAF Coltishall on 28 August and resumed operations over and across the North Sea.

HB835/SZ-G was the NMF Mustang III usually flown by No. 316 Sqn commander, S/Ldr Paweł Niemiec.

On 24 October it moved to RAF Andrews Field, where it replaced No. 315 Sqn, taking over its Mustangs. Its subsequent operations were mostly to escort daylight raids on Germany by heavy bombers. In mid-January 1945 the squadron was transferred to the control of No. 150 Wing RAF (which also included No. 122 Sqn RAF), but remained at the same airfield. In April 1945 it was joined at Andrews Field by No. 303 Squadron (now on Mustang IVs), making the 3rd Polish Wing a real force again. In mid-May the two squadrons moved to Coltishall, returning to Andrews Field on 10 August. At the end of November 1945 the 3rd Wing moved to RAF Turnhouse, and in early January 1946 to RAF Wick. In mid-March 1946 the two squadrons moved to RAF Hethel, where they then stayed until disbandment in December 1946.

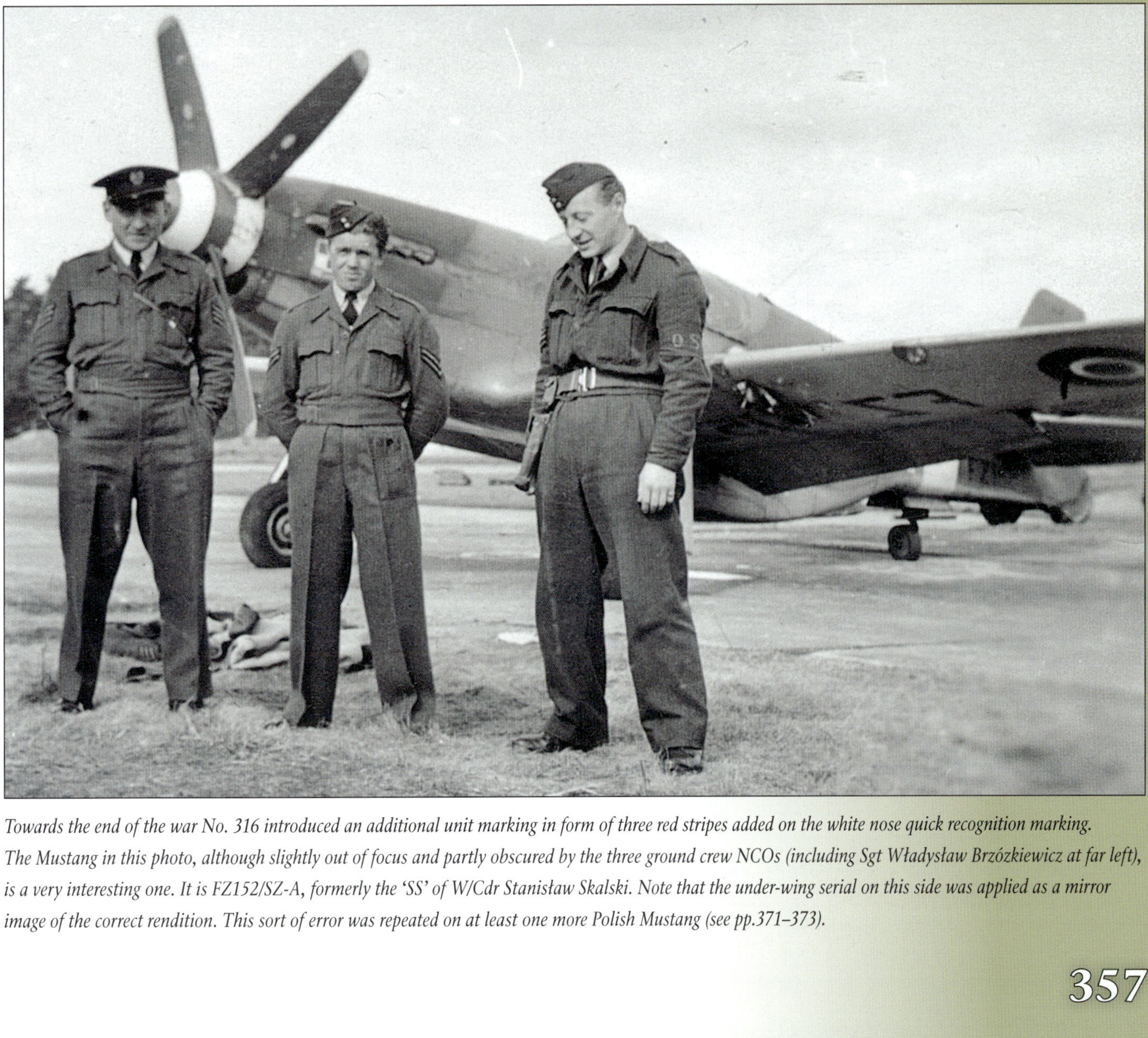

Towards the end of the war No. 316 introduced an additional unit marking in form of three red stripes added on the white nose quick recognition marking. The Mustang in this photo, although slightly out of focus and partly obscured by the three ground crew NCOs (including Sgt Władysław Brzózkiewicz at far left), is a very interesting one. It is FZ152/SZ-A, formerly the 'SS' of W/Cdr Stanisław Skalski. Note that the under-wing serial on this side was applied as a mirror image of the correct rendition. This sort of error was repeated on at least one more Polish Mustang (see pp.371–373).

Other Units

Several Polish pilots flew the variant with allied units: Nos. 19, 65 and 129 Squadrons RAF and the 355th and 356th Fighter Squadrons of the 354th Fighter Group USAAF.

Mustang IIIs were also flown by Polish pilots during training at No. 61 OTU, by Polish ferry pilots (both in service units and with the ATA), and by test pilots at the AAEE Boscombe Down.

Before any Polish unit re-equipped with the Mustang III, two pilots from No. 306 Squadron were attached to the Mustang-equipped No. 122 Wing RAF for experience on the type. On 2 March 1944 morning FZ190/QV-A of No. 19 Squadron RAF was flown by F/O Władysław Szajda during an escort mission for US heavy bombers. At the time of Szajda's flight the aircraft still carried the white quick recognition band across the fin and rudder, which was then obliterated before this photo was taken in April.

P-51B s/n 43-12199/AJ-H nicknamed 'Miss "El"' was flown by F/Lt Antoni Głowacki on 29 March 1944 during his exchange posting to the 356th Fighter Squadron 354th Fighter Group 9th Air Force USAAF. The aircraft was in standard USAAF camouflage of Olive Drab on upper surfaces and Neutral Gray underneath. At the time it displayed the white quick recognition markings of the Mustangs: the bands on the wings and tailplane and the white nose.

Mustang III FX953 was tested by the Aeroplane and Armament Experimental Establishment at Boscombe Down. Polish pilot S/Ldr Janusz Żurakowski flew it on various trials between April and June. Typically for RAF fighters allocated for testing, the aircraft was in standard Fighter Command camouflage and markings. Notably, however, this Mustang lacked the special recognition markings of the type: it featured no white bands across the wings and tail surfaces, nor the white nose.

Mustang III FB125 was delivered to No. 133 (Polish) Wing on 12 April 1944 by W/O Witold Krupa from No. 306 Sqn, but the aircraft spent its entire career with No. 129 'Mysore' Squadron RAF, which was part of the wing for much of 1944. This photo was taken soon after delivery, when it was coded DV-F. Subsequently recoded DV-C, FB125 was written off a year later, on 7 May 1945, in an accident of the unit's Polish pilot, W/O Edward Wojczyński.

By the end of the war in Europe Mustang IIIs had also been delivered to training establishments. The last generation of exiled Polish AF fighter pilots underwent training on these aircraft at No. 61 OTU at Rednal in 1945. The serial of this particular machine is not known, but in March 1945 Sgt Bronisław Jazownik logged a practice sortie there in a Mustang III coded UU-K.

North American P-51B-1-NA Mustang s/n 43-12478/AJ-Q, 356th Fighter Squadron, 354th Fighter Group USAAF, March 1944. Upper surface camouflage: Olive Drab; under surface colour: Neutral Gray. Standard US national markings. 'Sonava Buggar' personal name applied on the port side of the nose, victory markings (black swastikas in white fields) below the windscreen and 'sweep' markings above the exhausts.

The name 'Sonava Buggar' had been applied by early March 1944.

The markings near the cockpit of the Mustang: three victory symbols (black swastikas in white fields) and the names of the regular pilot (Capt. J. W. Edwards) and the ground crew (S/Sgt P. O. Kemf, Sgt L. S. Walker and Sgt R. E. Smith).

P-51B-1-NA s/n 43-12478/AJ-Q of the 356th FS, 354th FG of the 9th Air Force photographed probably in February 1944, when it still lacked the personal name, but already had the three victory markings. Note the white bands on the wing and tail. These were the quick recognition markings to help distinguish Mustangs from Messerschmitt 109s. F/Lt Antoni Głowacki flew this P-51B in late March 1944 during his exchange posting to the 354th FG.

'Mustangs and cattle': the other side of s/n 43-12478/AJ-Q seen in pastoral scenery.

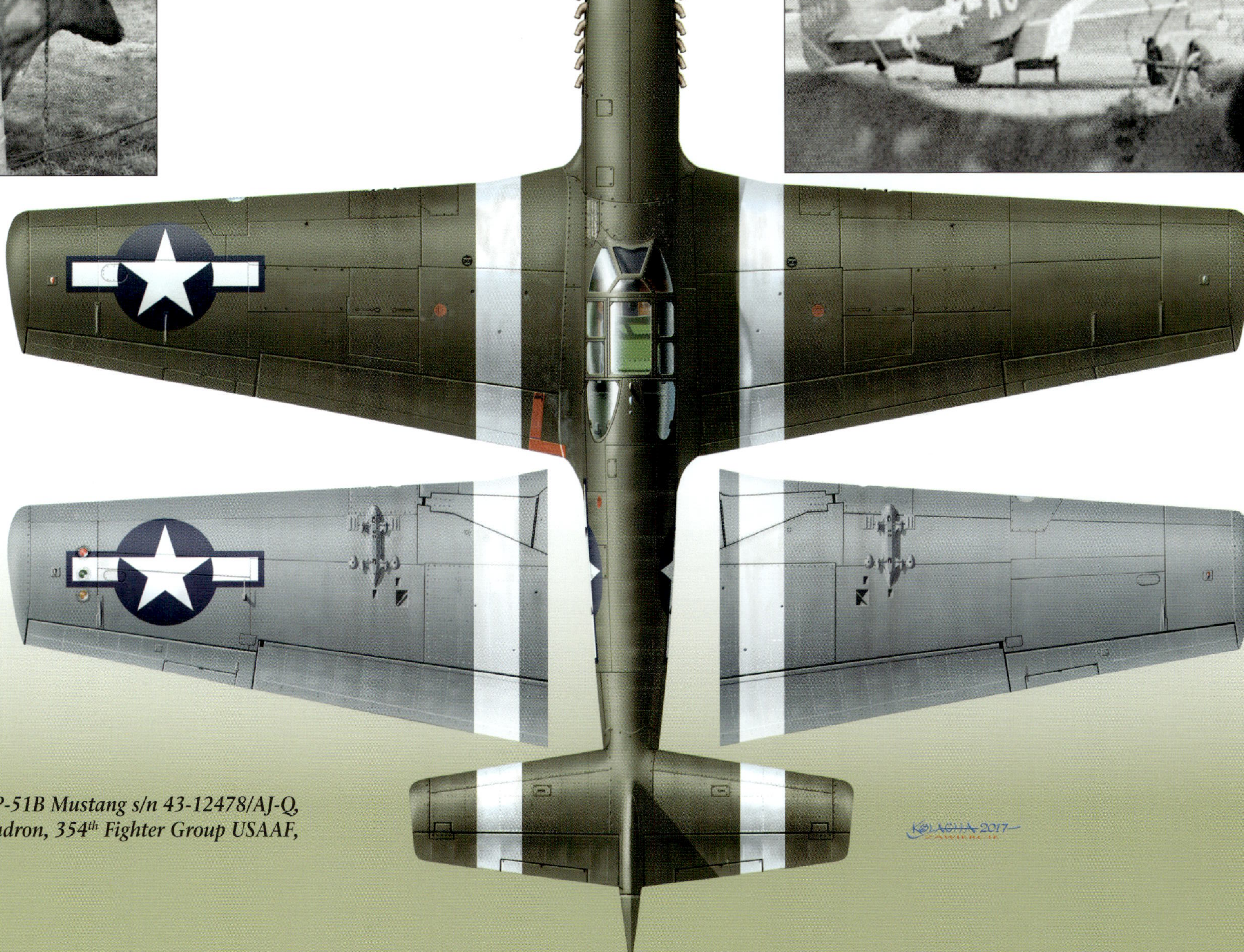

North American P-51B Mustang s/n 43-12478/AJ-Q, 356th Fighter Squadron, 354th Fighter Group USAAF, March 1944.

North American Mustang III (P-51B-5-NA, s/n 43-6533) FZ152/SS of No. 133 Wing Leader, W/Cdr Stanisław Skalski, June 1944. Upper surface camouflage colours: Ocean Grey and Dark Green ('B' pattern); under surface colour: Medium Sea Grey. Standard British national markings. Polish national marking on both sides of forward fuselage, with 'POLAND' stencil below. Full invasion markings in form of white and black bands on the fuselage and wings. Wing Commander's pennant and victory markings (crosses) on the port side of fuselage below the cockpit.

Mustang III FZ152 was the personal mount of W/Cdr Stanisław Skalski who led No. 133 Wing during spring and summer of 1944. Similar to the Spitfires he had flown when leading No. 131 Wing from Northolt, his Mustang displayed the pilot's initials as a personalised code. On 24 June 1944 Skalski was credited with two Messerschmitt 109s destroyed while flying this aeroplane. This photo, taken in June 1944, shows full white and black bands around the fuselage and wings. Note the white band on the horizontal tail surfaces. Note that the aircraft has no fuselage tank installed.

A different view of a similar scene with W/Cdr Skalski in the cockpit of Mustang III FZ152/SS. The D-Day bands are peeling off on the bottom surface of the flap, but so is the camouflage paint on the upper cowling of the engine! Note how the propeller blade roots have been oversprayed with white paint. It is also noteworthy that the tread pattern on each of the main wheel tyres is different.

North American Mustang III (P-51B-5-NA, s/n 43-6533) FZ152/SS of No. 133 Wing Leader, W/Cdr Stanisław Skalski, June 1944.

Close-up of W/Cdr Skalski in the cockpit of FZ152, showing his rank pennant, his scoreboard, a part of the personal code, and the white band on the fuselage (its front edge not quite straight). In this photograph the black crosses of the victory markings show as the same shade of grey as the camouflage, which makes the last four (without white outlines) virtually indistinguishable.

This photo, taken about a month before D-Day, shows Skalski and his freshly applied scoreboard: seventeen black crosses with white outlines plus four more in uncertain colour(s). The meaning behind these numbers of crosses is not certain, because by D-Day Skalski had been credited with sixteen plus two shared confirmed victories, two probables and four damaged.

North American Mustang III (P-51B-5-NA, s/n 43-6535) FZ154/PK-N, No. 315 Squadron, June 1944. Upper surface camouflage colours: Ocean Grey and Dark Green ('A' pattern); under surface colour: Medium Sea Grey. Standard British national markings. No. 315 Sqn badge below the windscreen, facing forward on both sides of the fuselage. Polish national marking on both sides of forward fuselage, with 'POLAND' stencil below. Full invasion markings in form of white and black bands on the fuselage and wings.

FZ154 was one of very few Mustang IIIs with original 'greenhouse' cockpit canopies used in Polish squadrons. This photograph was probably taken at Coolham ALG in the first weeks following the Normandy landings. At the time the aircraft displayed the full quick recognition invasion markings in form of white and black bands around the fuselage and wings. On 7 June F/Sgt Ryszard Idrian flew FZ154/PK-N when he claimed a Messerschmitt 109 destroyed.

Rearming the 0.5 in. guns of FZ154. Note that the codes had been masked during application of the D-Day bands, resulting in a narrow outline of camouflage colours. The bands were obviously applied rather roughly, with uneven edges. The black paint is already peeling off on the flap. Note that the aircraft has no fuselage tank installed.

North American Mustang III (P-51C-5-NT, s/n 42-103710) HB861/UZ-B, No. 306 Squadron, late 1944. Upper surface camouflage colours: Ocean Grey and Dark Green ('A' pattern); under surface colour: Medium Sea Grey. Standard British national markings. Polish national marking on both sides of forward fuselage, with 'POLAND' stencil below. Late-1944 invasion markings in form of white and black bands on the bottom of the fuselage only. 'Dancing girl' personal emblem below the windscreen, port side only.

Above: An anonymous ground crew member posing with HB861. The letters UZ-B look distinctively darker than the Sky band around the fuselage, even though Air Ministry Orders required the code to be applied in Sky on day fighters. Since the fuselage band had been applied before the aircraft was delivered for squadron use, it was probably in Sky proper. As there was not enough space between the band and the roundel for the letter B, it seems likely that squadron ground crews deliberately darkened the paint, so that the code stood out against the band. On 6 March 1945 S/Ldr Józef Jeka flew HB861 when he claimed a V1 destroyed.

Right: *The same airman posing by the main wheel with the aircraft's distinctive personal emblem visible in the background. The white quick recognition band on the undercarriage cover and the white bars painted on the wheel hub and tyre for easier checking of tyre creep are well visible. Note that the tread on the tyre is different from either of those on FZ152 (p. 358).*

Above: *Another airman posing with the same Mustang, and clearly focused on the personal emblem. The standard stencilled Polish national marking can be seen on the nose.*

Left: *Close up of the personal emblem. A very similar image of a dancing girl had earlier been applied on two Spitfire IXs, used by Nos. 316 and 302 Squadrons.*

North American Mustang III (P-51C-5-NT, s/n 42-103775) HB886/TN of No. 133 Wing Officer Commanding, G/Cpt Tadeusz Nowierski, October 1944. Upper surface camouflage colours: Ocean Grey and Dark Green ('C' pattern); under surface colour: Medium Sea Grey. Standard British national markings. Polish national marking on both sides of forward fuselage, with 'POLAND' stencil below. Late-1944 invasion markings in form of white and black bands on the bottom of the fuselage only. Group Captain's pennant on the port side of fuselage below the cockpit.

Mustang III HB886 was the personal mount of G/Cpt Tadeusz Nowierski who commanded No. 133 Wing throughout 1944. It displayed the pilot's initials as a personalised code. Note that when the D-Day markings were removed from the wings, the Mustang quick recognition white bands were reinstated there. The residue invasion markings were applied in No. 133 Wing at the time in form of just four bands: two white and two black, with the Fighter Command's Sky band around the rear fuselage replacing the rearmost white band. On 5 August 1944 G/Cpt Nowierski used this Mustang when he claimed a V1 destroyed.

North American Mustang III HB886/TN of No. 133 Wing Officer Commanding, G/Cpt Tadeusz Nowierski, October 1944.

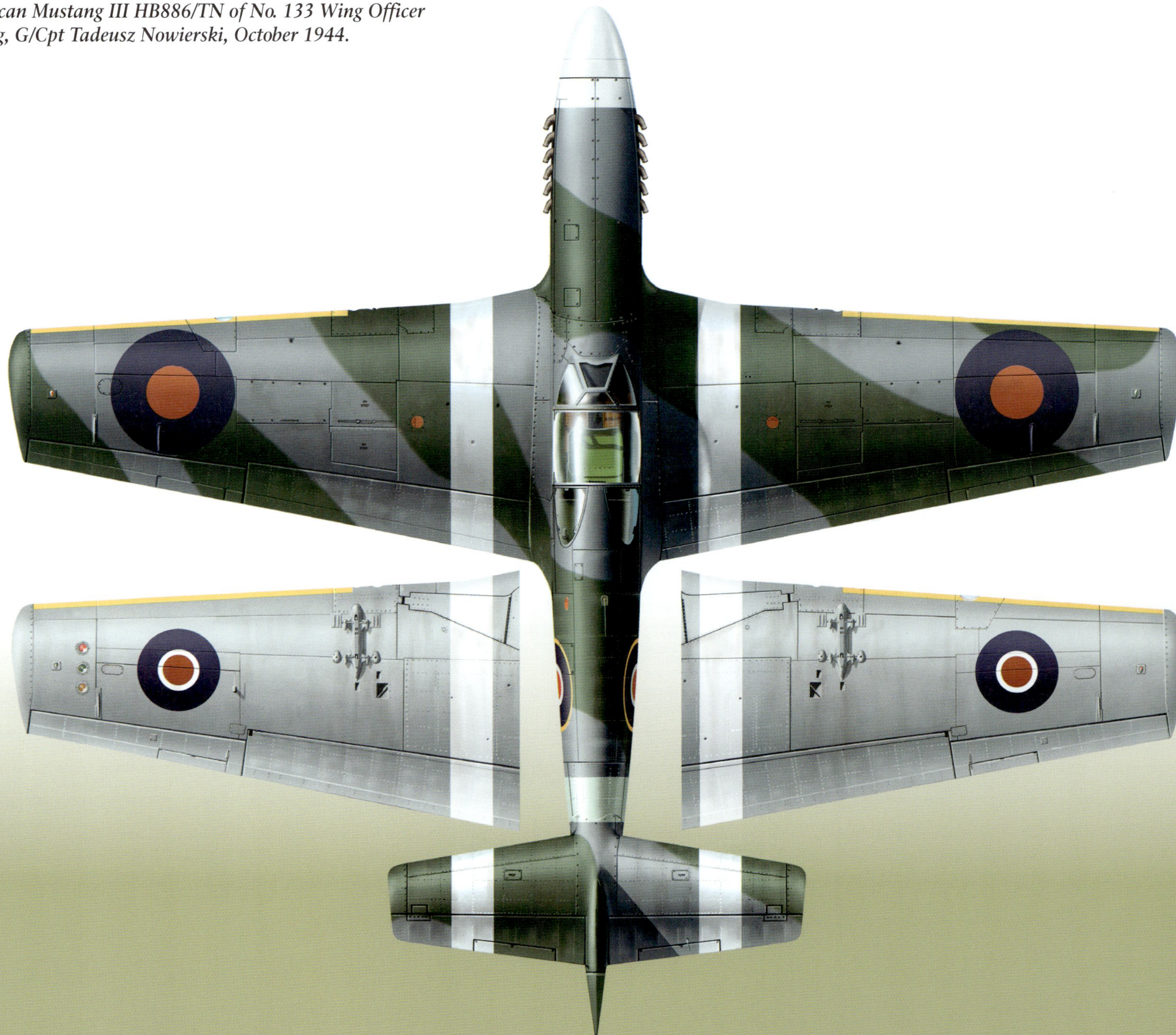

North American Mustang III (P-51C-10-NT, s/n 44-10999) KH574/WC-A, No. 309 Squadron, March–July 1945. Upper surface camouflage colours: Ocean Grey and Dark Green ('C' pattern); under surface colour: Medium Sea Grey. Standard British national markings. Polish national marking on both sides of forward fuselage, with 'POLAND' stencil below. (No. 309 Sqn badge below the windscreen, on the port side of the fuselage only.)

Mustang III KH574/WC-A was the personal mount of S/Ldr Antoni Głowacki, commanding No. 309 Squadron between March and July 1945. On 15 April it was also used by W/Cdr Kazimierz Rutkowski, No. 133 Wing Leader, during 'Ramrod 1541' to Swinemünde (Świnoujście). The aircraft was first delivered to an operational unit in February 1945 and should have had 'type C' (three-tone) roundels on upper wing surfaces from the outset, but the roundel in the photo seems to lack the white ring ('type B'). Note the prominent trace where the night flying exhaust glare shield was removed from the side of the cowling between the exhausts and the cockpit.

North American Mustang III (P-51C-10-NT, s/n 44-10930) KH528/SZ-L, No. 316 Squadron, April 1945–late 1946. Upper surface camouflage colours: Ocean Grey and Dark Green ('C' pattern); under surface colour: Medium Sea Grey. Standard British national markings. Polish national marking on both sides of forward fuselage, with 'POLAND' stencil below. No. 316 Sqn badge below the windscreen, facing forward on both sides of the fuselage. Additional unit marking: red and white stripes on the nose and propeller spinner.

Mustang III KH528 had been used by a number of RAF squadrons before it was delivered to No. 316 Squadron in April 1945, hence the prominent traces of repainting in the area where codes were applied. This aircraft, too, has had its night flying exhaust glare shields removed, like KH574. Three red bands were applied on the white nose and spinner, this being an additional identity marking of No. 316 Sqn as of early 1945. The Mustang was usually flown by F/Lt Tadeusz Kwiatkowski, the 'A' Flight commander. On 19 April it was slightly damaged during 'Ramrod 1545' to Munich, when flown by S/Ldr Zygmunt Drybański, commanding No. 316 Sqn.

North American Mustang III (P-51C-5-NT, s/n 42-103692) HB843/UZ-I, No. 306 Squadron, 1946. Natural metal overall. Standard British national markings. Polish national marking on both sides of forward fuselage, with 'POLAND' stencil below. No. 306 Sqn badge below the windscreen on both sides of the fuselage. Additional unit marking: forward section of the propeller spinner painted red.

A rare colour photo of HB843/UZ-I at RAF Coltishall in 1946. Note the red propeller spinner of the camouflaged Mustang in the background. This was an additional marking of No. 306 Sqn, introduced on its aircraft after the war.

An unidentified pilot with a natural metal Mustang III from No. 306 Sqn, possibly HB843/UZ-I, photographed in early September 1945. Note the Polish national marking, which seems to have no white at all, just the red parts of the insignia (the 'white' outline featuring a thin red border along the outer edge), with 'POLAND' also in red.

HB843/UZ-I landing at Coltishall. Note the bottom part of the under-wing serial ending ('43') visible on the main wheel cover.

The same Mustang taxiing at Coltishall. On this side the under-wing serial was positioned in such way that the very top of '43' can be seen on the main wheel cover. Note the white backgrounds painted on for the application/re-application of the Polish AF marking on the nose and the squadron badge below the windscreen.

The same pilot as on the previous page, this time in the cockpit of the natural metal Mustang III. Note that the windscreen and hood framing was painted a dark colour (possibly black), which has peeled off badly. The serial of the Mustang in the background looks like FX994, but it is probably in fact FX964.

North American Mustang IV

No. 303 Squadron 'City of Warsaw'

No. 303 Squadron re-equipped with Mustang IVs ((P-51D and P-51K aircraft delivered to the RAF under Lend-Lease, via USAAF inventory) in April 1945 at RAF Andrews Field, where it joined No. 316 Sqn (on Mustang IIIs) as part of the 3rd Polish Wing. Its first operation on Mustangs was flown on 23 April 1945, and the second on 25 April 1945. The latter proved the last operational mission flown by No. 303 and all other Polish Mustang squadrons, when they took part in the escort for several hundred Lancasters (including fourteen of the Polish No. 300 Squadron) that bombed Hitler's Alpine resort at Obersalzberg near Berchtesgaden. In mid-May the 3rd Polish Wing moved to Coltishall, but it returned to Andrews Field on 10 August. It then moved to RAF Turnhouse in late November 1945, to RAF Wick at the beginning of January 1946, and to RAF Hethel in mid-March 1946. No. 303 Squadron was disbanded there in December 1946.

KH663/RF-M was one of extremely few camouflaged Mustang IVs used by the Polish Air Force. It is shown here soon after delivery to No. 303 Squadron in early April 1945, before the Polish national marking was applied on the nose.

Mustang IV KH855/RF-A photographed after the take-off accident of F/O Julian Krok on 28 April 1945. Note the original wartime code letters (RF), the squadron badge under the cockpit and the Polish Air Force red-and-white chequered square on the nose. Nearly all Mustang IVs used by No. 303 Squadron were in natural metal finish (which, in fact, included quite a lot of surface finished with 'Aluminium' paint).

Air-to-air shot of Mustang IVs KH868 PD-E, KH747 PD-F and KH663 PD-L in late 1945 or early 1946. the latter is in the Day Fighter camouflage but with a replacement cockpit hood which the other two Mustangs are in natural metal finish. The codes of No. 303 Sqn were changed from RF to PD in early August 1945.

F/O Ryszard Górecki in the cockpit of Mustang IV KM 112/ PD-D. Note the form of No.303 Squadron's traditional 'Kościuszko' badge and its position in relation to the signal pistol firing port. It is sometimes claimed that the badge covered this opening on some Mustangs, but no photo to corroborate this is known.

Other units

No other Polish AF squadron re-equipped with the variant, but two more Mustang IVs were used by the exiled Polish units.

KH642 (P-51D, probably camouflaged), was used by W/Cdr Kazimierz Rutkowski, the 3rd Polish Wing Leader. According to documents its code was KR or KWR, but no photographs are known.

KM249 (P-51K) was transferred from No. 250 Sqn RAF to No. 318 Squadron in Italy in September 1945 to provide the latter's pilots with experience on the type. It is not clear if the aircraft was marked with No. 318 Sqn code letters (LW). In February 1946 it was transferred to No. 239 Wing HQ.

Mustang IVs were also flown by Polish ferry pilots (both in service units and with the ATA), and in testing at the AAEE Boscombe Down.

Mustang IV KM249/LD-J photographed by No. 318 Squadron member LAC Bolesław Preis. It was transferred from No. 250 Sqn RAF to No. 318 Squadron in Italy in September 1945, but it is not certain if it was ever marked with No. 318 codes or emblem. The aircraft was adorned with the 'Crusaders' Shield' badge of the 8th Army under the windscreen. Note that the blue ring of the wing roundel on this aeroplane looks so pale that it merges completely with the NMF wing finish in this black and white photo.

North American Mustang IV (P-51K-10-NT, s/n 44-12343) KM220/RF-B, No. 303 Squadron, April–July 1945. Silver/natural metal overall. Standard British national markings. Polish national marking on both sides of forward fuselage, with 'POLAND' stencil below. No. 303 Sqn badge below the windscreen on both sides of the fuselage.

Mustang IV KM220/RF-B soon after delivery to No. 303 Squadron in April 1945 at RAF Andrews Field. Only the codes had been applied by the time this photo was taken. The Polish AF marking on the nose and the squadron badge near the cockpit would be added soon afterwards.

W/O Jerzy Kmiecik poses with KM220/RF-B, leaning on the propeller blade with its original USAAF serial number, 44-12343.

Cpl Józef Klachacz (middle) and two other ground crew members posing on KM112 PD-D. No. 303 Sqn badge on the side of the fuselage, the kill markings below the windscreen and the Polish AF insignia on the nose can be seen.

Another group of ground crew with KM112 PD-D (LAC Zbigniew Więckowicz at far left). The scoreboard marked under the windscreen included eight black crosses with white outlines in the upper row to denote confirmed kills and three in the lower row, probably outlined in red, which denoted probables.

A group of pilots on KM112, probably during summer 1946 at RAF Hethel. On the main wheel is W/O Jakub Bargiełowski. Seated on the fuselage are, left to right: W/O Jan Talar, F/Sgt Zbigniew Zabłocki and F/O Ryszard Górecki, and on the wing root is F/Sgt Rudolf Falkowski. Note the aircraft letter D applied on the bottom cowling, and the serial number on the under surface of the port wing, the latter mistakenly painted on as a mirror image of the correct rendition! (Compare FZ152 on p.353). The Polish national insignia on the nose looks sharp but 'POLAND', stencilled in red below it, seems badly worn.

North American Mustang IV (P-51K-10-NT, s/n 44-12335) KM112/PD-D, No. 303 Squadron, February–November 1946. Silver/natural metal overall. Standard British national markings. Polish national marking on both sides of forward fuselage, with 'POLAND' stencil below. No. 303 Sqn badge below the windscreen on both sides of the fuselage. Victory markings (black crosses) on the port side of fuselage below the windscreen.

Mustang IV KM112 was the usual mount of S/Ldr Bolesław Drobiński, and then S/Ldr Witold Łokuciewski. This photo was taken after the latter took command of No. 303 Squadron in February 1946. In addition to the Polish national insignia on the nose and the squadron badge under the cockpit, the scoreboard of the pilot was applied under the windscreen. Note the worn appearance of the fuselage roundel and the badly faded blue ring of the wing roundel.

North American Mustang IV KM112/PD-D,
No. 303 Squadron, February–November 1946.

USAAF P-51D s/n 44-13332 was delivered to the RAF in June 1944, becoming its very first Mustang IV. The RAF serial number, TK589, was applied in a non-standard position and style on this aircraft (the USAAF number was applied where the RAF serial would normally be). The photos were taken in 1944, before the tail section was modified. Traces of the original USAAF number 413332 can still be seen.

North American Mustang IV (P-51D-5-NA, s/n 44-13332) TK589, Aeroplane and Armament Experimental Establishment, Boscombe Down, March 1945. Silver/natural metal overall. Standard British national markings. Traces of the USAAF serial no. on rear fuselage.

S/Ldr Janusz Żurakowski flew Mustang IV TK589 (ex s/n 44-13332) in trials at the Aeroplane and Armament Experimental Establishment at Boscombe Down in March 1945, by which time the fin fillet was fitted to this aircraft (this has become standard on RAF Mustang IVs).

Another photo of TK589 from the 1944 air-to-air session, showing the Mustang in unmodified form, without the fin fillet.

Other Mustang Variants

After it was decided that No. 309 Squadron would become a purely fighter one, several experienced Polish tactical reconnaissance pilots were posted in late 1944/early 1945 to RAF units still flying the Allison-powered Mustangs in this role: Nos. 2 and 268 Sqns. Their equipment at the time included Mustang IAs (RAF equivalent of the P-51) and Mustang IIs (P-51A). Both variants were flown by Polish pilots until the squadrons re-equipped with Spitfires (No. 2 at the end of 1944 and No. 268 in mid-1945).

Mustang IAs were also ferried by Polish pilots (both male and female).

Some of the first Merlin-powered conversions, labelled as the Mk X, were test flown by Polish pilots with the Air Fighting Development Unit and the Royal Aircraft Establishment in 1943.

AM208 was one of a number of Mustang Is converted in Britain by fitting Merlin engines. These conversions were known under the provisional designation of Mustang X. This aircraft was test flown at the RAE in August 1943 by F/L Kazimierz Kazimierczuk. It was finished in Temperate Land scheme on upper surfaces, with Sky under surfaces and the propeller spinner in black. It featured the yellow 'P in ring' prototype marking on the fuselage.

AL975 was a Mustang X flown by F/Lt Jerzy Solak at the Air Fighting Development Unit at RAF Duxford in April 1943, and the photo was taken about the same time. To balance the new nose section the aircraft featured an enlarged fin. In subsequent production variants the fin area was increased by adding a long fillet, but here the fin leading edge was extended forward. The standard day fighter quick recognition markings (the Sky fuselage band and propeller spinner) suggest the aircraft was in the Day Fighter (Dark Green and Ocean Grey) on top and Medium Sea Grey underneath. The pattern was probably 'A' originally, but was altered significantly during conversion work.

Left: A tactical recce Mustang II in the second half of 1944, with the Sky spinner and fuselage band, large two-tone roundels on wing upper surfaces, and residual invasion bands on the lower fuselage. Reconnaissance squadrons were not given any unit codes, only the aircraft letter being applied. The colour scheme looks like 'C' pattern. The Mustang is believed to be FR910/W of No. 2 Sqn in late summer 1944, quoted in a number of documents as lost on 10 August 1944. However, operational records continued to mention this serial with No. 2 Sqn until late 1944 and then with No. 268 Sqn until 1945, so either FR910 was not in fact lost, or its serial number was mistakenly recorded for its replacement aircraft. In any case, F/Lt Antoni Krąkowski flew 'FR910' with No. 2 Sqn in mid-October 1944, and F/Lts Gołko and Szyszko with No. 268 Sqn in December 1944.

Above: This No. 268 Sqn Mustang II, presumably FR918/U, displays the different appearance that was typical for 1945: black spinner, no fuselage bands of any kind, and upper wing roundels identical in form and size to the fuselage ones. The camouflage is most definitely in 'C' pattern. FR918 was flown by F/Lt Jerzy Gołko in December 1944 (still with the earlier set of markings), and then by F/Lts Szyszko and Lewkowicz between January and May 1945. Note that the 'greenhouse' cockpit canopy had been replaced by the 'Malcolm hood'.

Left: Mustang IA FD535/X of No. 268 Sqn RAF being de-iced in early 1945 at B.77 Gilze-Rijen, with the Sky band around the rear fuselage already obliterated with camouflage. The disruptive scheme appears to match the 'C' pattern. This aircraft was flown by F/Lts Jerzy Gołko and Jan Szyszko in late 1944 (still with the Sky fuselage band and Sky propeller spinner) and by F/Lts Janusz Lewkowicz and Tadeusz Galler in the spring of 1945.

Hawker Typhoon

No Polish squadron was ever equipped with the Hawker Typhoon, but numerous Polish pilots flew the type with various RAF units. Between 1942 and 1945 Polish fighter pilots continued to be posted individually or in small groups to various allied units, and these included Typhoon-equipped Nos. 1, 3, 4, 182, 183, 195, 268 and 609 Squadrons RAF.

No. 609 Squadron pilot F/O H. T. Skett and a friend posing with Typhoon IB R8888/PR-Y. The aircraft was flown on operations by F/O Antoni Polek and Sgt Tadeusz Turek between December 1942 and February 1943. It displays a perfectly standard set of regulation camouflage and markings, including a standard size fuselage roundel (compare R7713 PR-Z on page 386).

A propaganda photo of No. 609 Sqn Typhoon IB DN547/PR-S before an early dive bombing sortie. P/O Tadeusz Turek flew the aircraft on operations in May and June 1943. The standard camouflage and markings of the type included the underwing black and white bands introduced in December 1942 to prevent friendly fire incidents when Typhoons were mistaken for Focke-Wulf 190s. The rear portion of the propeller spinner was probably repainted Ocean Grey due to a misunderstanding of the AMO (Air Ministry Order) instructions, only the forward section being finished in Sky.

Air-to-air photos of No. 183 Sqn Typhoon IB DN275/HF-B. F/O Eugeniusz Gottowt flew the aircraft on operations in March 1943. The images show standard Day Fighter camouflage and markings of the type in 1943. Apart from the set of markings applied to all Fighter Command aircraft, Typhoons featured a set of quick recognition markings aimed at preventing friendly fire incidents caused by mistaking them for Focke-Wulf 190s. These included a 9 in. yellow band across the upper wing surface, aligned with the inboard cannon, and a set of black and white bands on bottom wing surface. The latter were supposed to consist of four 12 in. black and three 24 in. white bands with the outermost black band just outboard of the outer cannon, but on this aircraft it was misapplied just outboard of the inner cannon, so there was not enough space left for the innermost black band to be applied. Note that the port undercarriage leg cover seems to have been a replacement item from another machine where the bands were applied in the correct position.

The first of them was F/O Jerzy Solak, posted to No. 609 Sqn RAF in August 1942. In November he transferred to the Air Fighting Development Unit at Duxford, and served there until April 1943, flying Typhoons among other types.

Meanwhile, Sgt Tadeusz Turek joined No. 609 Sqn in October, and he was credited with two Fw 190s destroyed during December 1942. His 'kill' scored on the 16th while flying Typhoon I R7849/PR-U should have become the acclaimed 500th kill of the Polish AF and the one on the 20th in R8837/PR-M – the 501st. However, although the victories were subsequently duly recorded in his files, they were not given the official publicity by the Polish AF HQ at the time

No. 183 Sqn Typhoon IBs during Exercise 'Spartan' in March 1943 at Cranfield. The squadron was part of the 'Eastland' force, which played the role of the Germans defending against the forthcoming invasion of Western Europe. 'Eastland' aircraft bore prominent markings to differentiate them from the 'Southland' (the invading forces): broad white bands along the forward fuselage, black propeller spinner and black under surface of the port wing. The black and white bands were retained underneath the starboard wings of Typhoons, making their colour scheme even more striking than that of any other 'Eastland' type. The aircraft furthest from camera here, DN334 HF-D, was flown by both F/O Eugeniusz Gottowt and F/Lt Zbigniew Moszyński during 'Spartan'. On 6 March Gottowt was declared 'shot down' in this aircraft by the umpires of the exercise.

EK273/JE-DT, photographed during refuelling at RAF Ludham in the spring of 1943, was the personal mount of No. 195 Squadron Commander, S/Ldr Don Taylor. It displayed his personal emblem, Donald Duck with a red-hot poker in his arm, on the radiator housing. It also featured personalised code letters: see p. 383. Otherwise its camouflage and markings conformed with AMO regulations of the time. The Typhoon was repeatedly flown by F/O Zygmunt Nentwich in June 1943. On 6 July 1943 it was lost on operations with W/Cdr Alexander 'Sandy' Rabagliati, Coltishall Wing Leader, at the controls.

Typhoon IB R8938/JE-R photographed at the same spot with P/O Ken Trott (its usual pilot). The aeroplane was flown by F/O Zygmunt Nentwich several times between January and June 1943. Unlike EK273, it displayed no personalised code or emblem. Note the non-standard pattern of colours on the nose. The Typhoon had previously featured the all-white nose type recognition marking. This was then overpainted with camouflage colours without paying attention to the AMO-prescribed pattern.

Wrecked Typhoon IB JP921/QO-P of No. 3 Sqn guarded by a German soldier (and a dog?) after F/O Erazm Wardziński was downed in it by Flak on 29 March 1944, during a 'Ramrod' operation. The belly landing took place 12 km North-East of Eindhoven in Holland. Wardziński managed to evade capture in enemy-held territory and return – he eventually had the distinction of being the sole Polish fighter pilot to do that twice during the war! Although the quality of the photo is far from perfect, it can be seen that the aircraft featured standard camouflage and markings.

(the glory going to No. 306 Sqn Spitfire pilots instead). It is not clear if this was because Turek's claim's paperwork got stuck in bureaucracy channels during Christmas period, or if it was decided at the top levels of command that publicity for Polish squadrons was more important. F/O Antoni Polek joined No. 609 Sqn in December 1942, and he would enjoy a successful career on Typhoons with the unit.

No. 182 Sqn was the next Typhoon unit with a Polish contingent, when three Polish pilots were posted there in September 1942. Sgts Kazimierz Gawlewicz and Tadeusz Bubes would continue to fly with the unit for a long period, while F/O Antoni Polek transferred to No. 609 Sqn in December 1942, as mentioned above.

In October 1942 F/O Korneliusz Górniak was posted to No. 1 Sqn, but after a brief period there he was posted back to Polish No. 306 Sqn on Spitfires.

F/Os Mieczysław Wyszkowski and Zygmunt Nentwich were posted to No. 195 Sqn in November 1942. Wyszkowski left the unit in February 1943, going to Africa with the 'Skalski's

Following repairs of Category B damage suffered with No. 174 Sqn on 30 January 1944, Typhoon IB EK128 has its engine run up at No. 511 Forward Repair Unit at Odiham. On 26 April the Typhoon was ferried from that airfield to Eastleigh by 1st/Off Anna Leska, ATA. The aircraft is in standard Fighter Command camouflage and markings. The Typhoon-specific quick recognition markings were no longer applied at the time.

Hawker Typhoon IB R7713/PR-Z, No. 609 Squadron, late 1942. Upper surface camouflage colours: Ocean Grey and Dark Green ('A' pattern); under surface colour: Medium Sea Grey. Standard British national markings except on the wing under sides, where the pre-June 1942 pattern roundels were retained. Type quick recognition markings in form of black and white bands on the under side of the wings. No. 609 Sqn badge and victory markings (two black crosses and three steam engines) forward of the windscreen. Aircraft letter probably in yellow on the wing leading edge inboard of the cannon.

Right: *A pilot of No. 609 Sqn (probably F/O Peter James Nankivell; often misidentified as "P/O Gilbert") in the cockpit of Typhoon IB R7713/PR-Z. Note the squadron badge (the rose of the County of Yorkshire superimposed on two hunting horns, with the 'TALLY HO' motto below) and the victory markings (two black crosses and three steam engines) forward of the cockpit. The score was probably that of F/O Nankivell. The aircraft featured oversize fuselage roundels (42 in. outer diameter) obtained from the earlier 'A1' roundels by extending the roundel blue and roundel red to obliterate parts of the white and yellow rings.*

Right: *F/Sgt Alan Haddon (near the cockpit) and Sgt John George Wiseman (with the dog) on R7713/PR-Z. The Typhoon was flown by F/Os Jerzy Solak (in October 1942) and Antoni Polek (in February-March 1943), and Sgt Tadeusz Turek (in November-December 1942). The photo, taken between early December 1942 (when the underwing bands were introduced) and 14 February 1943 (when both Haddon and Wiseman were shot down and killed), shows a number of interesting features. The type recognition markings in form of four black and three white bands under each wing were applied with the two outer black bands extending onto the cannon. The fuselage roundel and the fin flash (the lowest part of both just visible beneath the wing trailing edge) are of the later style, as introduced in mid-1942, but the under-wing roundel is still in the so-called 'A' form, with the broad white ring. This was seen on a number of Typhoons at the time. The camouflage pattern on the nose is non-standard. The Typhoon had previously featured the earlier, all-white nose type recognition marking. When this was abandoned, the nose was repainted with camouflage colours without paying attention to AMO-prescribed pattern, and it seems that white was left on the under surface. The rear portion of the spinner was apparently repainted Ocean Grey, with only the forward section in Sky. Note the aircraft letter on the wing leading edge inboard of the cannon, probably applied in yellow. The yellow leading edge stripe looks very neat, especially when compared to the badly worn appearance of the inboard section of the wing.*

Hawker Typhoon IB EN273/JE-DT, No. 195 Squadron, 1942–1943. Upper surface camouflage colours: Ocean Grey and Dark Green ('A' pattern); under surface colour: Medium Sea Grey. Standard British national markings. Type quick recognition markings in form of black and white bands on the under side of the wings. Initials of the unit commander (S/Ldr Don Taylor) in place of the aircraft letter. 'Donald Duck' personal emblem on the nose.

Close-up of S/Ldr Don Taylor's personal emblem applied on the radiator housing: Donald Duck armed with a red-hot poker.

EK273/JE-DT, the personal mount of S/Ldr Don Taylor, was flown by F/O Zygmunt Nentwich several times in June 1943. The aircraft was in standard camouflage and markings, except for the aircraft letters, DT, applied in small size. The entire propeller spinner was finished in Sky.

Circus'. Nentwich continued to fly with No. 195 until July 1943, when he was posted to the Polish, Spitfire-equipped, No. 316 Sqn at Northolt. No. 195 Sqn saw its next Polish team when F/O Tadeusz Żurakowski (not to be confused with the famous test pilot Janusz Żurakowski) and Sgt Stanisław Domański joined it in December 1943. They would both serve with the unit until it disbanded in mid-February 1944, when they were re-posted to another Typhoon unit, No. 3 Sqn.

F/O Eugeniusz Gottowt was posted to No. 183 Sqn in December 1942. He would serve with the unit until his death in a flying accident in July 1943. In February 1943 he was briefly joined by F/Lt Zbigniew Moszyński, who was, however, posted to No. 318 Sqn just two months later.

No. 3 Sqn was the last Typhoon-equipped fighter unit of the RAF that had Polish pilots flying with it. F/Sgt Józef Fudala and F/O Erazm Wardziński were posted to it in December 1943. As already mentioned, F/O Żurakowski and Sgt Domański joined them in February 1944. This was not a good month for No. 3 Sqn's Polish contingent, though: Fudala was killed during a 'Roadstead' to Zeebrugge on the 23rd, while Wardziński was downed on the 29th. The latter managed to evade capture, however, and returned to Britain in early October. Żurakowski and Domański continued to serve with No. 3 Sqn after it converted to Tempests in May 1944.

Two more Polish pilots flew Typhoons on tactical reconnaissance operations: S/Ldr Jerzy Gołko with No. 268 Squadron between September and November 1944, and F/Lt Mieczysław Urban with No. 4 Sqn from October 1944 until January 1945.

Polish test pilots also flew Hawker Typhoons in trials with the Royal Aircraft Establishment at Farnborough. The type was flown by Polish ferry pilots as well. Among these, 1st/Off Anna Leska, a Polish 'Spitfire girl' flying with the ATA, ferried no fewer than 75 aircraft of the type.

Fighter-reconnaissace Typhoon FR.IB's of No. 268 Squadron at B.43 St Omer-Fort Rouge in liberated France, probably photographed on 11 September 1944, when crowds of local French population flooded the airfield. The rear fuselage and tail of Typhoon EK383/G can be seen at the right edge of the photo. This aircraft was flown by F/Lt Jerzy Gołko on operations in September and October 1944. The Typhoon coming towards the camera is presumably either EK180/R or EK196/M (the latter was ferried to B.43 that day, so it might be taxiing upon arrival). Both these aircraft were flown on operations by Polish pilots. F/Lt Gołko used EK196/M during his last Typhoon sortie, on 5 November 1944. EK180, on the other hand, was not flown by a Pole with No. 268 Sqn. However, F/Lt Mieczysław Urban flew it, now coded E, with the No. 4 Sqn in December 1944. Gołko was the only Polish pilot to fly Typhoons on operations with No. 268 Sqn, although both he and three other Poles flew fighter-reconnaissance Mustangs with the unit in 1944–1945 (some of these aircraft can be seen in the background of the photo). The Typhoons shown here are in Day Fighter camouflage and markings, but their propeller spinners are black (with the exception of JP371/A at far left). This photo offers a good view of the reconnaissance modifications of the type: both inboard cannon installations were removed; a forward looking camera was mounted inside the starboard cannon compartment, its lens aligned with the stub fairing, while three downward looking oblique cameras were fitted in the port compartment, that cannon fairing being removed completely.

Hawker Tempest

Poles flew Tempests on operations with Nos. 3 and 501 Squadrons.

As already mentioned, F/O Tadeusz Żurakowski and Sgt Stanisław Domański were flying Typhoons with No. 3 Sqn when it converted onto the Tempest in May 1944. Sadly, Żurakowski was killed on 27 May during a sortie off the French coast. Sgt Domański met his fate on 3 July 1944, when he was shot down in error by friendly AA fire while chasing a V1 flying bomb.

A well-known publicity photo depicting No. 3 Sqn pilots 'discussing next operation' around the tail of Tempest V JN812/ JF-M. The pilot at far right of the photo, near the rudder, is Sgt Stanisław Domański, who scored some V1s destroyed while flying with the unit, but was killed on 3 July 1944, falling to friendly AA fire. The Tempest displays quite neat D-Day bands around its fuselage and wings. Note the clear traces of unit code change in May 1944: the previous code of QO was replaced by JF and the patches where the previous letters were partly overpainted are quite prominent.

Tempest V EJ555/SD-Y of No. 501 Sqn RAF. The aircraft was flown on operations by W/O Edward Wojczyński in October 1944, a few days before this photo was taken. It displays Day Fighter camouflage scheme with a perfectly standard set of markings. Half a year later, upon disbandment of No. 501 Squadron in April 1945, F/Lt Józef Mierzejewski (serving with No. 1 Aircraft Delivery Flight RAF at the time) ferried this machine from Hunsdon (No. 501's last base) to No. 84 Group Support Unit at Lasham.

The last Tempest V but one, SN354, was used for trials with the 40 mm Vickers P anti-tank cannon installation in late 1945/early 1946. On 17 January 1946 F/Lt Antoni Majcherczyk of the AAEE at Boscombe Down suffered an engine failure in the aircraft immediately after the take-off. He managed to make a successful emergency landing, with the aircraft only slightly damaged. It seems the Tempest was in standard camouflage and markings of home-based operational RAF fighters.

Two Polish pilots were posted to No. 501 Squadron on Tempests in mid-August 1944: S/Ldr Piotr Ostaszewski-Ostoja and W/O Edward Wojczyński. At the time the unit converted from day to night fighter duties, intercepting the V1s. W/O Wojczyński enjoyed considerable success in these operations and he stayed with the unit until its disbandment on 20 April 1945, when he was re-posted to No. 129 Sqn on Mustangs. S/Ldr Ostaszewski was posted to No. 307 Sqn on Mosquitoes in late September 1944.

A number of Polish pilots ferried Tempests with RAF and ATA units. Polish pilots also flew Tempests occasionally at RAF training establishments in the period immediately following the end of hostilities in Europe.

At least two Polish Air Force test pilots: Janusz Żurakowski and Antoni Majcherczyk flew Tempests in trials at the AAEE Boscombe Down.

In the post-war years a number of Polish pilots flew Tempests with British and Pakistani air forces, but they were no longer in Polish Air Force service, so that is quite another story...

No. 33 Sqn Tempest V NV678/5R-M was flown by F/Lt Kazimierz Dolicher at No. 24 Armament Practice Camp at Sylt in April 1946. The aircraft, shown here among other machines of No. 33 Squadron, was finished in standard BAFO scheme and markings, including a black spinner, no Sky band around the fuselage, and large serial number on wing under sides.

Tempest II PR533 (the first aircraft of the type with the wings strengthened to carry two 1,000 lb bombs) was flight tested by S/Ldr Janusz Żurakowski at the AAEE between September and November 1945. Typically for production aircraft diverted for testing, it was left in standard camouflage and markings of home-based RAF fighters.

Hawker Tempest V EJ763/SD-X, No. 501 Squadron, late 1944. Upper surface camouflage colours: Ocean Grey and Dark Green ('A' pattern); under surface colour: Medium Sea Grey. Standard British national markings.

Two air-to-air shots of a trio of No. 501 Squadron Tempest Vs: EJ763/SD-X, EJ599/SD-W and EJ589/SD-J. W/O Edward Wojczyński flew EJ763/SD-X repeatedly on night anti-V1 operations. He used it to down two 'Divers' in October 1944: on the 14th at 03.45a.m. and on the 17th at 10.13p.m. Tempest EJ589/SD-J was flown several times by S/Ldr Piotr Ostaszewski.

Curtiss P-36/Mohawk & P-40/Tomahawk/Kittyhawk

No Polish squadron was ever equipped with the Curtiss fighters, but Polish pilots flew the type in combat with RAF and USAAF units in North Africa and China. Notably, in both theatres Polish pilots flew with famous units that adorned their Curtiss fighters with the distinctive 'sharkmouth' nose-art.

Curtiss Mohawk IV AX888 at No. 71 OTU, RAF Gordon's Tree, 1941. It was despatched from Takoradi on 5 November in a convoy of three Mohawks flown by Polish ferry pilots F/O Witold Jander, P/O Henryk Knapik and Sgt Stanisław Bujakowski, although the allocation of individual aircraft to pilots is not known. They arrived at Gordon's Tree on 9 November. Later it may also have been flown by Polish fighter pilots during their training at No. 71 OTU. The aircraft is in Temperate Land camouflage with Sky undersides.

Tomahawk IIB AK406 during assembly at Takoradi in mid-1941. Curtiss fighters sent by sea to West Africa were delivered in Temperate Land camouflage on upper surfaces, with Sky undersides. The camouflage pattern of Dark Earth and Dark Green areas is indiscernible in most photos. AK406 was a presentation aircraft, as shown by the decal on the fuselage. It was subsequently ferried across Africa (with RAF national markings applied) by F/Sgt Stanisław Szubka between 16 August and 4 September 1941.

With the RAF

Polish ferry pilots flew various aircraft of the P-36/P-40 family delivered to the RAF, both in the British Isles and overseas. Large numbers of these aircraft were ferried by Polish pilots on the trans-African route from Takoradi (on the Atlantic Coast) or Port Sudan to the Middle East. These included the Hawk 75 (similar to those flown by Polish pilots in the Battle of France – known as the P-36 in the USAAF and as the Mohawk in the RAF), the Hawk 81 (P-40A to C/Tomahawk) and the Hawk 87 (P-40D onwards/Kittyhawk). The Mohawks, Tomahawks and early Kittyhawks were from direct purchases, while later Kittyhawks were procured under Lend-Lease agreements.

In late 1941 a group of Polish ferry pilots in Africa volunteered for operational fighter service. They were first posted to No. 71 OTU at Gordon's Tree in Sudan, where they underwent training on Mohawks and Tomahawks.

In February 1942 they joined No. 112 Sqn RAF in Libya. By then it had been equipped with the Kittyhawk Is (P-40D), subsequently it also received Mk IAs (P-40E).

Even before the Polish group commenced operations with the squadron, F/O Czesław Matusiak was killed in a flying accident of Kittyhawk I AK584 (code unknown) on 12 February. Sgt Zbigniew Urbańczyk was the first Pole to fly on operations with the 'Flying Sharks', completing two patrols in AK702/GA-P on 14 February. Two Polish pilots were shot down on 21 February: Sgt Józef Derma crash-landed in AK894 but escaped unhurt, while F/O Witold Jander suffered injuries in AK814 and was hospitalised (he was eventually killed on 25 October when the *Luftwaffe* bombed a hospital where he was undergoing follow-on treatment).

During March 1942 No. 112 Sqn pioneered the use of single-seat fighters for ground attack dive bombing, which subsequently became one of the roles commonly flown by RAF and allied fighters in all theatres. Polish pilots took part in some of these initial 'Kittybomber' missions of the war. On 13 March Sgt Jerzy Różański was shot down in AK834, but he managed to crash-land safely near Tobruk. On 14 March the Polish group scored their only air-to-air success when Sgt Urbańczyk in AK913 shared with S/Ldr Clive Caldwell in the destruction of a Messerschmitt 109.

On 26 May P/O Henryk Knapik was hit by Flak and wounded in AK682/GA-U. He managed to land at El Gazala and was hospitalised. Most of the Poles left No. 112 Sqn by the end of May.

On 10 July the group suffered their last loss when F/O Feliks Knoll was shot down and killed in AK892/GA-T. P/O Knapik returned to No. 112 Sqn about that time and continued to fly Kittyhawks with it until mid-September.

A Curtiss Tomahawk ferried across Africa by a Polish pilot, photographed in flight from another machine of the same convoy. The aircraft is in barely discernible Temperate Land camouflage, with Sky undersides. The figure '5' on the side of the fuselage was applied temporarily for the ferry flight. When F/Sgt Szubka ferried AK406 it bore no. 5 in its convoy, so it may well be the same machine. The white rear fuselage spine (and horizontal tail upper surface) served as an additional marking to facilitate spotting the aircraft both in the air and on the ground, and particularly in the case of an emergency landing in deserted areas. Also the top of the cockpit canopy was painted white to screen the pilot from direct sunlight.

Curtiss Kittyhawk I AK578/GA-V of No. 112 Squadron was used by ace F/Lt Neville Duke to score a couple of victories in February 1942. It was also flown on operations by Poles, F/O Witold Jander and Sgt Jerzy Różański. The aircraft is shown in the initial finish of No. 112 Sqn Kittyhawks: with Desert camouflage on upper surfaces and Sky undersides. The Desert scheme was obtained by overspraying the Dark Green areas of Temperate Land pattern with Middle Stone (it seems that the fuselage roundel was partly obscured in the process). The serial number was left in a rectangular 'window' of the original Dark Green on the rear fuselage. The 'sharkmouth' motif was similar in general style on all aircraft of the squadron but differed in details. AK578 was one of a few initial Kittyhawks armed with just four machine guns in wings.

Kittyhawk AK637/GA-I taxies at a desert airfield with Sgt Różański seated on the wingtip. The huge nose of the Kittyhawk obscured forward view from the cockpit completely when taxiing, so the pilot needed a 'guide' on the wing. The aircraft displays the standard armament of most Kittyhawks: six wing-mounted 0.50 in. machine guns. It is finished in the Desert camouflage on upper surfaces with Sky undersides. Note the different shape of 'teeth' and 'eye' in the 'sharkmouth' artwork as compared to AK578. This Kittyhawk was flown on operations by F/O Feliks Knoll and Sgts Józef Derma, Stanisław Grondowski, Jerzy Różański and Zbigniew Urbańczyk.

Lt William B. Carlton with his P-40K, named 'Stinky', after it was damaged in the landing accident of S/Ldr Witold Urbanowicz on 8 December 1943. The 'sharkmouth' motif on the P-40s of the American 'Flying Tigers' in China was more elaborate than that in No. 112 Sqn RAF. The name of the usual pilot was displayed below the windscreen. As far as can be ascertained, Urbanowicz had no fighter assigned to him and flew other pilots' mounts.

With the USAAF

S/Ldr Witold Urbanowicz was the only Polish Air Force fighter pilot to fly in combat against the Japanese in the Far East. During his spell as an assistant air attaché at the Polish Embassy in Washington, DC, he managed to obtain an exchange posting to fly with USAAF units in China. He arrived in the theatre in late October 1943. Apparently he initially flew with the 26th Fighter Squadron of the 51st Fighter Group from Kunming.

The following month he joined the 75th FS of the 23rd FG (the "Flying Tigers") at Hengyang, serving with it until late December 1943. On 8 December he suffered a ground accident in the P-40K-1 usually flown by Lt William B. Carlton. On 11 December he was credited with two enemy fighters destroyed near Nanchang. These were listed as "Zeroes" in USAAF documents but they must have been army fighters in fact, probably Ki-44s (the Mitsubishi A6M "Zero" was a navy fighter, but the name was commonly misapplied at the time to any Japanese radial-engined single-seater).

Curtiss P-40K-1 named 'THE Deacon SAD SACK' parked with other aircraft of the 75th Fighter Squadron USAAF. This was the personal aircraft of Lt. Lyndon R. Lewis and in this photo it displays a single miniature Japanese navy ensign below the windscreen, denoting the victory he scored on 20 September 1943. S/Ldr Witold Urbanowicz flew at least one operational sortie in this aircraft. See pp. 394–395 for more details.

Curtiss Mohawk IV AX891/4, Polish Detachment at RAF Station Takoradi, October 1941. Upper surface camouflage colours: Dark Earth and Dark Green (probably 'A' pattern); under surface colour: probably Sky. Standard British national markings. Temporary ferry markings: white upper surface of the rear fuselage and horizontal tail and white number 4.

Below: *Two Mohawk IVs upon arrival at RAF Gordon's Tree, for service with No. 71 OTU. AX891 is in the foreground. It still features the white markings applied for the ferry flight and the convoy number 4. The unusual appearance of the fuselage roundel in this picture is due to the use of photographic material that rendered the yellow outline unnaturally dark.*

Above right: A poor but rare photo of Polish ferry pilots in Africa with an RAF Mohawk IV, probably AX891 (despatched from Takoradi on 24 October 1941). Standing second right is probably Sgt Stanisław Bujakowski. The aircraft is in Temperate Land camouflage scheme with, presumably, Sky undersides. The white patches on upper rear fuselage and on the cockpit canopy were applied with washable paint for the ferry flight across the jungles and deserts of Africa. Note the '4' in white applied on the side of the fuselage, partly obscured by Sgt Bujakowski. This was a temporary number that identified the aeroplane within a trans-African ferry convoy.

Curtiss Kittyhawk I AK772/GA-Y 'London Pride', No. 112 Squadron, spring 1942. Upper surface camouflage colours: Dark Earth and Middle Stone ('B' pattern); under surface colour: probably Azure. Standard British national markings. Theatre quick recognition markings in form of red propeller spinner. No. 112 Sqn marking in form of the 'sharkmouth' motif on the nose. Individual name 'London Pride' applied in small characters above the aircraft letter on the rear fuselage.

Kittyhawk I AK772/GA-Y with a 250 lb bomb with an extended fuse attached on the under-fuselage carrier. In the spring of 1942 No. 112 pioneered the use of single-seat fighters as dive bombers for close air support duties. Offensive operations against the enemy required more appropriate colouring of the under surfaces, the Sky finish was replaced by a much darker colour, probably Azure (Azure Blue). Note how the yellow outline of the fuselage roundel was partly obliterated with Middle Stone when the camouflage scheme was changed from Temperate Land to Desert. AK772 was flown by F/Lt Feliks Gazda in March and by P/O Henryk Knapik in April 1942.

Curtiss P-40K-1 (USAAF serial unknown)/169 'THE Deacon SAD SACK', 75th Fighter Squadron, 23rd Fighter Group, Hengyang, late 1943. Upper surface camouflage: Dark Olive Drab; under surface colour: Neutral Gray. US national markings limited to 'star and bar' insignia on top of the port wing and underneath the starboard wing. 23rd FG marking in form of the 'sharkmouth' motif on the nose. 75th FS markings in form of white forward section of the propeller spinner and white code number between 150 and 199. Parts of the rear fuselage and fin overpainted with unspecified dark green where previous markings were obliterated. Individual name 'THE Deacon SAD SACK' applied in white below the exhausts. The name and rank of the usual pilot, Lt. Lyndon R. Lewis applied in white below the windscreen with his score marked beneath in form of a Japanese navy ensign.

P-40K-1 no. 169 named 'THE Deacon SAD SACK' opens a line-up of the 75th Fighter Squadron USAAF. Patches of different camouflage colour can be discerned on the side of the fuselage and on the fin (particularly beneath the digits 6 and 9), marking the areas were previous markings had been overpainted. The main wheel hub is painted black with white edge. S/Ldr Witold Urbanowicz flew this aircraft at least once, on 4 December, on a mission to drop ammunition for Chinese troops at Tehshan (now Deshan) during the battle at Changteh (now Changde). Note that the next aircraft in line shows a disruptive pattern on the nose. Many P-40Ks used by the USAAF in China were diverted machines in RAF Temperate Land camouflage.

Lt. Lyndon R. Lewis in the cockpit of his P-40K-1 no. 169. The photo shows the pilot's details applied below the windscreen. The two Japanese navy ensigns denote two victories he scored while flying with the 75th FS: on 20 September and on 10 December 1943. Only the first of these (the rearmost one) was present when Urbanowicz flew this aircraft on 4 December 1943, although it is not impossible that he then flew no. 169 again after 10 December.

An interesting, if poor quality, shot of the other side of the 'THE Deacon SAD SACK', showing the name applied on this side and the 'star and bar' insignia on the starboard wing. Note the external fuel tank with the tail section cut off and blanked off. In such form it was used as a container for dropping supplies to ground troops.

Republic P-47 Thunderbolt

No Polish unit was ever equipped with the P-47, but numerous Polish pilots flew the type with various allied units and establishments.

With the RAF

F/Lt Jerzy Solak was in all probability the first Polish AF pilot to fly the Thunderbolt. In February 1943, while serving with the Air Fighting Development Unit at RAF Duxford, he flew P-47C s/n 41-6198, on loan from the USAAF to the RAF for trials.

Two years later, in 1945, S/Ldr Janusz Żurakowski flew several Thunderbolt I and II aircraft in trials with the Aeroplane and Armament Experimental Establishment at Boscombe Down.

Polish ferry pilots also flew the Thunderbolt, delivering the type to RAF units in South-East Asia.

Certainly the most famous Polish P-47 pilot: F/Lt Bolesław Gładych and his equally famous personal emblem: a cartoon penguin named 'Pengie'. Contrary to a popular myth, not all of Gładych's personal P-47s sported this emblem. This particular nose-art was applied on P-47D-22 s/n 42-26300/HV-V.

Below: P-47D-22 s/n 42-26300 was delivered to the USAAF in natural metal finish and was used as such by the 61st Fighter Squadron of the 56th Fighter Group, coded HV-V. The 'Radio Call Number' on the tail was, essentially, the USAAF serial number without the first digit or the dash ('226300' instead of s/n 42-26300). The red band at the front of the engine cowling was initially the 61st FS quick recognition marking, but was adopted by the entire 56th FG, following which the rudder in the same colour identified the 61st FS. The 'Pengie III' nose-art was applied on both sides of the nose. On D-Day (6 June) evening Gładych flew this P-47 when he was credited with an Me 109 destroyed. By that time, of course, the aircraft had been marked with the distinctive white-and-black bands around the fuselage and wings. A day later F/Lt Zbigniew Janicki used this Thunderbolt to claim a Focke-Wulf probably destroyed and another one damaged. This P-47D was destroyed in a ground fire at Boxted on 18 July 1944. Note that this natural metal 'Pengie III' has been misidentified in some publications as s/n 42-25836/HV-M (probably due to the popular myth that Gładych's personal Thunderbolts were invariably coded HV-M).

With the USAAF

In 1944 and 1945 a number of Polish fighter pilots obtained exchange postings to various USAAF units. Although the principal aim of these postings was to gain experience at various levels of command, a number of the pilots used the opportunity to fly on operations with American units.

The most famous Polish team flew with the 61st Fighter Squadron 56th Fighter Group of the 8th Air Force. This originated from the personal friendship between the squadron commander, Lt. Col. Francis Gabreski and a number of Polish pilots. Gabreski was an American pilot of Polish parentage (born as Franciszek Gabryszewski) who had earlier flown Spitfires with No. 315 Squadron at Northolt. W/Cdr Aleksander Gabszewicz was the first Pole to join the 61st FS temporarily in February 1944, soon followed by F/Lt Bolesław Gładych. Within weeks Gabszewicz returned to lead Polish wings, but Gładych would continue flying P-47s with the 56th FG until the end of the war. He was joined in March by S/Ldr Tadeusz Sawicz and F/Lt Tadeusz Andersz, and in May by S/Ldr Kazimierz Rutkowski and F/Lts Zbigniew Janicki and Witold Łanowski. Gładych was by far the most successful of the group and he was eventually officially credited with 10 enemy aircraft destroyed in the air while flying the Thunderbolt with the Americans (many more aerial victories were attributed to him in various non-official accounts). Łanowski and Andersz also scored

An interesting air-to-air shot of 61st Fighter Squadron P-47s during the summer of 1944. Although the formation looks pretty chaotic in this view, it consists of two neat sections in fact. The finger-four nearest camera is led by s/n 42-28520/HV-P with s/n 42-28623/HV-N at its port wingtip, while s/n 42-28834/HV-H is flown by the other element leader with s/n 42-25864/HV-Z as his starboard wingman. The other section is partly obscured. Its leader flies s/n 44-19718/HV-M (hiding here behind HV-H) with s/n 42-27224/HV-G as the port wingman, while the other element of that section is led by s/n 44-19739/HV-A, with s/n 42-26044/HV-Z (hidden behind HV-Z) as the wingman. Note the multitude of colour schemes. The USAAF adopted natural metal finish on its aircraft as standard pretty early on, but the 56th Fighter Group did not enjoy the concept, repainting their Thunderbolts in a variety of camouflage patterns. Several aircraft of this formation are known to have been flown by Polish pilots, although not necessarily on this occasion. s/n 42-26044/HV-Z and s/n 44-19718/HV-M are discussed in detail in subsequent pages. Both s/n 42-27224/HV-G and s/n 42-28834/HV-H are believed to have been flown on operations by F/Lt Witold Łanowski. s/n 42-25864/HV-Z was used by Łanowski to claim an Me 109 destroyed on 5 July 1944. The same Thunderbolt was also flown by F/Lt Zbigniew Janicki.

F/Lts Stanisław Socha (left) and Tomasz Rzyski (both from No. 303 Sqn) posing on Gładych's last personal Thunderbolt, P-47M s/n 44-21127/HV-M, in 1945. The meaning of the 26 crosses and the 'Yellow man' symbol is discussed on p. 400. On earlier aircraft the crosses were applied in various colours to denote different categories of victories, but they all appear uniform here. The colour of the crosses is not certain (probably red), but they are evidently paler than the black finish of the aircraft.

F/Lt Czesław Główczyński posing with a 366th FG P-47D-28 called 'Blitz Buggy'. Note the aircraft code letter Y on the cowling lip right next to his face. The pilot flew all of his P-47 operational missions with the 390th FS, but none in a Y-coded machine.

P-47D-22 s/n 42-26066/I7-E of the 493rd FS 48th FG about to take off from the A-4 airfield at Deux Jumeaux in Normandy in July 1944. F/Lt Jerzy Solak flew this aircraft on 24 July when he joined the 493rd FS on a fighter-bomber mission to St Lo area (by the time of that sortie the D-Day markings had presumably been reduced to lower surfaces of the airframe only).

air-to-air victories on P-47s. Janicki was credited with a probable and a damaged, but he was killed on 13 June in P-47D-16 s/n 42-76145 during an operational mission over France.

Polish pilots who flew P-47s with 9th Air Force units did not achieve such fame, but were also numerous. At least six such officers have been identified.

F/Lt Jerzy Solak (see above) was posted to the HQ of the 48th Fighter Group in May and regularly joined its three P-47 squadrons (the 492nd, 493rd and 494th FS) on operations. On 10 August 1944 he was shot down at Finchebray in P-47D-22 s/n 42-26334/F4-V (a 492nd FS machine). Following a short period in captivity he escaped and returned to service, but he did no more flying with the USAAF.

F/Lt Czesław Głowczyński obtained a posting to the 390th FS 366th FG in December 1944. He then flew P-47s with the squadron until July 1945.

Other Polish pilots who also flew P-47s with US units included F/Lt Stefan Łaszkiewicz (attached to the 9th Tactical Air Command), F/Lt Walerian Jasionowski (9th Air Defence Command), F/Lt Jerzy Zbrożek (9th Fighter Command) and F/Lt Józef Sobolewski (9th Air Support Command).

P-47D-28 s/n 42-29245/B2-B, photographed at Y-29 airfield at Asch in Belgium, was the aircraft in which F/Lt Głowczyński soloed on the type on 5 January 1945. On 18 January he used it again, during his first Thunderbolt operational sortie, which he described in his flying log book as 'Intercept. Maastricht – Aachen'.

Thunderbolt I FL844 (ex-P-47D-22 s/n 42-25792) was test flown by S/Ldr Janusz Żurakowski in take-off trials at the AAEE in April and May 1945. The aircraft was in standard RAF camouflage and markings of the time, although the roundel's yellow ring looks unnaturally dark due to the use of photographic material that enhanced warm hues.

Republic P-47D-11-RE s/n 42-75224/Q 'SOVEREIGN SENATORS / DEFENDER'/'Pengie III', 61st Fighter Squadron, 56th Fighter Group, Boxted, spring 1944. Upper surface camouflage: Dark Olive Drab; under surface colour: Neutral Gray. Standard US national markings. No squadron code. Group marking: red band around the nose. Squadron marking: the rudder in red. Victory markings on the port side of fuselage below the cockpit. Personal emblem 'Pengie III' on both sides of the engine cowling.

Left: *F/Lt Bolesław Gładych boarding his personal camouflaged razorback P-47. The box below the windscreen displays his name as the pilot, followed by those of his trusted ground crew. The victory markings in the upper row all seem to include black crosses (in the original photo the colour of the crosses can definitely be seen as slightly darker than the surrounding finish of the aircraft). Only the first cross in the lower row looks as dark as the upper ones, while the next three are slightly paler than the camouflage. These must have been applied in a different colour, to denote a lesser victory category, such as 'probably destroyed' or air-to-ground kills.*

Opposite page: *A general view of the same aircraft. It was one of several P-47s funded by the New York lodge (known as the 'Sovereign Senators') of an organisation called the 'Knights of Pythias'. All these aircraft bore similar presentation inscriptions, with 'SOVEREIGN SENATORS' followed by an individual name – 'DEFENDER' in this case (arguably the most well known of these P-47s was 'SOVEREIGN SENATORS / K. of P.', delivered to the USSR under Lend-Lease Act). Due to the presence of the large presentation name in the usual location of the squadron code, s/n 42-75224 displayed only the aircraft letter Q on the port side of the fuselage. This aircraft has been portrayed in other publications as 'Pengie II', but recently unearthed photographic evidence shows that the Roman numeral in the nose-art was in fact 'III'. This photo was taken after D-Day, by which time Gładych had another personal P-47D, s/n 42-26300/HV-V (also named 'Pengie III', see p. 396), but s/n 42-75224/Q still displayed his score and nose-art. The scoreboard can be seen to consist of ten crosses in the upper row, with four more crosses in the second row, followed by the 'yellow man' and another cross. The initial set of 14 crosses was probably applied at the time when the P-47 was allocated to Gładych (soon after 8 March 1944). The eleven black crosses corresponded to 'confirmed destroyed' (eight claimed with Polish squadrons during 1941–1943 plus three with the 61st FS until 8 March 1944.). The meaning of the three coloured crosses that followed is unclear, but these must have referred to 'lesser successes' (possibly two 'probably destroyed' scored with Polish units plus one ground kill with the 61st FS on 6 March 1944). The 'yellow man' and the 15th cross were then added after the air combat on 27 March south of Angers, when a German pilot baled out of his Messerschmitt 109 before Gładych even opened fire on that aircraft. Note that this Olive Drab 'Pengie' has been misidentified in some publications as s/n 42-75410/HV-M (probably due to the fact that the latter was written off when flown by Gładych, and also to the myth about all his Thunderbolts being coded HV-M).*

SOVEREIGN SENATORS
DEFENDER

Republic P-47D-22 s/n 42-26044/HV-Z 'Silver Lady', 61st Fighter Squadron, 56th Fighter Group, Boxted, 1944. Natural metal finish overall. Standard US national markings. Group marking: red band around the nose. Squadron marking: the rudder in red. Full invasion markings in form of white and black bands on the fuselage and wings. Victory markings on the port side of fuselage below the cockpit. Personal name 'Silver Lady' and victory markings on the port side of fuselage below the cockpit. Crown personal motif on both sides of the engine cowling.

Polish AF pilots of the 61st Fighter Squadron USAAF photographed at Boxted in mid-June 1944. Left to right: F/Lt Bolesław Gładych, S/Ldr Tadeusz Sawicz, Lt. Col. Frank Gabreski (the 61st FS commander), S/Ldr Kazimierz Rutkowski (often misidentified as "Janicki", who had been killed before this photo was taken), F/Lt Tadeusz Andersz and F/Lt Witold Łanowski. Backdrop is provided by P-47D s/n 42-26044/HV-Z 'Silver Lady' with the distinctive golden crown nose-art on the side of the cowling.

A later photo of ground crew members on the P-47, now fitted with the 'Malcolm hood'. The photo shows details of the name 'Silver Lady'. Note that Maj. Smith's score had been obliterated by then.

'Silver Lady' during routine pre-flight maintenance, photographed about the same time as the group photo of Polish pilots on previous page. Note the D-Day bands on the wing and fuselage, and the oversize 'star & bar' national insignia on the bottom of the port wing. The crown nose-art was applied with golden (not yellow!) paint on both sides of the cowling. S/n 42-26044 had been the assigned machine of Maj. Leslie C. Smith until he finished his first tour of duty, and was then frequently flown by Polish pilots, who used it to claim a number of victories. Gładych was credited with two 'kills' in it: an Me 109 on 5 July and a Ju 88 on 12 August. Łanowski scored an FW 190 destroyed on 18 November. The tail of s/n 42-74620/HV-B can be seen on the left – that Thunderbolt was also flown by F/Lt Łanowski in June and July 1944.

S/n 42-26044/HV-Z during June 1944, with full D-Day bands. At the time it still displayed Maj. Leslie C. Smith's seven 'kill' symbols below the cockpit, although he had left the squadron by then. The name 'Silver Lady' referred to the aircraft's natural metal finish – it was, apparently, the first unpainted P-47 delivered to the unit at the time when all its fighters were still in factory-applied camouflage. This name is often shown as yellow in artistic renditions, but there are colour photographs that show it as greyish blue (clearly more fitting for the 'Silver' appellation). The black codes were outlined in red, the group and squadron identification colour.

Republic P-47D-28 s/n 44-19718/HV-M, 61st Fighter Squadron, 56th Fighter Group, Boxted, autumn 1944. Upper surface camouflage: probably dark green; under surface colour: natural metal/grey. Standard US national markings. Group marking: red band around the nose. Squadron marking: the rudder in red. Late-1944 invasion markings in form of white and black bands on the bottom of the fuselage only. Victory markings on the port side of fuselage below the cockpit.

Left: *Gładych posing with P-47D s/n 44-19718, his first personal 'Bubbletop', accompanied by his crew chief, S/Sgt Richard Moffat. The Thunderbolt was originally delivered in natural metal finish and its camouflage was applied in the 56th FG. Although the colour is not certain, it was most probably a dark green. It is sometimes incorrectly shown as black or nearly black, but the black crosses in the pilot's scoreboard are visibly darker than the surrounding camouflage n this photo.*

Above: *F/Lt Łanowski arrives in s/n 44-19718/HV-M at RAF Andrews Field in January 1945 to visit his friends in the Mustang-equipped No. 133 (Polish) Wing based there. The absence of any nose-art on the cowling is obvious in this view, even though this Thunderbolt is often claimed to have been 'Pengie IV'. Note the oversize US insignia on the bottom surface of the port wing and the under-fuselage D-Day bands (with the forward white one much shorter than the other four). It seems that the wing under surface was repainted grey.*

Middle photo: *Bolesław Gładych and Tadeusz Andersz in front of s/n 44-19718. The scoreboard on this P-47 was applied in rows of four crosses. The upper six rows denoted victories claimed by Gładych before he was allocated this machine: the top sixteen crosses (with white outlines) were for enemy aircraft destroyed and the eight below these (with dark outlines, presumably red) for the 'lesser victories'. The two white-outlined crosses at the bottom must have been added after he claimed two FW 190s destroyed on 21 September 1944 while flying this Thunderbolt. The 'yellow man' was now applied separately, not among the 'kill' symbols. By the time this P-47 entered service with the 61st FS the white-and-black identification bands had been reduced to the bottom of the fuselage only. The forward white band reached only as high up as the prominent panel line there, while the other bands extended up to the star-and-bar insignia.*

Republic P-47M-1 s/n 44-21108/HV-Z, 61st Fighter Squadron, 56th Fighter Group, Boxted, early 1945. Upper surface camouflage: black; under surface colour: natural metal. Standard US national markings. Group marking: red band around the nose. Squadron marking: the rudder in red. Cockpit framing painted golden. Personal emblem (an armoured knight's hand crushing a German fighter) on the engine cowling. A horseshoe attached below the windscreen. Unpainted dorsal fin fillet.

Left: The well known photo of F/Lt Łanowski's personal P-47M in 1945, after the dorsal fillet was painted to match the rest of the airframe. Note that the fuselage US insignia has a pale outline, but that on the wing upper surface has not.

Below: P-47M-1 s/n 44-21108/HV-Z, with its unmistakable personal emblem on the cowling, photographed at RAF Andrews Field in early April 1945 among the Mustangs of the Polish squadrons there. Note the unpainted dorsal fillet and the absence of US insignia on the bottom of the port wing.

Left: Close-up of Łanowski's personal emblem which showed the Polish AF national marking (a white and red chequered square) with a superimposed image of a knight's hand in a gauntlet crushing a Luftwaffe fighter. A narrow outline was added to the upper left section of the square so that it did not blend in with the 56th FG red cowling band.

Polish Night Fighter and Intruder Units Alongside the RAF

No. 307 Squadron was established by orders dated 24 August 1940. Kirton-in-Lindsey was its first base and it was initially equipped with Boulton Paul Defiant I turret fighters. The unit's role was purely air defence, in the face of mounting air attacks by German night bombers against British cities.

In late July 1941 the squadron received its first Bristol Beaufighter IIFs. The re-equipment entailed personnel movements as the other crew member was now a radar operator rather than a gunner. Some of the gunners retrained in the new role, while some experienced Defiant crews transferred to RAF units still flying the type. To gain experience in the entirely new kind of night fighter flying some crews were also attached to RAF units equipped with radar-equipped aircraft.

For twin-engined flying training the squadron also used some Blenheim Is (as well as non-fighter types, such as the Oxford).

In May 1942 the unit took delivery of its first Beaufighter VIFs.

A number of crews excelled in the night air defence, scoring multiple victories on the Beaufighters. The crew of Sgts Bolesław Turzański (pilot) and Henryk Ostrowski (radar operator) were in a class of their own, credited with four confirmed 'kills' in just four engagements with enemy aircraft!

Just before Christmas 1942 the squadron started conversion onto the Mosquito II, the 'Wooden Wonder'. Unlike in the Beaufighter, the radar-operator/navigator was now seated side-by-side with the pilot, which ensured close co-operation of the crew.

Standard finish of a Defiant of No. 307 Squadron: matt black overall, with standard British national markings, light grey codes and the Polish red-white square beneath the cockpit.

A Beaufighter IIF of No. 307 Sqn in standard finish: Special Night overall.

F/O Grzegorz Bukowiecki (not to be confused with F/O Zdzisław Buchowiecki of the same unit) on a Beaufighter IIF of No. 307 Sqn. Note the stencil-applied Polish marking.

In May 1943 the squadron commenced intruder missions over enemy airfields in occupied Holland and France, and Ranger sorties, but it also continued to fly air defence patrols due to lack of crews trained in offensive operations.

In June No. 307 Sqn commenced daylight section-strength patrols over the Bay of Biscay, as part of the anti-U-boat warfare. In early August 1943 the unit was attached to to Coastal Command and for the next three months flew no other missions but patrols over the Biscay by formations of between three and twelve Mosquitoes (usually no more than six). The aim was to intercept any German long range aircraft to protect allied air patrols against U-boats. During that time the unit operated a mix of Mosquito IIs and VIs.

Bristol Beaufighter VI X8005 EW-R in Special Night finish provides backdrop for a parade during the visit of Gen. Władysław Sikorski, the Polish C-in-C, in No. 307 Sqn in September 1942. Note the pale area aft of the cockpit: the Polish Air Force national marking and three swastikas denoting the victories credited to F/O Gerard Ranoszek, the usual pilot of this aircraft.

The same Beaufighter VI X8005 EW-R in the subsequent colour scheme (introduced in October): Medium Sea Grey with Dark Green areas on upper surfaces. The Polish marking and the pilot's scoreboard were re-applied on the refinished aircraft. Four swastikas can be seen aft of the cockpit, denoting Ranoszek's aerial victories scored while flying this Beaufighter. The pilot used the machine to claim three enemy aircraft destroyed and one damaged.

At the beginning of November 1943 the squadron moved to Scotland, to operate against German long range aircraft over the North Sea and the Atlantic. Some crews were detached to Sumburgh in the Shetlands to provide longer radius of action. During that period operations were not limited to intercepting enemy aircraft over the sea, offensive missions were also flown against German installation in occupied Norway.

In late January 1944 No. 307 Squadron re-equipped with Mosquito XII and XIII night fighters. The next month it moved to Lincolnshire and resumed night operations. In May No. 307 Sqn moved to Yorkshire, and from there it flew intruder missions over the Continent in preparation for the Normandy landings. During July 1944 No. 307 Squadron was responsible for night fighter defence of the entire eastern coast of Britain north of No. 11 Group, with sections of aircraft detached to other airfields.

De Havilland Mosquito NF.II of No. 23 Squadron in the Intruder scheme of Dark Green/Ocean Grey areas on upper surfaces with the under surfaces painted Night (black). This and other Mosquitoes of the unit in this scheme were flown by Polish crews from Malta.

In late September 1944 No. 307 Sqn commenced re-equipment with the Mosquito XXX. The new mission was to provide support to night bombers, and training for the new role continued until early December. In late January the unit moved to Cambridgeshire. Increased fuel tankage allowed sorties to areas as distant as Austria, Czechoslovakia or Berlin. The last operation mission was flown on 9 May 1945 (one day after the VE-Day!) in support of the re-capture of Jersey.

No. 307 Squadron continued to fly training sorties until the end of 1946. Like other Polish units, it never returned to its homeland, but was disbanded in early 1947.

It is noteworthy that, although nominally a night fighter unit, No. 307 Sqn achieved about half of its victories in daylight operations in the Battle of the Atlantic.

No. 307 Squadron was the most 'high-tech' unit of the exiled Polish Air Force, as since 1941 it operated top-secret radar-equipped aircraft. The knowledge and experience of its air and ground crews would have been invaluable for the post-war Polish aviation had Poland regained her freedom in 1945. It is noteworthy that the communist-controlled post-war Polish Air Force did not receive its first radar-equipped aircraft until 1955!

Douglas Havoc Turbinlite in the two-tone night fighter scheme (Medium Sea Grey/Dark Green) provides backdrop for a parade at Northolt on 23 February 1943, led by W/Cdr Wojciech Kołaczkowski and S/Ldr Franciszek Kornicki (saluting). The location (where a Polish Wing was based) and presence of Polish fighter pilots have led to a myth that this aircraft was used by No. 307 Squadron. It may have, in fact, belonged to No. 1422 Flight, based at RAF Heston (Northolt's satellite airfield).

No. 307 Squadron de Havilland Mosquito NF.II DZ271 EW-R (and another aircraft of the type in a distance) in the two-tone night fighter scheme. The aircraft displays victory markings of F/Lt Gerard Ranoszek, who can be seen in the cockpit, and a stencil-applied Polish marking. Its location and colour layout was standard for No. 307 Sqn Mosquitoes. Note the extremely worn condition of the finish. The five swastikas denote Ranoszek's five victories: three destroyed and a damaged he had scored with No. 307 Sqn, plus one damaged before that, with No. 306 Sqn in a Hurricane. No Polish fighter was credited with five confirmed night 'kills'.

No. 305 (Bomber) Squadron was the other Polish unit equipped with Mosquito FB.VI fighter-bombers and engaged in intruder operations. It converted from North American Mitchells to the Mosquitoes at the end of 1943 while based at RAF Lasham. This involved significant personnel reshuffle as the air crews were reduced from four to just two men: a pilot and a navigator.

From early 1944 on, 20 Mosquitoes and 24 crews were employed on night operations over France, flying intruder patrols against German communications. After the invasion, the nature of combat operations remained unchanged, although daytime operations were also undertaken. Enemy communication lines and troops were attacked.

On 19 November the squadron moved to Epinoy airfield near Cambrai in liberated France. The crews continued to support the ground troops in their advance. On 22 February the squadron took part in 'Clarion', the largest combat operation in the history of air warfare, involving thousands of aircraft that attacked communication lines throughout Germany. No. 305 Sqn was deployed over the northern part of the Reich, near the Danish-German border.

In mid-1944, because of high losses, one flight of No. 305 Sqn was re-formed entirely of British and Allied air crews. It took until July 1945 before the squadron was re-established as an all-Polish unit, by which time it was training in peacetime conditions.

After the end of the war No. 305 Squadron became part of the occupation forces in Germany. From March until October 1946 it was based at Cologne-Wahn. Apart from the usual military activities, aircraft of the squadron flew courier missions to Nuremberg bringing documents for the trials of German war criminals.

In October 1946 the squadron mover to the Polish bomber base at RAF Faldingworth, where it subsequently disbanded.

Throughout the war Polish night-fighter/intruder crews flew with a number of RAF units, including Nos. 23, 25, 85, 96, 125, 151, 153, 219, 255, 264, 418, 533, 604 and 605 Squadrons RAF. The types they flew included various marks of the Defiant, Beaufighter and Mosquito, as well as the Bristol Blenheim and Douglas Boston/Havoc/Turbinlite aircraft.

Training of Polish night fighter crews took place in relevant RAF establishments. Their operational training took place at Nos. 13, 51, 54 and 60 OTUs.

Polish crews also flew various types of night fighter/intruder aircraft at trials establishments and in second-line roles, including ferrying and post-overhaul testing.

Camouflage and Markings of Night Fighters Used by Polish Air Crew Alongside the RAF

Similar to day fighters, Polish night fighter aircraft followed RAF regulations in regard to camouflage schemes and RAF national insignia plus various quick identification markings. There is no need to discuss these in great detail here. The following is a brief summary of principal camouflage schemes and identification markings applied to the aircraft flown by Polish crews. Details of the finishes and markings are covered in the subsequent part that discusses individual aircraft types.

RAF Camouflage Regulations that Applied to Polish Units

The early Boulton Paul Defiants converted for the night fighter role were still finished in the Temperate Land scheme of day fighters, as described in vol. 1.

In October 1940 a new colour scheme was introduced for RAF night fighters: Matt Black overall. In March 1941 Matt Black was replaced by the smooth Special Night (black) finish. The all-black scheme was used on Defiants and Beaufighter IIs and VIs of No. 307 Sqn until mid-1942.

On 1 October 1942 a new scheme was introduced for RAF night fighters: Medium Sea Grey overall with irregular areas of Dark Green on upper surfaces. In No. 307 Sqn this scheme was introduced on Beaufighter VIs in late 1942 and then used on all versions of Mosquitoes until the unit was disbanded.

At the beginning of March 1942 the RAF decided that the intruder aircraft (those used on offensive night fighter-bomber operations) would be camouflaged in line with the Day Fighter scheme

Mosquito NF.XXX NT280/G / EW-S displaying the standard set of codes and British national markings. The '/G' suffix at the serial number meant that the aircraft included sensitive equipment (air interception radar in this case) and therefore required special security while on the ground.

(Dark Green/Ocean Grey on upper surfaces with Medium Sea Grey under surfaces). In October 1942 the colouring of the intruder aircraft was changed: they would retain the Day Fighter scheme (Ocean Grey/Dark Green) on upper surfaces, but the under surfaces were to be painted black. The serial numbers in this scheme would be Dull Red. As far as can be ascertained neither of these schemes was applied to aircraft of Polish units. Numerous Polish crews, however, flew aircraft in such camouflage with allied units.

The special intruder scheme was abandoned in December 1942, replaced by the standard two-tone night fighter scheme of Medium Sea Grey and Dark Green. Therefore, when No. 305 Squadron converted onto Mosquito FB.VIs in late 1943, their aircraft were finished in a similar manner to those of No. 307 Sqn, even though the role of each unit was quite different.

RAF/Allied Identification Markings

As explained in vol. 1, RAF recognition markings were applied on aircraft of the exiled Polish AF throughout their service (1940–1946). The main reason for that was to avoid confusion of the square-shaped Polish national markings with the German crosses.

Until 1945 all aircraft of night fighter units featured red and blue (the so-called 'B' type) RAF roundels on wing upper surfaces. The outer diameter was 56 in. (1,422 mm) for the Defiant, 63 in. (1,600 mm) for the Beaufighter, and 54 in. (1,372 mm) for the Mosquito. In January 1945 these were modified to the so-called 'C' type, with a narrow white ring separating the red and blue areas.

From 1940 until the end of April 1942 the fuselage roundels were red, white, blue and yellow ('A1' type) with the proportion of diameters of the respective areas of 1/3/5/7. The outer diameter was 42 in. (1,067 mm) on the Defiant and 35 in. (889 mm) on the Beaufighter. Then the 'C1' type roundels were introduced. Their dimensions were the same on the Beaufighter and the Mosquito: red/white/blue/yellow diameters of 12/16/32/36 in. (305/406/813/914 mm), respectively.

Similarly, the fin flash was originally made up of three stripes of equal width, but as of May 1942 the white portion was reduced in width, the other stripes extended inwards.

Unlike on day fighters, there were no special quick recognition markings on night fighter or intruder aircraft.

The serial numbers were initially grey. At the beginning of January 1941 it was decided that the serial numbers in this scheme should be Dull Red.

Unit markings consisted of two-character 'codes', plus an individual character for each aircraft in the unit. These were initially applied in light grey on the Defiants in the Temperate Land and Matt Black schemes. Then they were applied in Dull Red on night fighter of No. 307 Squadron in all subsequent schemes. No. 305 Mosquitoes initially featured their code letters in Sky, and from

Mosquito NF.XXX MT497/G / EW-O after the end of the war, showing large black serial number on wing under surface.

A Mosquito FB.VI of No. 305 Squadron displaying the standard form and position of the Polish national marking as applied in that unit.

August 1945 these were applied in yellow, the squadron colour (at the same time the propeller spinners were also repainted yellow).

The serial numbers on the sides of the rear fuselage were black on aircraft in the Temperate Land scheme. In the all-black scheme these were initially grey, but as of January 1941 Dull Red was specified. With the introduction of the two-tone night fighter scheme the serial numbers on the fuselage reverted to black. After the war ended, similar to day fighters, serial numbers were applied in large characters in black on lower surfaces of night fighters.

All senior officers (from Squadron Leaders up) were allowed to apply their rank pennants on their aircraft. A few Polish Wing Commanders used this privilege on their Mosquitoes.

Polish Markings

The Polish Air Force national marking, a white-red chequered square, was applied on the Defiant below the cockpit canopy and on the Beaufighter on the fuselage spine aft of the cockpit glazing. Available photos suggest that not all aircraft of these types displayed this marking. The application of the Polish marking was certainly standardised in No. 307 Squadron on the Mosquito: it was applied on both sides of the fuselage, beneath the windscreen, with the upper left field white.

The standard form on the Mosquitoes of No. 305 Squadron was with the word POLAND applied above the square and well forward of the windscreen. The colour layout of the square varied between aircraft.

Mosquito FB.VI NT227 SM-M of No. 305 Sqn displays the invasion markings as re-introduced in late 1944 on twin-engined aircraft. At the time they were applied on the fuselage only, obscuring the squadron code letters.

Mosquito FB.VI RS559 SM-L of No. 305 Squadron with the black propeller spinners introduced in early 1945.

Mosquito FB.VI NS649 SM-Z in the final colour scheme of No. 305 Squadron aircraft introduced in August 1945: with the spinners and codes in yellow as additional unit identification markings.

Boulton Paul Defiant

No. 307 Squadron 'City of Lwów'

No. 307 Squadron, formed in early September 1940 at RAF Kirton in Lindsey, was the only Polish Air Force unit equipped with Boulton Paul Defiants. Its first complement of 18 of these aircraft was delivered between 14 and 19 September 1940. The aircraft were in Temperate Land camouflage (at the time the standard scheme for day fighters). Night flying and air gunnery training at the Sutton Bridge range commenced in mid-October.

On 7 November 1940 the squadron took its 16 Defiants (two had been damaged in accidents) plus two trainers, a Fairey Battle I and a Miles Master, to RAF Jurby in the Isle of Man. Serious engineering problems at Jurby (lack of spares and tools for the Defiants) affected the serviceability. Doubts as to the night-fighting capability of No. 307 Sqn was voiced on 30 November, when No. 9 Group notified it "that the Squadron is to train for day operational state and not for night operations and that the present aircraft (Defiants) are to be retained".

On 3 December 1940 No. 307 Squadron was declared operational (by day) and the next day it was assigned for convoy protection duties.

It took until early 1941 before a detachment of five Defiants, equipped with new VHF radios, started to operate from RAF Squires Gate providing night defence for Liverpool. The first five

Three members of No. 307 Squadron (Sgts Maksymilian Trawicki, Lucjan Szempliński and Jan Woźny) photographed on 14 December 1940 at RAF Jurby in the Isle of Man. The Defiant I in the foreground is in Temperate Land scheme with Sky under surfaces and 'A' style roundels. The propeller spinner is in Sky, in line with the new quick recognition markings for RAF day fighters introduced at the time (which also included a Sky band around the rear fuselage and black under surface of the port wing. The first Defiants were delivered to No. 307 Squadron in these colours and markings. Note the triple kidney-shaped exhausts (one per two cylinders).

The gun turret of the Defiant with No. 307 Squadron code letters. Note the style of the EW as applied on the Defiants, with the peculiarly shaped W.

Another shot of the Defiant I shown on the previous page with the K aircraft code applied in light grey between the roundel and the turret. All aircraft delivered to No. 307 Squadron were brand new, factory fresh machines coming via No. 19 and 24 Maintenance Units. Clearly, in the early period (at least until December 1940) these aircraft were in the Temperate Land as prescribed for day fighters.

No. 307 Squadron ground crew members in front of a Defiant finished in a disruptive scheme on upper surfaces with black undersides. A part of the aircraft letter I or L in a pale colour can be seen behind the head of the man on the left. Note also the absence of yellow tips on the propeller blades, the six individual exhaust tubes, and the dirty engine cowling.

modified Defiants (N3315, N3435, N1809, N3391 and N3401), painted black overall, were collected from Jurby on 6 and 7 January. It was at that time that Polish national markings were applied for the first time on the all-black aircraft, below the cockpit. The Defiant Is used by No. 307 Squadron had no radar fitted and had to be guided by ground controllers using radio.

On 9 January 1941 the squadron suffered its first fatality. Sgt Antoni Joda lost his bearings over the sea due to problems with radio communication and when he attempted to land near the coast the aircraft overturned in soft sand. The bodies of Sgt Joda and his gunner, Sgt Wiktor Gandurski, were found in their Defiant N3401, which lay on its back off Barmouth, half submerged in the sea.

12 January 1941 saw the decision to fit all No. 307 Sqn Defiants with VHF radios and to move completely to RAF Squires Gate on 20 January. Within the next few days the squadron despatched most of its Defiants to No. 6 Maintenance Unit for modification and received ten new ones, but the move from Jurby to Squires Gate had to be postponed due to snowfall and violent winds. When three Defiants attempted to reach Squires Gate, one was forced to land in a field, and another one was damaged. The rest of the squadron reached Squires Gate four days later, after the weather improved.

On 3 February 1941 the entire squadron was placed at readiness and ordered to maintain half of its strength on alert during the day and the other half during the night. 17 February saw another tragedy: N3314 crashed following aerobatics during formation flying, killing Sgts Kazimierz Bocheński and Kazimierz Frąckiewicz.

Seven patrols were flown along the 'George South' line (Formby-Denbigh) over the Liverpool Bay on the night of 12 March and about 10.00 p.m. the crew of Sgts Franciszek Jankowiak and Jerzy Karais fought the squadrons first air combat, claiming a Heinkel 111 damaged.

On 26 March 1941 the squadron was transferred to No. 10 Group and moved to RAF Colerne, Wilts. Night patrols and extensive training from that station commenced on 6 April 1941.

The unit's first confirmed kill was scored by the crew of Sgts Franciszek Jankowiak and Józef Lipiński in Defiant N3315/EW-C on 12 April at 1.35 a.m. A piece of the wing of the He 111P-2 from the 9./KG 27 was subsequently nailed to the door of the 'A' Flight hut as a trophy.

A still from a cine film, showing a Defiant I of No. 307 Squadron (presumably EW-O or EW-Q) most probably at RAF Church Stanton in August 1941. Note the position of the codes: the squadron letters applied near the tail and the aircraft letter near the turret.

A nice air-to-air shot of an all-black Defiant I coded EW-E or EW-F (serial unknown). The aircraft is in all-black finish of night fighters. Note the position of the Polish national marking near the cockpit and No. 307 Squadron code letters below the turret.

On the night of 15 April F/O Maksymilian Lewandowski and Sgt Mieczysław Zakrocki managed to engage an He 111, which was credited as damaged.

On 26 April the squadron moved to Clyst Honiton airfield, about 4 miles north-east of Exeter. On the night of 11 May the airfield was attacked by bombers and No. 307 Sqn took part in defence. One of the patrolling sections was ordered to scramble at the moment when the second wave of bombers started dropping their load. Only one crew, Sgts Jerzy Malinowski and Stanisław Jarzembowski in Defiant N3403, managed to take off. While flying at about 1,000 ft they spotted an He 111 against the clouds. After a long chase they made a beam attack and the gunner hit the bomber in the middle of the fuselage. When the German turned and gradually entered a dive, the gunner fired again and then the He 111 turned upside down and hit the sea. This was the squadron's second confirmed kill.

In July 1941 No. 307 Sqn resumed convoy protection duties, which outweighed night operations for a short period. The last two Defiant patrols were flown on the night of 15 July, and the last practice 'cooperation' sorties (with Hurricanes) on 26 August.

Between September 1940 and August 1941 No. 307 Squadron operated a total of 60 Boulton Paul Defiants. Five were lost in operational or training flights and one was destroyed during the air raid on Exeter on the night of 11 May 1941.

No. 307 Squadron was credited with two confirmed victories and four enemy aircraft damaged while flying the Defiants.

No. 307 Squadron ground crew members with Defiant I N3336 in the hangar at RAF Exeter during an overhaul in June 1941. The ending of the serial number can be seen on the rear fuselage.

Other Units

No. 307 Squadron crews were attached to other night fighter squadrons. For example, two crews: P/Os Witold Gayzler and Włodzimierz Pfleger, and P/O Stanisław Reymer-Krzywicki with F/O Kazimierz Bokowiec, flew Defiant Is between February and April 1941 with No. 151 Squadron RAF. During that period the unit operated both the Defiant Is and Hawker Hurricane Is, the latter type being phased out gradually. Polish crews were also posted to No. 255 Squadron: Sgts Kazimierz Thiesler and Józef Erdt in March, and Sgt Józef Feruga with F/Sgt Władysław Serafin in April 1941.

Nos. 54 and 60 OTUs that trained night fighter crews, used Defiants (among other types), which were also flown by Polish pilots and air gunners who were then posted to No. 307 Squadron.

P/O Grzegorz Bukowiecki photographed in the summer of 1941 at No. 60 OTU against all-black Defiant I with large code number 54 applied in light grey near the tail. The serial, L7023 or L7029, can be discerned, partly obliterated by the '4' in the code number.

Two all-black Defiant Is of No. 60 OTU photographed between June and August 1941. The aircraft seem to have no code letters or numbers. V1109 is in the foreground, with N1580 (or N1680) behind. The latter has the rear fuselage fairing in the lowered position, to allow turret movement.

As the Defiants were withdrawn from first line squadrons, they were allocated to air gunner schools, such as Nos. 2 and 4 AGS, where they were flown by Polish staff pilots and used by Polish instructors.

The fighter version of the Defiant I was also flown by Polish pilots in anti-aircraft co-operation and ASR units. F/O Stanisław Józef Sowiński was posted in April 1942 to one of the latter, No. 281 Squadron. He graduated as an operational pilot there in July 1942. Before specialised ASR versions of the Defiant were introduced, he flew fighter type Defiant Is. On 20 August 1942 he flew T4036 during a search for the crew of a Beaufighter that crashed off Acklington. On 3 September 1942 he was posted missing with his Canadian air gunner F/Sgt Jean Gererd Pelletier in Defiant I N1804.

Another all-back Defiant I of No. 54 or 60 OTU. In this case the code number 25 was applied near the turret.

Defiant I N3459 was flown by the Polish crew of P/Os Witold Gayzler and Włodzimierz Pfleger with No. 151 Squadron on 13 April 1941. At the time it was coded DZ-G. This photograph of the aircraft was taken at No. 10 Air Gunners School in 1942. By that time the RAF markings had been changed to the 'C' style – note the fuselage roundel partly visible in the photo (and the bottom part of the code number/letter applied forward of the roundel). Members of the Polish Air Force flew as staff pilots and as instructors with the unit in 1942.

Boulton Paul Defiant I N3333, delivery to No. 255 Squadron RAF, 27 November 1940. Upper surface camouflage colours: Dark Earth and Dark Green; under surface colour: Sky. Standard British national markings.

On 27 November 1940 F/O Bohdan Arct of No. 10 (Polish) Ferry Pool delivered Defiant I N3333 to No. 255 Squadron, where it became YD-B as shown in this photo. The unit was forming at the time and the newly delivered aircraft was still in Temperate Land scheme with Sky undersides, similar to the initial Defiants of No. 307 Sqn. Arct subsequently ferried several more Defiant Is, including N1794 to No. 151 Squadron, which was later flown in the unit by a Polish crew.

Boulton Paul Defiant I N3437/EW-K, No. 307 Squadron, Exeter, spring 1941. Upper surface camouflage colours: Dark Earth and Dark Green; under surface colour: Special Night RDM 2A. Standard British national markings. Squadron codes grey, serial number black. Polish national marking below the cockpit.

Defiant I N3437/EW-K in the night fighter scheme. Bottom surfaces were evidently black (Night). It is not certain if the upper surfaces were also repainted black, or left in the Temperate Land (this latter option is suggested by the serial number N3437 standing out quite well against the surrounding area). Shown in the photos are (standing near the wing) Sgts Franciszek Jankowiak (pilot) and Józef Lipiński (gunner), and (near the tail) Cpl Leon Witkowski (ground crew). The aircraft was delivered to the unit on 1 February 1941 and is certainly not the same EW-K that was shown in Temperate Land scheme on pages 415–416.

Boulton Paul Defiant I N1772/EW-P, No. 307 Squadron, Exeter, spring 1941. Special Night RDM 2A overall. Standard British national markings. Squadron codes grey, serial number Dull Red. Polish national marking below the cockpit.

A formation of No. 307 Squadron Boulton Paul Defiant Is photographed in flight from another machine. The aircraft nearest camera, coded EW-O (serial unknown), has the rear fuselage ventral aerial mast fully extended. The other aircraft are EW-M (N3330 or N3336) and N1772/EW-P. All these Defiants feature light grey codes, but their serial numbers appear to differ in colour. These should have been applied in red according to regulations, but light grey cannot be ruled out, particularly on EW-M.

Boulton Paul Defiant I N3328/DZ-Z, No. 151 Squadron, April 1941. Special Night RDM 2A overall. Standard British national markings. Squadron codes and serial number Dull Red. Individual marking in form of the 'sharkmouth' motif on the nose.

One of the most unusual Defiant Is, adorned with a 'sharkmouth' on the nose. The aircraft, N3328/DZ-Z, belonged to No. 151 Squadron RAF. A Polish crew, P/Os Witold Gayzler and Włodzimierz Pfleger, flew a training sortie in it on 13 April 1941, and the following day P/O Gayzler flew it with another gunner.

Boulton Paul Defiant I N3398/BA-A, departure from No. 277 Squadron RAF, 20 May 1943. Upper surface camouflage colours: Extra Dark Sea Grey and Dark Slate Grey with heavy retouching in unspecified camouflage hues; under surface colour: Sky. Code letters in non-regulation colour, probably Sky or white. Standard British national markings.

Boulton Paul Defiant I N3398/BA-A in No. 277 Squadron in 1942. 2nd/O Jadwiga Piłsudska ferried the aircraft from Gravesend to Kirkbride on 20 May 1943, on its way out from that unit to No. 44 MU. Although Red was specified in RAF regulations as the correct colour for code letters on Air Sea Rescue aircraft, it is clear these were much paler here, probably Sky or white.

Bristol Blenheim

Blenheim IF coded YP-H used by No. 23 Sqn RAF. It was photographed at Grangemouth in the second half of April 1941, when Polish crews in that unit were undergoing twin-engined conversion training on Blenheims to eventually fly Douglas Havocs.

Poles first flew the type in November 1940, while flying with anti-aircraft co-operation units. F/O Leon Suryn flew both Mk I and Mk IV variants with No. 6 AACU.

No. 23 Squadron was among the initial RAF units that specialised in modern night fighter duties. It re-equipped with the Blenheim IF fighters in 1939. The first success on the type was scored on 18 June 1940 (with the crew of Sgt A. Close and LAC L. R. Karasek). The unit continued to use the Blenheim until May 1941. It was in May 1941 that first Polish crews posted to fly Douglas Havocs with No. 23 Sqn had their initial introductory sorties in Blenheim IFs L4934 and L1302. These aircraft were finished black overall with the squadron YP code letters.

No. 307, the sole night fighter squadron unit of the exiled Polish Air Force was the only Polish unit to have Blenheims on charge. A few of these aircraft were used for twin-engined conversion training from the Defiants. L8438 was the first of these, delivered on 12 August 1941. The aeroplane was written off on 21 December 1942. More Blenheim Is arrived during August–October 1941: nos. L6737 (ex-23 Sqn) and L6837 (ex-23 Sqn YP-B, ex-406 Sqn), and possibly one more, Mk. IV V6017, apparently coded 'Z', although it has proved impossible, so far, to ascertain beyond doubt that the latter aeroplane was indeed on charge of the Polish unit. There are similar doubts regarding Blenheim I L1186, which was damaged on 21 October 1941 when flown by P/O Stefan Maxymowicz-Raczyński. Documents suggest that in certain periods (i.e. October 1941) the squadron had three Blenheims at the same time.

As the type was withdrawn from front line units and earmarked for auxiliary and training duties, more and more Blenheims were delivered to schools of air gunners, navigators and bomb aimers. Night fighter pilots and radar operators were trained, among others, at Nos. 51, 54, 58 and 60 OTUs, and in most these units all versions of Blenheims, as well Bisleys and Beauforts, were flown by Polish air crews under training as well as by the few Polish instructors.

Fighter Blenheim IF and IVF aircraft were also flown by Polish ferry pilots, both in Britain and the Middle East, delivering these aircraft to front line or training units. The Blenheims and Bisleys they delivered were then used by home-based OTUs as well as by Nos. 70 and 71 OTUs at Ismailia in Egypt. Aircraft of the type (in fighter, as well as bomber and reconnaissance versions) were also flown by Polish test pilots at the Royal Aircraft Establishment at Farnborough.

Blenheim IF K7159 YX-N used by No. 54 OTU. Polish radar operators were trained in the unit in such aircraft of the type. Also L6737, delivered to No. 307 Squadron from No. 23 Sqn RAF in September 1941, presumably featured a similar set of radar aerials and overall black finish.

Bristol Blenheim I L8438, No. 307 Squadron, Exeter, August 1941. Temperate Land camouflage with Sky under sides. Black serial number. No codes, no Polish national markings.

The nose of one of three Blenheim Is used by No. 307 Squadron in 1942 with the colour division line clearly visible below the cockpit glazing.

Blenheim I dual, L8438, slightly damaged after the unfortunate landing of P/O Marceli Neyder and F/Sgt Bolesław Turzański on 20 August 1941, at RAF Exeter, the base of No. 307 Squadron. The aircraft is in Temperate Land camouflage with Sky undersides.

Bristol Beaufighter IIF

No. 307 Squadron 'City of Lwów'

The first Beaufighters, in the Merlin XX-powered Mk II variant, were delivered to No. 307 Squadron in late July 1941, while the unit was based at RAF Exeter.

The new type was a marked improvement over the Defiants. The twin-engined fighter was fitted with a radar system that allowed it to locate enemy aircraft without the necessity of visual contact. This resulted in significant changes among the flying personnel. Unlike in the Defiant, in the Beaufighter it was the pilot who operated the powerful armament (four 20 mm cannon and six 0.303 in. guns), while the other crew member operated the 'AI' (Airborne Interception) system, as the air-to-air radar was known. Most air gunners eventually transferred to Wellington-equipped Polish bomber squadrons, while some retrained to become radar operators.

The first victories on the type were scored by No. 307 Squadron on the first night of November 1941, when the crew of Sgts Bolesław Turzański (pilot) and Henryk Ostrowski (radar operator) was credited with the destruction of two Dornier 217s. By the end of November this and two other crews were credited with two more German bombers destroyed plus one damaged. Following a winter lull, five destroyed, three probably destroyed and a damaged were claimed within two weeks in late April/early May 1942. This number included four Junkers 88s credited as destroyed between 1.40 and 2.55 am on 4 May.

Despite the successful engagements, the Merlin XX-powered Mk II was not a popular variant of the Beaufighter, being prone to failures and accidents. R2315 was the unit's first write-off, when

Sgt Władysław Illaszewicz and F/O Zbyszko Lissowski posing with their individual emblem, most probably applied on Beaufighter IIF T3042 EW-D. While flying this aircraft they claimed two Ju 88s destroyed and one probably destroyed in April–May 1942, which was marked by the allegory of a bird throwing thunderbolts at three swastikas. This is the only individual emblem on a Beaufighter IIF of No. 307 Sqn known from photos. F/O Lissowski is holding the fairing of the camera gun. The latter piece of equipment can be seen in few photographs from the unit.

Two ground crew members (LAC Henryk Walenty Mietelski on the left) with a Beaufighter IIF that displays a pale code letter E on the nose. It was most probably grey or red. The photo shows to advantage the different types of black paint used. The propeller spinners were painted with the smoother DTD 308 while the rest of the aircraft with the regulation Special Night (R.D.M. 2) that appears more matt. The latter finish also proved less resistant, as shown by the wear. Bristol Beaufighter IIF R2449 was officially taken on charge by the RAF on 31 July 1941. AI Mk IV radar was fitted at No. 19 Maintenance Unit, and on 14 August 1941 it was delivered from there to No. 307 Sqn at Exeter, where it received individual code letter E. Having flown a number of operational sorties, its career ended several minutes after midnight on the night of 2 April 1942. 5 minutes after take-off for an operational mission the Beaufighter suffered an engine fire and crashed at Kenton near Exminster. Bodies of both crew members, P/O Grzegorz Bukowiecki and P/O Stanisław Puzyna, were found in the partly burnt out wreck.

it crashed at Exeter on 30 August 1941 due to an engine failure. The crew of Sgts Jerzy Malinowski (pilot) and Zygmunt Modro (radar operator) escaped unhurt.

The first fatality came on 27 September, when R2442 crashed into high ground at Widecombe in low cloud, killing the crew of F/Os Witold Gayzler and Włodzimierz Pfleger. Less than a month later, on 23 October S/Ldr Jerzy Antonowicz and F/O Lech Karwowski were killed in T3025 when it crashed at Exeter due to an engine failure.

Mid-February 1942 proved particularly tragic. On the night of 11 February T3035 crashed into trees while landing in bad visibility, killing the crew of Sgts Kazimierz Thiesler and Edward Podgajny. R2446/EW-P crashed on the night of 13 February, killing F/Os Zdzisław Kurek and Józef Skrouba. The following day R2445/EW-A crashed during a daytime training sortie, P/O Stefan Maxymowicz-Raczyński (pilot) was killed, while F/O Jerzy Łazarowicz (radar op.) was seriously injured and had to have his leg amputated.

Another fatal crash near Exeter came on the night of 2 April, when F/Os Grzegorz Bukowiecki and Stanisław Puzyna were killed in R2449/EW-E. Ten nights later F/Lt Roman Smok and F/O Mieczysław Świerz were lost off Beer Head on a night sortie in R2457.

Altogether, during eight months the unit lost thirteen air crew members killed and one seriously injured in a total of 27 accidents. At the same time nine enemy aircraft were credited as destroyed, three as probably destroyed and two as damaged.

Other Units

The Beaufighter IIF was also flown by Polish pilot, Sgt Zbigniew Dunin-Rzuchowski, with No. 600 Squadron 'City of London' (with an RAF radio-operator, Sgt Dixon) between 2 December 1941 and March 1942.

Polish crews flew Beaufighter IIFs in training at No. 54 OTU.

Members of the Polish Air Force test flew Beaufighter IIs at British research establishments.

Polish pilots also ferried these aircraft and test flew them at overhaul facilities. Sgt Stanisław Jednaki was killed while test flying T3445 at 30 MU on 8 September 1942.

Two Beaufighter IIFs photographed at Exeter, most probably in May 1942: EW-B (most probably T3009) and T3382/EW-K. The aircraft display the British national markings introduced in May 1942. Both aircraft took part in combats on the night of 4 May 1942 and their crews scored against Junkers 88s. T3382/EW-K was also used by the crew of F/O Mieczysław Pietrzyk – F/O Czesław Krawiecki to claim a Ju 88 probably destroyed on 26 April 1942.

The most popular photo of a No. 307 Squadron Beaufighter IIF. It shows clearly the aerials on the starboard wing and the open radar-operator's escape hatch. T3048 was officially taken on charge by the RAF on 12 October 1941. No. 19 Maintenance Unit transferred it on 15 December 1941 to No. 307 Sqn (officially taken on charge there the following day), where it was given code letters EW-O (often misinterpreted in the photo as EW-U). The style of the code letters in the squadron differed quite significantly between aircraft, especially that of the 'W'. In this case it has a sharp central tip. T3048 left the Polish unit on 7 May 1942 going to No. 96 Squadron RAF (officially taken on charge there on 9 May). Its career has then taken it to the Far East: in September 1943 it was sent to Ceylon aboard s/s 'Behar'.

Bristol Beaufighter IIF R2396/BQ-E, No. 600 Squadron RAF, Predannack, December 1941–March 1942. Special Night RDM 2A overall. Standard British national markings. Code letters: Medium Sea Grey. Serial number: Dull Red.

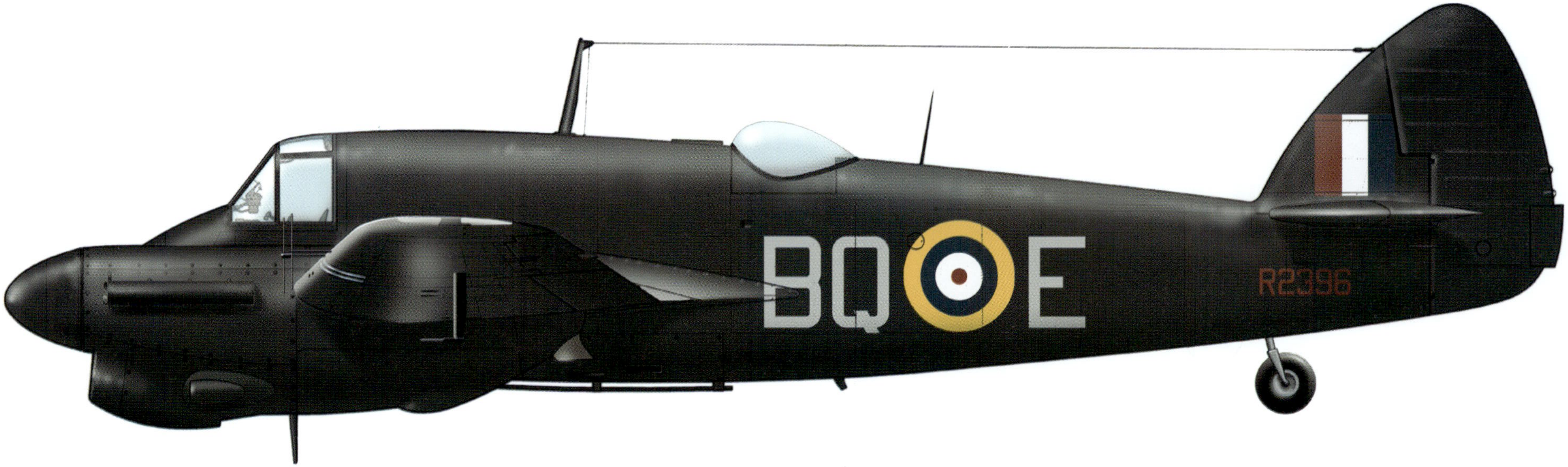

R2396/BQ-E, one of few documented Beaufighter IIFs of No. 600 Squadron RAF. This aircraft was flown in early 1942 by Polish pilot Sgt Zbigniew Adam Józef Dunin-Rzuchowski with his radio-operator Sgt Dixon.

Bristol Beaufighter IIF R2445/EW-A, No. 307 Squadron, Exeter, August 1941–April 1942. Special Night RDM 2A overall. Standard British national markings. Code letters: Dull Red. Serial number: Dull Red. Polish national markings on the fuselage.

The only known photo of a No. 307 Squadron Beaufighter with the early 'A' type British national markings, as used until May 1942. The Polish red-and-white chequer marking can be seen on the fuselage. The aircraft is Beaufighter II R2445/EW-A undergoing maintenance at Exeter. On 14 February 1942 an experienced crew of P/O Stefan Maxymowicz-Raczyński and F/O Jerzy Łazarowicz, crashed in this Beaufighter IIF. The pilot was killed, while the seriously injured F/O Jerzy Łazarowicz was taken to hospital where he had a leg amputated. The aircraft was used by the Polish unit from 17 August 1941 and has flown a total of 125 hours 20 minutes (of which 122.5 hours in the squadron). It was used on five operational sorties, including three flown by P/O Maxymowicz: twice with F/O Jerzy Łazarowicz and once with F/O Zbigniew Domański.

Bristol Beaufighter IIF R2390/EW-U, No. 307 Squadron, Exeter, August 1941–April 1942. Special Night RDM 2A overall. Standard British national markings. Code letters: Dull Red. Serial number: Dull Red. No Polish national markings.

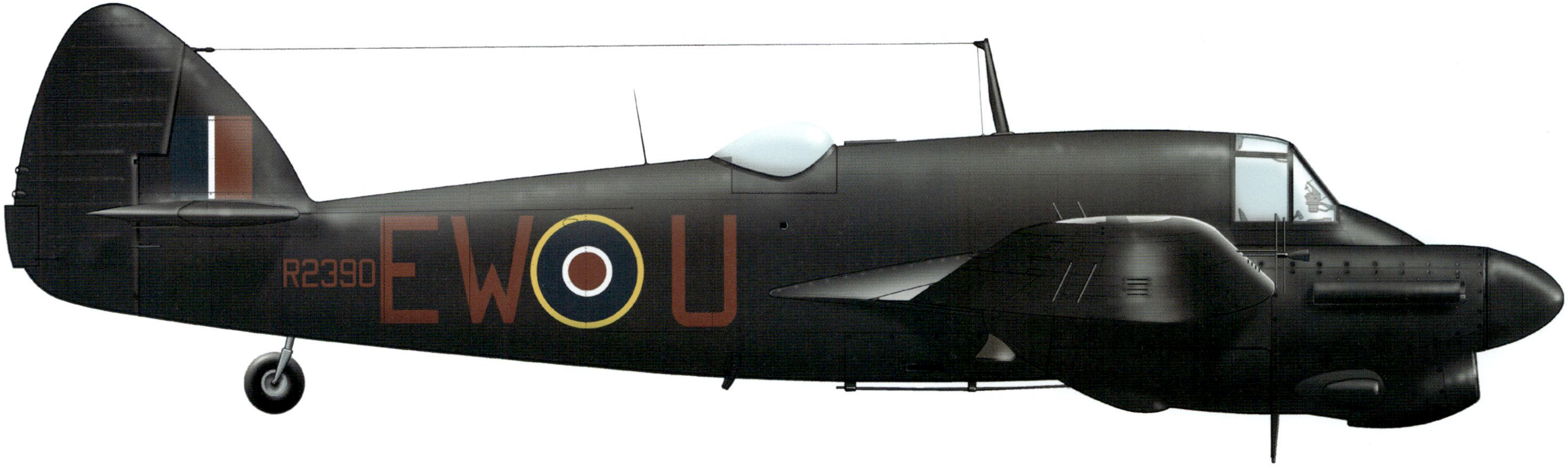

A formation of No. 307 Squadron Beaufighter IIFs in flight, most probably on 2 April 1942. As can be seen none of the aircraft featured the Polish red-and-white chequer insignia. R2390 was only used by No. 307 Sqn between 23 March and 7 May 1942. During this period the 'B' Flight Authorisation Book has recorded day time exercise that involved formation flying of five aircraft on 2 April, taking off from Exeter at 15.00. The formation was led by S/Ldr Maksymilian Lewandowski with Sgt Tadeusz Śliwak in T3030/EW-N. On his starboard wing Beaufighter IIF R2390/EW-U can be seen, with the crew of F/Sgt Bolesław Turzański and Sgt Henryk Ostrowski. The photo was most probably taken from T3048/EW-O flown by F/O Jerzy Damsz, who had two other crew members on this occasion: radar-operator F/O Witold Sylwestrowicz, and F/Lt Zdzisław Radomski (recently posted as Operations Room controller for No. 307). The aircraft to the port of the leader were R2392/EW-R with the crew of F/O Mieczysław Pietrzyk – F/O Czesław Krawiecki and T3358/EW-S with F/Lt Marceli Neyder – Sgt Jan Woźny. During the same flight Lewandowski, Pietrzyk and Turzański have also performed an exercise of firing at sea targets. T3030 had commenced its No. 307 Sqn service on 27 October 1941 and was used on 18 operational sorties by the unit. On 19 May 1942 T3030/EW-N was ferried to No. 96 Squadron RAF at Wrexham by the crew of F/Os Stanisław Kohut and Czesław Borzemski, alongside three other machines. All aircraft in this photo displayed British markings as introduced in May 1942. The Beaufighter IIFs would soon be replaced by Mk VIFs with radial engines.

Bristol Beaufighter IIF R2390/EW-U, No. 307 Squadron, Exeter, August 1941–April 1942. Special Night RDM 2A overall. Standard British national markings. Code letters: Dull Red. Serial number: Dull Red. No Polish national markings.

Bristol Beaufighter IIF R2390/EW-U in flight. The aircraft features the camera gun fairing on the fuselage spine aft of the cockpit. This was not seen on other machines, nor in the other photo of the same aircraft that was taken on an earlier occasion. Note the clearly paler wing and tailplane leading edges. The pale area on top of the port tailplane might be a repair or a gas patch. The aircraft had an interesting career: it was originally delivered to No. 307 Sqn on 27 August 1941, but the same day it was transferred to the Fighter Interceptor Unit, where it then underwent operational trials. It returned to No. 307 Sqn in March 1942.

Bristol Beaufighter IIF R2390/EW-U, No. 307 Squadron, Exeter, August 1941–April 1942.

Bristol Beaufighter IIF V8164/VX, No. 54 OTU, Winfield, June 1943. Overall Medium Sea Grey with Dark Green disruptive pattern. Standard British national markings, Black serial number. Code letters: Dull Red.

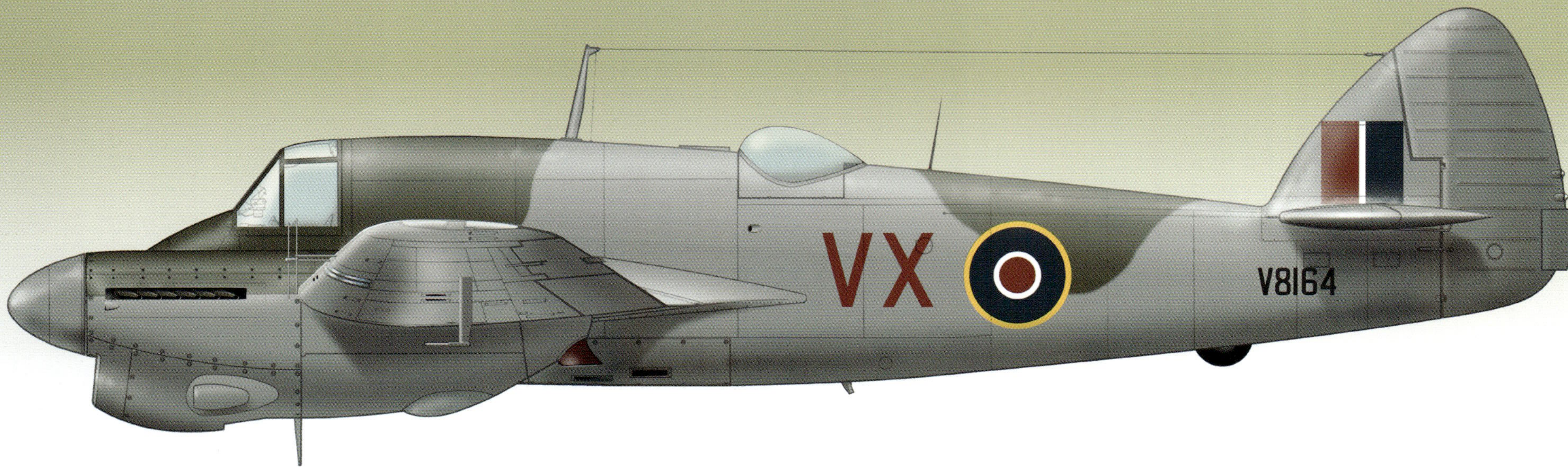

Bristol Beaufighter IIF V8164/VX of of 'B' Squadron No. 54 OTU at Winfield. On 12 June 1943 the aircraft was flown by the crew of F/Sgt Jan Górski – F/O Eric Thomason during air firing exercise.

Bristol Beaufighter IIF V8164/LX-E of No. 54 OTU at Winfield in the pre-October 1942 colour scheme. A number of Polish air crews flew with the unit at the time, including P/O Antoni Dzięgielewski, F/O Czesław Krawiecki, P/O Jan Mika, Sgt Jan Pacholczyk, F/O Karol Rach, P/O Tadeusz Śliwak.

Bristol Beaufighter VIF

No. 307 Squadron 'City of Lwów'

In May 1942 the unit took delivery of its first Beaufighter VIFs, a more reliable variant with Bristol Hercules VI radials.

First success on the new aircraft came on the night of 27 June, when three crews claimed a total of one German bomber destroyed and two damaged. The last successful combat on the Beaufighter VI was fought by No. 307 Squadron on the night of 24 September, when a Dornier 217 was credited as destroyed by the crew of F/O Gerard Ranoszek and F/Lt Stanisław Sawczyński.

Sgt Władysław Illaszewicz and P/O Zbyszko Lissowski were the first fatal casualties while flying the new variant. They were killed on the night of 17 July 1942, when X8131 crashed into the sea while returning from a patrol. Radar operator Sgt Stanisław Jarzembowski was killed in a crash of X7935 during a test flight on 1 August, while the pilot and a passenger were injured. The last fatal incident on the Beaufighters took place on 8 November 1942, when X8149/EW-A crashed during a training sortie. The pilot, S/Ldr František Rypl (Czech) was injured while Sgt Wacław Gajek, the radio operator, lost his life.

On the night of 29 July the crew of P/O Stefan Podgórski and F/Lt Stanisław Sawczyński baled out of X7932/EW-U over sea. They were rescued after four hours in the dinghy, the first crew of No. 307 Sqn to bale out safely and the first one rescued from the sea.

The night of 4 August 1942 was the most successful for No. 307 Squadron: the crew of S/Ldr Gerard Ranoszek and Sgt Jerzy Trzaskowski claimed two Junkers 88s destroyed, and another one was claimed by F/O Stanisław Szablowski and Sgt Henryk Gajewski. Altogether, the crews of No. 307 Squadron were credited with six enemy aircraft destroyed and four damaged while flying the Beaufighter VI.

In mid-December 1942 the squadron started conversion onto the Mosquito. The last Beaufighter patrol was flown on 31 January 1943.

An artistic impression of an all-black Beaufighter VIF with the code letter Z on the nose beneath the aerials. This is EL154, one of two (alongside EL146) in the Polish squadron from the batch of 260 aircraft delivered to the RAF by the Old Mixon Shadow Factory at Weston-Super-Mare between June and October 1942. It was soon sent back to its parent factory for re-camouflaging, this being done on a large scale in October 1942.

Other Units

Members of the Polish Air Force also flew the variant with RAF units.

The crew of Sgt Zbigniew Dunin-Rzuchowski and Sgt Dixon in No. 600 Sqn flew Beaufighter VIFs between February and August 1942. In September the squadron moved to the Mediterranean, while Sgt Dunin-Rzuchowski was posted to No. 307 Sqn, where he continued to fly Beaufighter VIFs.

A number of Polish crews were posted to No. 219 Squadron RAF for operational flying (see 'Other Beaufighter Variants'). The crew of S/Ldr Antoni Alexandrowicz and F/O Zbigniew Domański was killed on 14 February 1943, when their Beaufighter VIF V8551 hit high ground at Ireleth (Cumbria).

Polish crews also served briefly with No. 153 Sqn during its conversion from Beaufighter Is to VIs.

The last successful air combat of a Beaufighter VI with a member of the Polish Air Force in its crew took place on the night of 8 August 1944 over Italy. F/Lt Włodzimierz Bereżecki, a Spitfire pilot of No. 318 Squadron, joined a No. 225 Squadron crew (F/O Bruce Brerethon and F/Lt Walter Cunningham) on a night sortie during which they claimed a Junkers 88 downed near Ancona.

Polish Air Force pilots test flew Beaufighter VIs at British research establishments. Polish pilots also ferried these aircraft and test flew them at overhaul facilities. P/O Stanisław Cieliński, ferry pilot of No. 3 Delivery Flight, died of his injuries following an accident of Beaufighter VIF X7887 on 18 April 1943.

Beaufighter VIF X7952/EW-K adorned with four swastika kill markings of the crew of Sgt Bolesław Turzański. In No. 307 Squadron diary this photograph accompanied the entry for the first success of the crew of Sgts Turzański and Ostrowski, with the caption 'Brave ground crew of the victorious Beaufighter'. This image has been incorrectly captioned previously, the identity of the aircraft mistaken, but the memorabilia of Bolesław Turzański preserved by his relatives include a similar print captioned by the pilot on the back 'Exeter 1942 / My Krysia' (Krysia is a Polish girl's name, equivalent to Christy). For Turzański the code letter of his aircraft was 'K for Krysia'. Beaufighter VIF X7952 EW-K was his usual aircraft in the summer of 1942. X7952 was delivered to No. 307 Squadron on 1 May 1942 and initially had no aircraft code letter. Out of the 30 operational sorties it flew with No. 307 before being transferred to No. 488 Squadron RNZAF in February 1943, 16 were completed by Turzański with his radar-operators: first Sgt Henryk Ostrowski and then Sgt Jan Woźny. The photo shows four swastikas, denoting Turzański's four kills, and a pale square, which might be an overpainted fifth swastika, related to a victory credited as probable. The victory markings were most probably applied on the occasion of the Squadron Day on 10 September 1942.

Right: *Re-fitting the tail on a brand new Beaufighter VI X8108. The position and style of the serial number, typical for Beaufighter VIFs built at Weston-Super-Mare, are clearly visible. The aircraft was delivered to the Polish unit on 5 May 1942 and its code letters EW in red feature on the fuselage. The initial months of operation of these aircraft in No. 307 Sqn saw many instances of the tail being replaced and the cracking longerons being welded in the rear area, which entailed dismantling the entire tail surfaces.*

Left: *A Beaufighter VIF with the squadron code on the rear fuselage and the Polish marking near the cockpit shown to advantage. The code letters on Beaufighter VIs differed in style, with no sharp central tip in the W. It has proved impossible to identify the serial number of the aircraft or its code letter (D, E, N or P). Note the wear of the matt black finish in the areas walked on, and the place on the fuselage where a large chunk had peeled off. The roundel shows no traces of overpainted early 'A' type one which might suggest this was one of the last aircraft of the type delivered to the squadron.*

Right: *Beaufighter VIF X8013/EW-S was delivered to the Polish unit on 1 May 1942 from a Maintenance Unit. The brand new aircraft featured the old style British national markings, which were then repainted to comply with the new pattern introduced at the end of April 1942. Traces of this can be seen clearly both on the fuselage and in the fin flash. The aircraft has flown a total of 32 operational sorties in the squadron and was initially flown most often by the crew of F/Lt Marceli Neyder – Sgt Jan Woźny, who completed 10 sorties in it, and subsequently by F/O Jan Bieńkowski – Sgt Leslie Alexander William Smith (7 sorties).*

No. 307 Squadron members (mainly the air crew) photographed with Beaufighter VIF X8209/EW-H on 21 July 1942, during the farewell to W/Cdr Stanisław Brejnak, the departing squadron commander. Similar to a number of other photos, the image shows prominent traces of overpainting the large early roundel to modify it into the smaller late one. The new paint is clearly different, seemingly smoother and glossier than the standard night fighter finish. All No. 307 Sqn Beaufighter VIFs were used with late style British national markings, as introduced as of 15 May 1942: 36 inch 'C1' roundels and 'C' style fin flash with the reduced 2 inch central white area in a 24 inch square. X8209 was used by the Polish unit from 21 June 1942 until 7 January 1943 when it was transferred, along with several others, to No. 488 Squadron RNZAF. It was one of the most used aircraft and it completed 33 operational sorties, flown most often by Sgt Lucjan Szempliński, who accounted for 16 sorties with his radar-operators: Sgt Aleksander Mossor, and then P/O Jan Mika.

Arrival of the Polish Commander-in-Chief Gen. Władysław Sikorski to Exeter on 10 September 1942 in Beaufighter VIF EL146/EW-V. The head-on view reveals a small V code letter on the nose beneath the aerials.

Polish Commander-in-Chief Gen. Władysław Sikorski leaves Beaufighter VIF EL146/EW-V upon his arrival at Exeter on 10 September 1942.

Beaufighter VIF EL146 built by Bristol at Weston-Super-Mare was officially taken on charge by the RAF on 5 July 1942. According to its Movement Card it went to No. 19 MU, and from there it was delivered on 17 August 1942 to No. 307 Sqn, receiving the code EW-V. A repair on site was recorded on 14 January 1943, and on 20 January it was transferred from the Polish unit to No. 406 Squadron RAF. It was struck off charge by the RAF on 24 July 1945.

A seldom depicted moment when the Polish C-in-C enters Beaufighter VIF EL146/EW-V, recorded on film as the only known image of the starboard side of the squadron commander's aircraft, with the code letter V expanded into 'Victory'. Before entering the Beaufighter Gen. Sikorski was provided with seat-type parachute harness that displayed the regular user's initials on the back: JB. These match the names of no less than four No. 307 Squadron members at the time.

'Somewhere in England', i.e. at Exeter. No. 307 Sqn members, left to right: radar-operator Sgt Stanisław Sadowski, pilot Sgt Ludwik Steinke and radio mechanic LAC Bolesław Grzyb. The Bristol Beaufighter VIF behind them is X8149/ EW-A, usually flown by the crew of Sgts Ludwik Steinke and Stanisław Sadowski, who completed 16 night sorties in it.

Beaufighter VIF X8148/ EW-T on trestles during maintenance at Exeter, with canvas covers on the engines and cockpit. The Polish national marking can be partly seen aft of the cockpit. The aircraft was used by No. 307 Squadron from 6 May 1942 to 26 February 1943. On the night of 31 January 1943 it flew No. 307 Squadron's last Beaufighter VIF operation, the crew of F/Sgt Edward Wojczyński and Sgt Emil Słuszkiewicz taking off at 20.10 for the two-hour sortie.

A ground crew team (left to right): LAC Józef Leśnik, LAC Jan Siodłak, Cpl Włodzimierz Gryc and LAC Wojciech Wesoły with the same Beaufighter VIF X8148/EW-T as the backdrop. The aircraft was flown by the crew of Sgts Jan Pacholczyk and Tadeusz Więckowski when they damaged a Junkers 88 on the night of 4 September 1942.

__Above left and right:__ X8025 was a brand new Beaufighter VIF delivered to the Polish unit on 1 May 1942, and most probably one of the first things was to overpaint the large old-style roundels on the fuselage to match the new pattern. X8025/EW-L was used by the squadron until 23 January 1943 and it completed 40 operational sorties in the hands of 14 crews. The aircraft was one of those most often used by the crew of S/Ldr Jerzy Damsz – F/O Witold Sylwestrowicz until their EW-Z for Zocha arrived (see below). The crew of P/O Antoni Beda – F/Sgt Maksymilian Trawicki has flown the highest number of sorties in EW-L for Love. Note the tiny letters applied next to the code letter L to form the inscription MY LOVE just visible in the photos. LAC Jan Kaszubowski, LAC Ferdynand Stefan Lasoń and Cpl Michał Herczuk pose in the upper photo.

__Left:__ Ground crews posing with Beaufighter VIF X8155/EW-F during maintenance of the Bristol Hercules VI engine. Note the aircraft letter on the fuselage and the pale fin-tailplane fillets.

Ground crew members play cards under the wing of Beaufighter VIF X8155/EW-F. The fin-tailplane fillets of the aircraft were finished in a pale colour after the tail was re-assembled. The aircraft was used by No. 307 Sqn from 1 August 1942. Its first operational sortie was flown on the night of 6 August 1942 by the crew of Sgts Franciszek Jankowiak and Jerzy Karais. That crew flew it most often: they completed eight out of its 34 sorties. After No. 307 Squadron re-equipped with Mosquitoes, the aircraft was transferred to No. 488 Squadron RNZAF on 7 February 1943.

Bristol Beaufighter VIF X8023/BQ-I, No. 600 Squadron RAF, Predannack, June 1942. Special Night RDM 2A overall. Mixed British national markings (early style fin-flash, late style roundels). Code letters: Dull Red. Serial number: Dull Red.

Bristol Beaufighter VIF X8023/BQ-I of No. 600 Squadron, which was flown on a night patrol on 3 June 1942 by the international crew of Sgt Zbigniew Dunin-Rzuchowski – Sgt Dixon. Several days later the aircraft was transferred to No. 406 Squadron RCAF. Note the incorrect (unmodified) fin-flash while the British national markings on the fuselage are already in the late 'C' type, introduced in May 1942.

Bristol Beaufighter VIF X7887/BQ-K, No. 600 Squadron RAF, Predannack, June 1942. Special Night RDM 2A overall. Standard British national markings. Code letters: Dull Red. Serial number: Dull Red.

Beaufighter VIF X7887/BQ-K in the foreground was delivered to No. 600 Squadron RAF from No. 19 MU at St Athan on 31 January 1942. The aircraft was in the standard scheme of night fighter Beaufighters as used until October 1942. The photo was retouched by a censor who has obliterated all aerials rather crudely, resulting in somewhat unusual nose shapes of the Beaufighters and the strange-shaped K code letter on the fuselage. On 21 June 1942 the aircraft with the crew of Sgt Zbigniew Dunin-Rzuchowski – Sgt Dixon took part in formation flying and air firing exercise. On 17 July 1942 the same crew flew an uneventful night patrol. The aircraft has another Polish connection: it crashed on 18 April 1943 off Bradda Head due to an engine failure when flown by F/O Stanisław Cieliński. The ex-No. 153 Squadron machine was ferried from Jurby, Isle of Man. The Polish pilot was picked up by a Royal Navy destroyer, but he died from his injuries.

Bristol Beaufighter VIF X8005/EW-R, No. 307 Squadron, Exeter, May–September 1942. Special Night RDM 2A overall. Standard British national markings. Code letters: Dull Red. Serial number: Dull Red. Polish national markings and three swastika kill markings on the fuselage.

The visit of Gen. Władysław Sikorski, Polish Commander-in-Chief, at Exeter on 10 September 1942. During the solemn mass backdrop was provided by a Beaufighter VIF with the code letter R on the nose. This was X8005/EW-R, used by F/O Gerard Ranoszek to score three enemy aircraft confirmed destroyed and a damaged. At the time the aircraft was in the all-black scheme, with the Polish national marking applied aft of the cockpit on the both sides and three 'kill' symbols on the port side only, as shown here.

Bristol Beaufighter VIF X8005/EW-R, No. 307 Squadron, Exeter, October–December 1942. Overall Medium Sea Grey with Dark Green disruptive pattern. Standard British national markings. Serial number: Black. Code letters: Dull Red. No Polish national markings. Four swastika kill markings on the fuselage

***Right:** Beaufighter VIF X8005 built at Weston-Super-Mare was officially taken on charge by the RAF on 17 March 1942. According to the Aircraft Movement Card it was delivered from No. 19 MU to No. 307 Sqn on 3 May 1942, although the unit records show it as early as 2 May. In No. 307 Sqn it was coded EW-R. On 19 September 1942 S/Ldr Władysław Różycki ferried the aircraft to its parent factory at Weston-Super-Mare, and on 22 September 1942 the aircraft in its new two-tone finish was brought back to No. 307 Sqn by the crew of P/O Stefan Podgórski – F/O Jerzy Lewandowicz. It was transferred from the Polish unit to No. 125 Squadron RAF on 10 January 1943 and until the end of that year it was used by further night fighter squadrons: Nos. 96, 409 and 406, ending its career in the Far East, sent there in mid-1944.*

***Left:** F/O Gerard Ranoszek poses for a photograph standing on the wing of the Beaufighter with four swastikas applied aft of the cockpit. X8005 was delivered to No. 307 Sqn on 3 May 1942. Coded EW-R, it was used by the crew of F/O Gerard Karol Ranoszek and Sgt Jerzy Trzaskowski to claim a Do 217 damaged over Devon on the night of 28 June 1942, and two Ju 88s destroyed on 5 August 1942.*

***Left:** F/O Gerard Karol Ranoszek with his radar-operator F/Lt Stanisław Sawczyński and ground crews by the side of their aircraft. The crew of Ranoszek-Sawczyński flew the aircraft on 24 September 1942 when they were credited with a Do 217 shot down into the Channel. This was the pilot's fourth victory on Beaufighters, hence the four white swastikas on the fuselage of X8005/EW-R.*

Bristol Beaufighter VIF EL154/EW-Zocha, No. 307 Squadron, Exeter, October–December 1942. Overall Medium Sea Grey with Dark Green disruptive pattern. Standard British national markings. Serial number: Black. Code letters: Dull Red. No Polish national markings.

Beaufighter EW-Z for Zocha refuelled under the watchful eye of LAC Alojzy Gorgoń. In October 1942 the aircraft received the new two-tone camouflage: on 8 October P/O Stefan Podgórski flew it, with F/O Jerzy Antoni Lewandowicz and F/Sgt Tadeusz Zygmunt Stępniewski on board, from the factory at Weston-Super-Mare to Exeter after it was re-camouflaged. This photo shows it with the brand new finish still looking immaculate.

Another view of Beaufighter VIF EL154/EW-Z. The pilot S/Ldr Jerzy Damsz is posing with the aircraft. Zocha was the name of his wife, applied on both sides of the fuselage. The crew of S/Ldr Jerzy Damsz – F/O Witold Sylwestrowicz flew the aircraft on operations most frequently, completing five operational sorties and a lot of non-operational flying during the short time the aircraft spent with No. 307 Sqn.

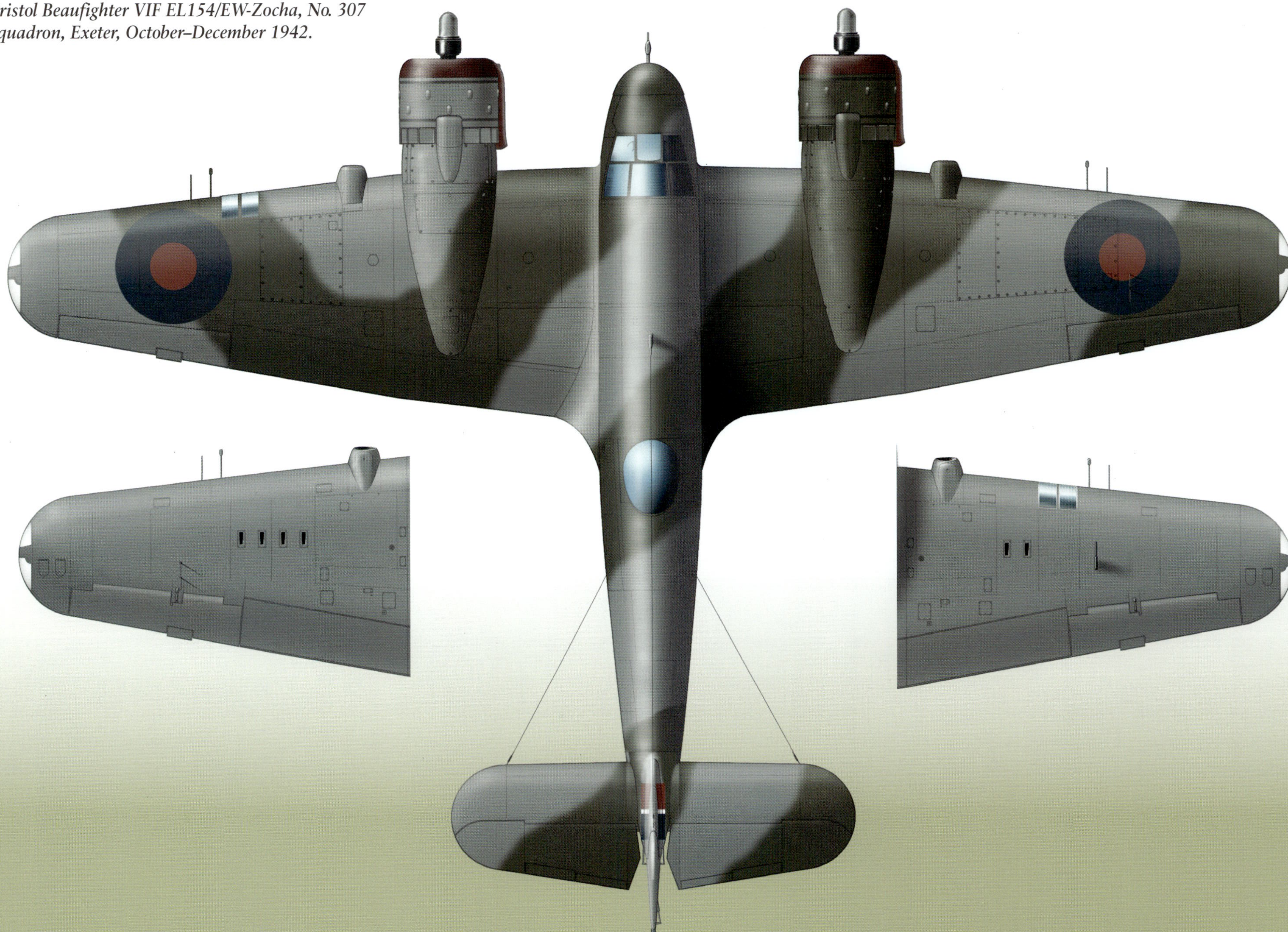

Bristol Beaufighter VIF EL154/EW-Zocha, No. 307 Squadron, Exeter, October–December 1942.

Bristol Beaufighter VIF EL154/EW-Zocha, No. 307 Squadron, Exeter, October–December 1942. Overall Medium Sea Grey with Dark Green disruptive pattern. Standard British national markings. Serial number: Black. Code letters: Dull Red. No Polish national markings.

Beaufighter VIF EL154/EW-Z for Zocha of Jerzy Damsz with the ground crew. It is not by accident that the men are positioned so as not to obscure the code letter Z expanded into the name ZOCHA. This was one of the shortest used Beaufighters in No. 307 Squadron, and its entire career did not even last one year. It was delivered via Nos. 30 and 29 MUs. Delivered to the Polish unit on 7 September 1942, it was transferred to No. 488 Squadron RNZAF on 13 February 1943. In that unit it suffered two accidents, on 8 and 21 June 1943, the latter resulting in writing it off.

Bristol Beaufighter VIF KV975/K, No. 54 OTU, Winfield, November 1943. Overall Medium Sea Grey with Dark Green disruptive pattern. Standard British national markings. Serial number: Black. Code letters: Dull Red.

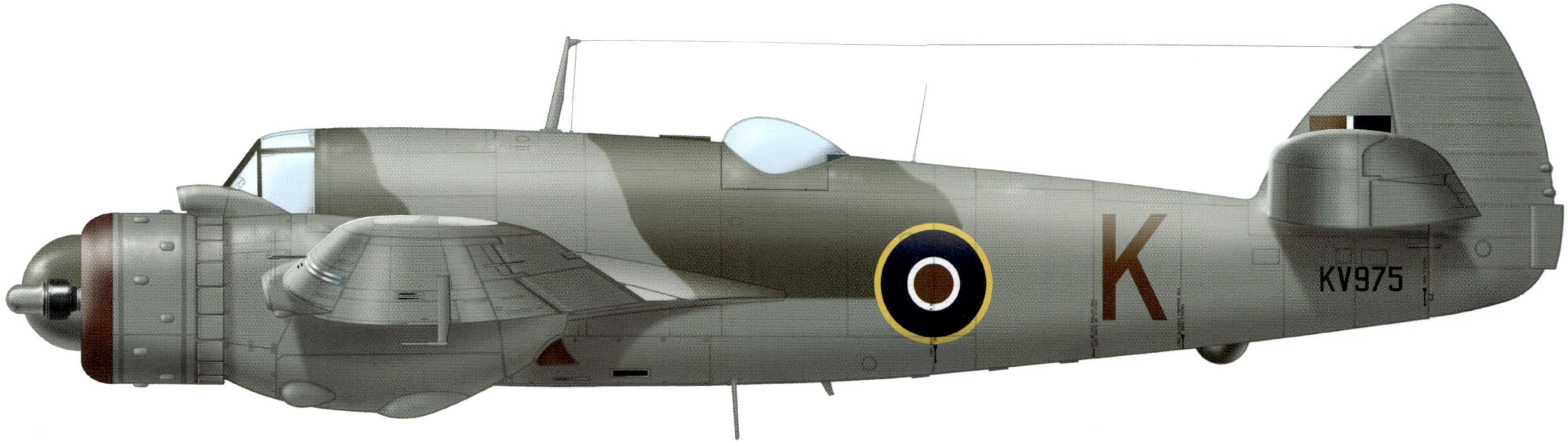

Bristol Beaufighter VIF KV975/K of 'C' Squadron No. 54 OTU at Winfield. On 12 November 1943 the aircraft was used by the crew of F/Lt Michał Drzazga – F/O Henryk Łuczak for training with AI Mk VII radar. The aircraft was in the standard night fighter scheme introduced in October 1942. Note the dihedral of the tailplane and the spherical nose fairing introduced with the new radar system

Other Beaufighter Variants

A number of Polish crews flew Beaufighter Is with No. 219 Squadron RAF. S/Ldr Antoni Alexandrowicz and P/O Zbigniew Domański scored three confirmed 'kills' with that unit in early June 1942, all in X7683. They continued to serve with the unit after it re-equipped with the Beaufighter VI (which see).

Polish crews flew Beaufighter Is in training at 54 OTU.

Polish Air Force pilots test flew various versions of Beaufighters at British research establishments.

Polish pilots ferried various versions of the Beaufighter, both in Britain and overseas. 1st/O Stefan Czyżewski, ATA, was killed on 21 July 1942 in the crash of Beaufighter I X7764. Polish pilots of No. 1 Air Delivery Unit delivered 13 (out of 337) Beaufighters in various versions across Africa. Poles also led convoys of Beaufighters on the trans-African route.

Beaufighter IF T4639/FK of No. 219 Squadron, photographed at Tangmere during late 1941 or early 1942, when the first Polish crews of Sgt Marian Ideć and S/Ldr Antoni Alexandrowicz joined the unit. Photographs of other aircraft of the type in service with No. 219 Squadron RAF from the same period show just the squadron code letters on the fuselage, which suggest that this was the rule, in which case neither Sgt Ideć's usual Beaufighter IF T4647 nor the victorious Beaufighter IF X7683 of the crew of S/Ldr Antoni Alexandrowicz – F/O Zbigniew Domański featured individual code letters on the fuselage.

Bristol Beaufighter IF R2268, Royal Aircraft Establishment, Farnborough, October–December 1942. Upper surface camouflage colours: Dark Earth and Dark Green; under surface colour: Black. Standard British national markings. Prototype marking (capital P in a ring, in yellow) on both sides of the fuselage. Serial number: Black.

In the spring of 1941 a modified Beaufighter I prototype with twin fins and rudders was flown. The new tail cured the lateral stability problems that had troubled the Beaufighter but its increased weight and consequential shift of the centre of gravity led to longitudinal stability problems. Eventually the option was abandoned, but the prototype, no. R2268, continued to be modified and tested at the Aeroplane and Armament Experimental Establishment, Boscombe Down, and the Royal Aircraft Establishment, Farnborough. In October 1942 the twin-tail Beaufighter was test flown at Farnborough by F/O Kazimierz Kazimierczuk. Photos suggest that the aircraft was fitted with the radar system from the outset. It was finished in the Temperate Land scheme (Dark Earth/Dark Green) on upper surfaces with black under surfaces.

When Polish pilot F/O Kazimierz Kazimierczuk flew the twin-tail Beaufighter on 27 October 1942 at Farnborough the aircraft featured additional rear-fuselage strakes as shown here. By that time the British national markings had been altered to the late style.

Bristol Beaufighter X EL393, Royal Aircraft Establishment, Farnborough, May 1943. Upper surface camouflage colours: Medium Sea Grey and Dark Green; under surface colour: yellow. Standard British national markings. Prototype marking (capital P in a ring, in yellow) on both sides of the fuselage.

Beaufighter X EL393 was test flown by F/Lt Roland Kalpas at the Royal Aircraft Establishment at Farnborough in May 1943. Here it is pictured at the AAEE Boscombe Down a year later. The colour scheme was probably unchanged: upper surfaces in the Night Fighter Scheme (Dark Green and Medium Sea Grey) with yellow undersides and the 'P in ring' marking denoting a prototype or a test aircraft.

Douglas Boston/Havoc/Turbinlite

Two Polish crews: P/O Stanisław Reymer-Krzywicki, F/O Kazimierz Bokowiec, F/O Andrzej Strasburger and F/O Władysław Różycki, P/O Stefan Gębicki, P/O Edward Ryciak were posted in early May 1941 to No. 23 Squadron at RAF Ford. Altogether the Polish crews of No. 23 Sqn flew twenty one black Havoc Is (with transparent noses), ten Boston III (Intruder) aircraft (fitted with flame-dampers on the exhausts and armed with four 20 mm Hispano cannon) and three Turbinlites.

Their most successful operation took place on the night of 6 December 1941. The crew of F/O Reymer-Krzywicki, F/O Strasburger and F/O Bokowiec saw an airfield with its lights on near Gilze and soon encountered several enemy aircraft coming in to land. They were credited with one destroyed and one damaged.

On 12 February 1942, Boston III W8365 was damaged on landing due to faulty brakes at the end of a delivery flight from a Maintenance Unit to No. 23 Squadron at Ford by P/O Kazimierz Kazimierczuk.

During a similar period, between June 1941 and August 1942, another group of Polish air crews were attached to No. 85 Squadron RAF, also equipped with Boston IIIs and Havoc Is (with unit code VY).

Havoc I (Intruder) BJ496 in the experimental camouflage of night-fighting aircraft composed of Dark Green and Extra Dark Sea Grey disruptive pattern, developed during March–April 1941 at the RAE. The aircraft was subsequently converted and allocated to No. 1422 Flight at Heston, No. 1451 Flt at Hunsdon, and then No. 1454 Flight at Colerne, where in August and October 1941 it was flown by a Polish crew of P/O Jan Krzyżanowski and P/O Leon Michalski on night sorties in co-operation with Hurricanes of No. 87 Squadron.

The Turbinlite Havoc was an unarmed variant fitted with a searchlight in the nose to illuminate targets for other night fighters. Initially these aircraft were organised in flights (grouped in the Air Target Illumination Unit) that co-operated with Hurricane and Defiant night fighter squadrons. Hurricanes of No. 87 Squadron (described in *Polish Fighter Colours* vol. 1) co-operated with No. 1454 Flight at Colerne. In August 1941 the unit had Polish air crews, and incidentally pilots of No. 87 Squadron joined it to get acquainted with the type. The flight was expanded into No. 533 Squadron in September 1942 and at the time it had two Polish crews: P/O Stanisław Szkop – P/O Ryszard Zwoliński and P/O Jan Krzyżanowski – P/O Leon Michalski.

Boston III (Intruder) aircraft were also used on operations until 1943 by Nos. 418 RCAF and 605 Squadrons. Pilot F/O Juliusz Frey and his navigtor F/O Jan Waciński, and F/Lt Bolesław Orliński flew the

Above and right:
F/O Władysław Różycki at Ford, playing with dogs. Havoc I of No. 23 Squadron, coded R, can be seen in the background.

TH-coded aircraft of the Canadian unit. The only Polish 'kill' scored in a Boston was credited to No. 605 Squadron's Sgt Jerzy Brochocki. On 16 February 1943, flying with Sgt Frederick Charles Haver Johns and F/Sgt Albert Henry Wettone in Boston III W8399/UP-X he claimed an unidentified twin-engined enemy aircraft near Evreux airfield.

Various Boston versions were also ferried by Polish air crews across the Atlantic and over Africa. The Bostons and Havocs flown on operations by Polish crews were from direct purchases for the RAF, while those ferried included aircraft procured under Lend-Lease agreements.

Douglas Havoc I BD112/YP-T in which a Polish crew of No. 23 Squadron: F/O Władysław Różycki, P/O Stefan Gębicki and P/O Edward Ryciak flew a successful sortie to bomb Lannion on 7 September 1941. The same aeroplane was used on the night of 6 December 1941 by the crew of P/O Stanisław Reymer-Krzywicki, F/O Kazimierz Bokowiec and F/O Andrzej Strasburger when they claimed a Luftwaffe *aircraft (probably Ju 88) destroyed and another damaged over Gilze-Rijen airfield. The aircraft was painted black overall, although the matt finish looks rather worn. The grey squadron code letters YP can be seen on the rear fuselage and the aircraft letter on the nose. The latter was also applied in small size at the bottom of the tail. This was typical for aircraft of the type in No. 23 Squadron RAF. These shots show clearly the poor condition of the matt finish, trodden by the ground crew when maintaining the engines.*

Douglas Havoc I BD121/YP-F, No. 23 Sqn, Ford, September 1941. Special Night RDM 2A overall. British national markings with reduced yellow ring. Dull Red serial number. Code letters: Grey. No Polish national markings

Havoc I BD121/YP-F showing the absence of roundels on the wing under sides and the 'B' type roundels on the upper surfaces. This aircraft was flown by the crew of F/O Różycki, P/O Ryciak and P/O Gębicki in July and August 1941 on night operations over France. The photographs were taken in the second half of 1941. The aircraft is often shown in artwork with red code letters, but in fact it did not differ in this respect from other Ford-based aircraft during the same photo session (see above). The only difference on this aircraft was that the yellow outer ring on the fuselage roundel was reduced in width.

Douglas Havoc/ Turbinlite AW400/A, No. 1454 Flight, Colerne, September 1942. Special Night RDM 2A overall. Standard British national markings. Dull Red serial number. Code letters: Dull Red. No Polish national markings.

31 Havocs were converted to the Turbinlite variant. AW400 was flown by the crew of P/O Jan Krzyżanowski and P/O Leon Michalski soon after its conversion with No. 1454 Flight at Colerne.

de Havilland Mosquito NF.II

No. 307 Squadron 'City of Lwów'

No. 307 Sqn, based at Exeter, started to receive Mosquito NF.IIs on 20 December 1942 and by Christmas Eve it had 21 aircraft of the type on charge. The Mosquitoes were fitted with the AI Mk IV radar, with the characteristic arrow-shaped aerials. The Polish crews were delighted with the flying characteristics and performance of the new type. Due to insufficient numbers of skilled Polish staff, especially the radar operators, No. 307 Sqn flying personnel had to be reinforced with British air crew. Mixed Polish-British crews would continue to fly with No. 307 until April 1946!

The first Mosquito operational sortie was flown by S/Ldr Gerard Ranoszek and F/O Czesław Krawiecki in DZ271/EW-R on 14 January 1943, taking off at 20.00.

On the night of 15 February F/O Ryszard Zwoliński and Sgt Henryk Gajewski, flying a patrol in DZ289, had No. 307 Sqn's first engagement in a Mosquito, claiming a Ju 88 probably destroyed.

Introduction of the new type entailed some accidents. The most tragic one was on 21 March, when W/Cdr Jan Michałowski, flying with F/O Stanisław Szkop, stalled DZ261/EW-V during a single-engine approach after a training sortie and both were killed in the crash.

In April 1943 the squadron moved to Fairwood Common. Three sorties on the night of 15 May included a 'Ranger', the first one flown by No. 307 Sqn: F/O Roman Grzanka and F/O Konrad Małuszek in DZ266/EW-K flew over France, but failed to locate any target due to ground mist. The following night two crews flew the first 'Intruder', heading for the Dutch coast: F/O Jerzy Damsz–F/O Witold Sylwestrowicz in DZ288/EW-Z, and F/O Roman Grzanka–F/O Konrad Małuszek in DZ266/EW-K. Their mission was part of extensive diversionary operations coinciding with the famed raid of No. 617 Squadron against the dams at Möhne, Eder and Sorpe. The main difference between the 'Ranger' and 'Intruder' offensive operations was that 'Intruder' sorties were ground controlled and aimed against specific enemy air activity (known or expected), while 'Ranger' sorties were planned ahead and intended to generally harass the enemy, without directions from ground control.

As shown in this photograph, some Mosquito NF.IIs delivered to No. 307 Squadron in late 1942/early 1943 were still in all-black finish, even though by that time the two-tone disruptive camouflage had been introduced. Unfortunately, it has not been possible, so far, to find enough photographic reference to reconstruct the appearance of any such aeroplane in No. 307 Squadron.

On the night of 18 May F/O Antoni Dzięgielewski and F/O Adam Węgiel were killed in DZ288/EW-Z, this being the first operational loss on Mosquitoes. F/Sgt Edward Wojczyński and Sgt Emil Słuszkiewicz were more fortunate on 21 May 1943 when they ditched in the Bristol Channel in DD729/EW-U – they were quickly picked up and soon resumed flying. On the night of 27 May F/O Jan Mieczysław Fusiński and F/O Stefan Tabaczyński were shot down and killed in DZ758/EW-O by Flak near Lahn (North-West Germany).

The nose of a Mosquito NF.II from No. 307 Squadron with the Polish white-and-red square markings in the position that was typical for that unit. Note the AI Mk IV radar aerials. The Serrate II system was fitted in the compartment previously occupied by four machine guns, as shown by the blanked over gun ports. Serrate was an allied radar detection and homing device used by night fighters to track Luftwaffe *night fighters and bombers equipped with the earlier versions of the Lichtenstein radar.*

Due to increased *Luftwaffe* activity over Brittany and the Bay of Biscay the squadron was ordered to maintain three crews at Predannack as of 4 June, and to take over night patrols in the Portreath Sector from No. 264 Squadron RAF. In the first half of June 1943 No. 307 Sqn commenced 'Instep' patrols over the Bay of Biscay. The purpose of these was to protect allied anti-U-boat aircraft from long-range *Luftwaffe* fighters. On 14 June, during the squadron's second 'Instep' patrol, S/Ldr Stanisław Szablowski and F/Sgt Henryk Gajewski in HJ648/EW-B led a section of four Mosquitoes when they spotted five surfaced U-boats. They seriously damaged two, U-68 and U-155, which had to return to Lorient for repair. On 19 June three Mosquitoes of No. 307 and one from No. 410 Sqn RCAF, led by S/Ldr Stanisław Szablowski on another 'Instep' out of Predannack, spotted a Bv 138 flying boat and promptly shot it down. On 6 July the detached section of three Mosquitoes returned from Predannack to Fairwood Common.

In late July 'Flower' patrols were undertaken, these operations being flown near enemy airfields to prevent aircraft taking off. On 2 August 1943 F/Lt Jan Bieńkowski and F/Lt Czesław Borzemski, while returning from 'Flower' patrol in HJ700/EW-E, were forced to ditch off the French coast due to a fuel system problem. The pilot drowned, while Borzemski was taken PoW as the first member of No. 307 Sqn.

On 7 August the entire No. 307 Sqn moved to Predannack, exchanging bases and aircraft with No. 264 Squadron RAF, and coming under Coastal Command control. On 21 August No. 307 received six long-range Mosquito FB.VIs to complement its Mk IIs. On 22 August an 'Instep' patrol led by S/Ldr Maksymilian Lewandowski–F/Lt Czesław Krawiecki in DZ761 encountered four Fw 190s. The crew of F/Sgt Tadeusz Eckert–F/O Konrad Małuszek in HJ655 were shot down and killed by an Fw 190 near Land´s End. On 11 September Polish crews had two successful engagements with the enemy, credited altogether with one Messerschmitt 110 destroyed, two probables and three damaged in the first one, followed by four Junkers 88s destroyed and one damaged in the second one – of these the 110 probable and three damaged were scored in an FB.VI, the rest going to Mk II crews.

A Polish Mosquito II during an overhaul in a hangar at Predannack. The Mosquito NF II was inherited from No. 264 Squadron RAF who had used that RAF station before No. 307. The four oval cannon ports on the bottom of the fuselage have been carefully covered with fabric, this being common practice as shown in other photos.

25 September saw another combat, during which two Mk II crews were credited with a Ju 88 destroyed, another probable and two damaged, but F/Sgt Leslie John Lowndes and F/Sgt Ivor Cotton (both RAF) were shot down and killed in HJ658. On 26 October W/O Stanisław Łoś and Sgt Isser Lejb Posner failed to return from 'Instep' south-west of Scilly Isles in DD781/EW-J.

On 9 November No. 307 Sqn moved to Drem and was thus transferred to the control of the Air Defence of Great Britain (ADGB), leaving its Mosquitoes at Predannack for No. 157 Sqn RAF. From 16 November three aircraft were based at Sumburgh in the Shetlands, flying reconnaissance patrols over the Atlantic. The Sumburgh section was credited with downing a He 177 on 22 November, a Ju 88 on the 26th, and another Ju 88 on 9 December. On 20 December F/Lt Jan Pfeiffer and P/O Kazimierz Kęsicki were killed when their Mosquito NF.II DD618/EW-X crashed at Sumburgh Head during a non-operational sortie.

W/O Lucjan Szempliński and P/O Frank Tillman RAF were killed on 13 January when their DZ243 hit high ground in bad weather during a navy co-operation practice. Six days later four crews flew a 'Rhubarb' over Norway, claiming a Junkers W 34 shot down plus several Bv 138C flying boats strafed to good effect on water.

Scrambles on the night of 11 February saw No. 307 Sqn's last three Mosquito NF.II sorties and also the first NF.XII one.

No. 23 Squadron RAF

Based at Ford, No. 23 Sqn RAF pioneered unique offensive Mosquito intruder operations. Having earlier flown such missions over Germany, Belgium and the Netherlands in Douglas Boston/Havoc aircraft, the squadron re-equipped in June 1942 with modified Mosquito NF.IIs, their radar system removed.

Several members of the Polish Air Force flew with the unit at the time: F/Os Władysław Różycki (pil.), Stanisław Reymer-Krzywicki (pil.), Andrzej Strasburger (nav.), Edward Ryciak (r/op.), Kazimierz Bokowiec (nav.) and Stefan Gębicki (nav.) Between April and August 1942 most of the

Mosquito F II (Intruder) DD712/YP-R with red code letters. On 27 August 1942 F/O Mieczysław Kałuża and Sgt Roberts suffered an accident in Mosquito II DD688 which looked similar, with the same code and painted matt black, such finish reducing the top speed by no less than 20 mph!

Poles transferred to other units, including No. 307 Sqn, replaced by others, who had just completed conversion training on Mosquitoes. F/O Mieczysław Kałuża was one of them, formerly a Beaufighter pilot of No. 307 Sqn who had trained on Mosquitoes in No. 54 OTU. Soon after joining No. 23 Sqn in August, F/O Mieczysław Kałuża, flying with Sgt Peter Alfred Roberts, crashed in Mosquito II DD688/YP-R on the 27th. The Pole was unhurt, but Roberts was injured. In October F/Os Kałuża and Strasburger flew non-operational sorties with 23 Squadron.

Another ex-No. 307 Sqn pilot, F/Lt Marceli Neyder, commenced operational flying with No. 23 Squadron in September 1942 with his navigator, F/O Sydney John Cornes. On the night of 7 September they flew DZ229/YP-C to Beauvais, and on 13 September to Twente in DZ236/YP-F. It was on 13 September that No. 23 Sqn moved to Bradwell Bay. Another Polish crew joined the unit at the time: F/Lt Jerzy Orzechowski and F/O Ignacy Szponarowicz.

In December 1942 No. 23 Squadron moved to Malta. The aircraft were ferried by air, making stops at Gibraltar and Maison Blanche. The squadron included two Polish crews on arrival, although both had mishaps. Orzechowski–Szponarowicz in DD691/YP-O suffered an engine failure when still 60 miles from Malta and were then unable to get the undercarriage down as they arrived on the 27th, while the tail of DZ238/YP-H of Neyder–Cornes was damaged on landing when they flew in on the 29th.

The Polish crews flew nearly 50 sorties between January and March 1943, mostly over Sicily. Neyder's crew achieved such good results against trains and steam engines that 'Neyder treatment' became the squadron's slang word for attacks on railways. F/Lt Neyder and F/O Cornes failed to return from a sortie on 21 February 1943. The crew of Orzechowski–Szponarowicz left Malta on 28 March 1943, going to No. 307, where Orzechowski was soon appointed the Squadron Commander.

Other Units

The crew of F/Os Włodzimierz Zykun and F/O Franciszek Kalinowski were attached to No. 151 Squadron RAF for three months, joining it in late February 1943 and flying first sorties on 5 March 1943. They flew with the unit until early June, both as duty readiness crew and in air-to-air gunnery training.

F/Sgt Julian Nowak flew with No. 25 Sqn RAF from late May 1943. He was killed on 12 August 1943 with his British navigator W/O Charles Godfrey Kendall when their Mosquito NF.II DD637 crashed at Sigglesthorne, Yorks.

Polish pilots test flew Mosquito NF.IIs at the Royal Aircraft Establishment at Farnborough.

De Havilland Mosquito NF.II HJ932/EW–L, No. 307 Sqn, Exeter, 28 March 1943. Overall Medium Sea Grey with Dark Green disruptive pattern. Standard British national markings, Black serial number. Code letters: Dull Red.

An excellent example of a No. 307 Squadron Mosquito NF.II with the radar. Although the variant was in use with the unit for over a year, there are not that many photographs to show these aircraft. HJ932/EW–L was first flown on operations on 27 January 1943 by the crew of P/O Antoni Beda–F/Sgt Maksymilian Trawicki, who then flew most sorties in this machine, although in March and April 1943 the aircraft was mostly flown by P/Os Jan Pacholczyk and Leon Michalski.

***Right:** Frames from colour film shot on 28 March 1943 at Exeter when F/O Jerzy Damsz (left) flew the Mosquito II to Tangmere and back to bring the Czech pilot F/Lt Hugo Hrbaček (in long coat) who had been shot down over the Channel and picked up by a boat. Mosquito NF.II HJ932/EW-L provides the backdrop, displaying the red codes.*

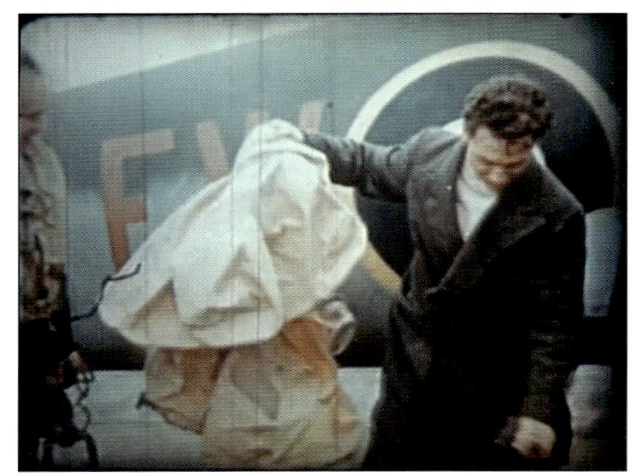

De Havilland Mosquito NF.II DD636/EW–B, No. 307 Sqn, Predannack, 10 October 1943. Overall Medium Sea Grey with Dark Green disruptive pattern. Standard British national markings, Dull red serial number. Code letters: Dull Red.

These photographs taken on 10 October 1943, during the visit of Gen. Kazimierz Sosnkowski, the Polish C-in-C, at Predannack, depict No. 307 Squadron ground crew at work on Mosquito NF.II DD636/EW–B. The photos show the layout of code letters and the position and style of the Polish national marking near the cockpit. Two days earlier the aircraft flew a patrol over the Biscay with a mixed Polish-British crew of F/Sgt Ryszard Kiełczewski and Sgt Jonathan Walker Kirkbride. Aircraft used in these missions had their radar systems removed. Note that the aircraft features serial number, poorly visible here, in Dull Red, the colour retained initially after the new disruptive camouflage was introduced by orders of 1 October 1942. A portion of the rear fuselage shows signs of overpainting the large code letters of the previous operators.

De Havilland Mosquito F.II (Intruder) DZ238/YP–H, No. 23 Sqn, Luqa, February 1943. Upper surface camouflage colours: Medium Sea Grey and Dark Green. Smooth Night Black (DTD 308) undersides. Standard British national markings, Black serial number. Code letters: Dull Red.

De Havilland Mosquito F.II (Intruder) DZ238/YP–H, No. 23 Sqn, Luqa, February 1943. Upper surface camouflage colours: Medium Sea Grey and Dark Green. Smooth Night Black (DTD 308) undersides. Standard British national markings, Black serial number. Code letters: Dull Red.

Mosquito F.II (Intruder) DZ238/YP–H in the camouflage scheme introduced for intruder aircraft. This aeroplane was flown to Malta by the crew of F/L Neyder and F/O Cornes and used as their machine during nearly all of their sorties from Luqa. They failed to return on 21 February 1943 when flying another Mosquito, DD793/YP-X. These photos were taken after DZ238 returned to Britain. The individual name 'Babs' can be made out on the nose. Note that on some Mosquitoes, for example DZ228/YP-D shown on p. 409, the intruder scheme introduced in December 1942 was obtained by adding grey and green areas on all-black finish, and the serial number in red was retained on black background. But in this case the serial is black on disruptive camouflage on both sides, proving that this aeroplane was originally finished in the two-tone night fighter scheme, its under surfaces then resprayed black to obtain the intruder scheme.

De Havilland Mosquito NF.II HJ652/EW-M, No. 307 Sqn, Predannack, 10 October 1943. Overall Medium Sea Grey with Dark Green disruptive pattern. Standard British national markings, Black serial number. Code letters: Dull Red. Polish national markings on the nose. Victory markings (crosses) on the port side of the nose.

Mosquito NF.IIs of No. 307 Squadron include some that deserve special attention. During the visit of Gen. Kazimierz Sosnkowski, the Polish C-in-C, at Predannack on 10 October 1943, souvenir photos were taken in front of HJ652/EW-M, adorned with black cross 'kill' markings. Just before the VIP visit four black crosses were applied below the Polish AF marking on the aircraft parked in front of a hangar. It is not clear if the crosses were meant to refer to the score of a paricular crew. The aeroplane was used to achieve only two credited victories: on 11 September, in an engagement with six Messerschmitt Bf 110s, S/Ldr Jerzy Damsz and F/Lt Witold Sylwestrowicz in HJ652/EW-M were credited with one probably destroyed, two weeks later W/O Franciszek Jankowiak and F/Sgt Jerzy Karais were credited with a Ju 88 damaged. W/Cdr Jerzy Orzechowski was the only member of No. 307 Sqn at the time who could boast four victories (one probable and three damaged) and he flew at least two combat sorties in this aircraft just before the event.

de Havilland Mosquito FB.VI

No. 307 Squadron 'City of Lwów'

No. 307 Squadron used the Mosquito FB.VI for a short while. On 21 August 1943 six long-range FB.VIs were delivered (HP854, HX859, HX860, HX861, HX862, HX863) in addition to the squadron's Mosquito IIs. On 30 August 1943 S/Ldr Maksymilian Lewandowski flew the squadron's first Mosquito FB.VI operational sortie. Although the weather in September was not very good, the squadron had some very successful encounters with enemy aircraft over the Bay of Biscay. During the first ten days of September uneventful patrols and Fighter Direction Operations in co-operation with the navy were flown. On 11 September Polish crews fought two victorious air combats. During the first of these four Mosquitoes, led by W/Cdr Jerzy Orzechowski and F/Lt Ignacy Szponarowicz in FB.VI HX859/EW-O, guided from HMS *Sheffield* by F/O Jan Maliński, attacked six Bf 110s. Two Mosquito II crews claimed one destroyed and one probable, while Orzechowski was credited with a probable and three damaged. The next patrol was flown by Mosquito IIs only.

Another successful combat was fought by four Mosquitoes led by S/Ldr Jerzy Damsz and F/Lt Ignacy Szponarowicz during an 'Instep' patrol on 25 September. They encountered eight Ju 88Cs from the V./KG 40. Two destroyed, one probable and three damaged were claimed by three crews, of which one, that of S/Ldr Damsz, flew Mosquito FB.VI HX859/EW-O. One Mosquito II was lost with its crew.

Between 5 and 8 October No. 307 Squadron transferred all its Mosquito FB.VIs to No. 60 OTU.

No. 305 Squadron 'Wielkopolska Province'

During late 1943, No. 305 Squadron converted onto the Mosquito FB.VI at Lasham. On 3 December 1943 the squadron was ordered to cease flying their Mitchell IIs and the following day they started conversion onto the Mosquito. This was a significant change for the unit, which switched from medium bombers with multiple air crew members to the two-seat Mosquitoes. Instead of performing daylight level bombing of substantial targets in formation they were now going to fly attack missions, often by single aircraft, against pinpoint targets. 'Ranger' operations against targets of opportunity would also be flown.

Mosquito FB.VI NS999 with fresh paintwork from a Maintenace Unit, upon delivery to No. 305 Squadron in October 1944. The colour scheme can be seen clearly: overall Medium Sea Grey with a disruptive pattern of Dark Green areas on upper surfaces. This was a standard finish on most aircraft of the unit at the time.

Mosquito FB.VI HP913 SM-W beautifully adorned with multiple mission markings. Only the last digit of the serial number has not been obliterated by the invasion markings. It was most often flown by the Polish crew F/O Aleksander Gertner – F/O Wacław Andruszko. During a sortie over Germany on 25 November 1944 the crew of P/O Tomasz Wilczewski and F/Sgt Zygmunt Haas received Flak fire while flying this aeroplane over the Ruhr, which caused failure of the electric system. The navigator was unable to see his maps, so they flew southwards (to avoid having to bale out into the sea) and after using up all the fuel they baled out. It turned out that they had landed in Champagne that was in American hands. The Polish crew met some Polish emigrants who helped them get in touch with the US military police. The story was described by Wilczewski upon their return to the unit a few days later. What he did not say at the time was that they lost an aeroplane worth thousands of pound sterling because they did not have a two shilling torch!

No. 305 Squadron's crews first flew the Mosquito FB.VI on 19 December 1943. The first combat operation on the new type was flown on 25 January 1944 by two Mosquitoes: LR313/SM–B and NS823/SM–H. The target, V1 launch installations, were not found due to bad weather, though.

'Ramrod-Intruder' operations were flown in early 1944, usually by pairs of aircraft. As more and more Polish air crew members were nearing the end of their tours, a British flight was formed in No. 305 Squadron pending arrival of newly trained Polish crews. The forming of the flight commenced on 14 April. It was commanded by S/Ldr Michael J. Herrick, who previously served as a staff officer with No. 138 Wing HQ.

Operations with use of the GH radar were commenced by No. 305 Squadron on the night of 9 April 1944, when three crews flew their first 'Night Ranger' against German airfields at Chartres, Conches and Beaumont. The first major scale attack was conducted on 18 April 1944 when twelve Mosquitoes led by W/Cdr Kazimierz Konopasek destroyed heavy artillery positions at Ouville-la-Rivière.

The only purely fighter episodes in the history of No. 305 Squadron were two sorties by W/Cdr John Robert Daniel Braham DSO DFC in the unit's Mosquitoes. He was Wing Commander Night Operations at the HQ No. 2 Group, 2nd TAF. On 13 April 1944 W/Cdr Braham and his navigator F/Lt William Gregory flew No. 305 Squadron's LR313/SM–B when he claimed an He 111 and an Fw 58 destroyed. On 29 April he flew MM422/SM–H when he claimed an Fw 190 North West of Poitiers.

During May 1944 No. 305 Squadron flew 108 night sorties and only one in day time. On D-Day, 6 June, the squadron had just 14 airworthy Mosquitoes, six less than the regulation establishment. The only day time 'Ranger' operation in June was flown on the 16th by S/Ldr Michael J. Herrick with his Polish navigator F/O Aleksander Turski. They were intercepted by a German fighter, shot down and killed off Denmark.

On 2 August 1944 No. 305 Squadron performed its famed attack on the German saboteur and spy training establishment at Château de Maulny near Le Mans. 31 August saw No. 305 Squadron's other most famous operation, when fuel tanks (13 million litres of petrol) at Nomexy near Epinal in Vosges were destroyed. The pinpoint attack caused no casualties among the French population of Nomexy, whose homes were left intact. For some reason, though, the local people believed this precision attack was performed by Canadian crews.

As it was planned to move the squadron onto the Continent, a rehearsal move to Hartford Bridge was carried out during 23–25 October, following which the squadron returned to Lasham, only to move to Hartford Bridge again on the 30th. On 19 November No. 305 Squadron moved again, this time overseas, as part of No. 138 Wing. The new base, code named A–75, was located at the village of Epinoy in northern France, about 50 km north of Lille, between the cities of Cambrai, Douai and Arras. This move reduced the cruising time during sorties: it now took about two hours to reach the Ruhr, instead of four hours from England.

The first operation from the new base was flown on the night of 21 November. Nine crews of No. 305 Squadron patrolled the area of Kevelaer – Wesel – Düsseldorf – Heinsberg – Venlo.

During 1944, No. 305 Squadron Mosquitoes have flown 1,636 sorties in a total time of 4,295 hours, dropping 907 tonnes of bombs.

22 February 1945 saw the largest allied daylight air operation of the entire war: Operation 'Clarion'. About 7,000 aircraft of various types were employed to paralyse the German communication system. They attacked railway, road and inland water transport installations throughout the Third Reich territory. No. 305 Squadron sent 19 crews, including six Polish ones, to the area between Hamburg, Wesermünde (now Bremerhaven) and Meldorf.

During April 1945 they continued to fly interdiction operations over Germany. No. 305 Squadron flew its last operation on the night of 25 April: 12 Mosquitoes patrolled the area of Westerland – Flensburg – Eckernförde – Neuhausen – Ording – Westerland attacking targets of opportunity.

The most frequent colour of the propeller spinners on the Mosquito FB.VI: Medium Sea Grey, the same as the basic overall tone of the aeroplane. This photo, taken in October 1944, shows the invasion markings around the fuselage.

Mosquito FB.VI with pale spinners, finished in Sky, typical for the day fighter scheme. Few Mosquitoes taken over from No. 613 Squadron RAF featured this marking. Note also the upper surface camouflage clearly different than the under surface colour, as shown below and aft of the Polish square.

Mosquito FB.VI HR145/SM-E with black spinners, as introduced after the war, photographed at an airfield in the occupied Germany. Note how the black paint peeled off in use.

TA496, photographed after the war with No. 51 Maintenance Unit at Lichfield, provides an excellent example of the yellow propeller spinners and code letters, as introduced in August 1945.

No. 305 Squadron's total effort in 1945 amounted to 813 sorties in 2,441 hoours, 279 tonnes of bombs were dropped.

After cessation of hostilities the squadron continued to be based at Epinoy until the end of July 1945. On 30 July it moved to B-80 Volkel in Germany. In September it moved to Gilze-Rijen (B–77) in the Netherlands and in November to Melsbroek (B-58) near Brussels in Belgium. In January 1946 the unit spent two weeks on gunnery training on Sylt in Germany.

On 11 March 1946 the squadron was transferred to the British Air Forces of Occupation and moved to B-119 Wahn near Cologne. Their Mosquitoes used it for frequent courier flights to England, delivering documents related to the Nuremberg trials of the Nazi German war criminals.

The squadron returned to Britain on 1 October 1946, moving to Faldingworth. In November it was transferred back to Bomber Command control. At the same time it started handing back its aircraft. The last Polish Mosquito FB.VI was flown from Faldingworth to the de Havilland factory airfield at Hartfield on 2 December 1946.

Altogether No. 305 Squadron used 117 Mosquito FB.VIs, losing forty on operations and in accidents.

Other Squadrons

In April 1943, three Poles served on Mosquito FB.VIs with No. 418 Squadron RCAF: pilots S/Ldrs Bolesław Orliński and Juliusz Frey, and navigator F/O Jan Waciński. Frey stayed with the Canadian unit until December 1943. S/Ldr Orliński later flew Mosquito FB.VIs with No. 305 Squadron as its commander, and F/O Waciński was a navigator on the type with No. 307 Squadron.

No. 23 Squadron RAF was the next unit in which Polish air crews flew the fighter-bomber variant of the Mosquito. The unit took delivery of its first Mosquito FB.VI, HJ672, on 17 May 1943. F/O Władysław Różycki and F/O Edward Ryciak joined No. 23 Sqn in Malta when they ferried Mosquito FB.VI HX947/YP-J, leaving Lyneham on 21 October 1943 and arriving at Luqa on the 26th. Although the allies had invaded Italy by then, No. 23 Squadron was still based on Malta. The following day the Polish crew flew to a forward airfield at Pomigliano near Naples. At the time No. 23 Squadron's Mosquitoes flew night harassment sorties against withdrawing German troops. On 7 December 1943 the Polish crew moved to another advanced airfield, at Alghero in North-West Sardinia. The intensity of operations was decreasing constantly and even operations over Southern France failed to bring significant success. The Poles ended their tour with No. 23 Squadron on 1 March 1944.

Mosquito FB.VI HX947/YP–J with F/O Władysław Różycki, who ferried the aircraft from Lyneham, leaving on 21 October 1943 and reaching Pomigliano near Naples in Italy on the 26th. The crew F/O Władysław Różycki – F/O Edward Ryciak flew this aircraft, among other, on interdiction sorties over enemy territory until March 1944. The aircraft was finished in the standard Intruder scheme with two-tone upper surface camouflage and black under surfaces, with Dull Red code letters.

Comparison of two photographs showing two different post-war schemes on No. 305 Squadron Mosquitoes. The rear view of FB.VI HR113/SM-R shows clearly the camouflage scheme on the wings and the 'Gee' aerial protruding from the rear section of the cockpit glazing. The other shows FB.VI TA378/SM-N with the yellow markings introduced in August 1945, showing here as spinners and code letters in the same pale tone. Both photos show the post-war small-size roundels with the white and yellow ring.

P/O Zbigniew Dunin-Rzuchowski, a pilot credited with a night victory while with No. 307 Squadron in 1943, flew with No. 604 Squadron from January until March 1945. In March 1945 he was posted to No. 605 Squadron. He was killed in that unit, with his navigator F/Lt Leslie Alexander William Smith, in de Havilland Mosquito FB.VI RS603/UP–F, during an intruder sortie on 19 March 1945, when they were shot down into the sea by a German fighter.

Polish ferry pilots also flew these aircraft. For example, Polish 'ATA girl' 1st/Off Anna Leska delivered a couple of Mosquito VIs in January 1944 to No. 613 Sqn RAF at Lasham. Other Polish ATA pilots who flew Mosquitoes included 1st/Off Leon Jaugsch, who was demoted to 3rd Officer for six months in March 1945 when he 'deliberately flew above cloud on a ferry flight from Edzell to White Waltham, became lost and found himself over France'. Luck certainly was not with him that month, because on 30 March 1945 he baled out of Mosquito FB.VI RF847 when he thought the starboard engine was on fire. Subsequent investigation of the wreckage proved there was no technical fault, and it was concluded that he must have mistaken static electric discharges or exhaust flame for an engine fire. He was ferrying the Mosquito from RAF Kirkbride to No. 404 Squadron RAAF at Banff.

Polish ferry pilots also delivered Mosquitoes to the Far East. S/Ldr Edward Peterek's last and longest ferry operation during the war was flown in March 1945 in FB.VI RF698 from Egypt via Habbaniyah, Karachi, to Poona in India. The Mosquito subsequently went to No. 84 Squadron RAF at Yelahanka in central India, which had been in the process of converting from Vengeance dive bombers since February 1945.

Polish test pilots at the RAE Farnborough flew Mosquito FB.VIs in trials

De Havilland Mosquito FB.VI HJ675/YP-V, No. 23 Sqn, Pomigliano, October 1943. Upper surface camouflage: Medium Sea Grey and Dark Green. Smooth Night Black (DTD 308) undersides. Standard British national markings. Black serial number. Code letters: Dull Red.

Mosquito FB.VI HJ675/YP–V, flown on several operational sorties by the Polish crew of F/O Władysław Różycki – F/O Edward Ryciak. This was an aeroplane from the first batch of FB.VIs that arrived in Malta to replace No. 23 Squadron's intruder Mosquito IIs. Similar to its predecessors, the aircraft was given black under surface finish applied on the standard two-tone camouflage.

De Havilland Mosquito FB.VI HX859/EW-O, No. 307 Sqn, Predannack, September 1943. Overall Medium Sea Grey with Dark Green disruptive pattern. Standard British national markings. Black serial number. Code letters: Dull Red. Polish national markings and Wing Commander pennants on the nose.

Mosquito VI HX859/EW-O was the personal aircraft of W/Cdr Jerzy Orzechowski, who flew it with his navigator F/Lt Ignacy Szponarowicz (both posing here). The aircraft displayed Wing Commander pennants on both sides of the nose, below the Polish AF squares. This was the sole documented case of applying rank pennants on Polish Mosquitoes in Nos. 307 or 305 Squadrons. On 11 September 1943 W/Cdr Jerzy Orzechowski flew the Mosquito FB.VI when he was credited with a Messerschmitt 110 probably destroyed and three more damaged. During an 'Instep' patrol on 25 September S/Ldr Jerzy Damsz and F/Lt Ignacy Szponarowicz damaged a Ju 88C and destroyed another while flying this Mosquito FB.VI.

De Havilland Mosquito FB.VI LR365/SM-J, No. 305 Sqn, Lasham, 30 March 1943. Upper surface camouflage: Ocean Grey and Dark Green. Medium Sea Grey under surfaces. Standard British national markings. Black serial number. Code letters: Dull Red. Polish national markings on the nose.

Mosquito FB.VI LR365/SM-J, photographed on 30 March 1944, was one of the longest-lasting Mosquitoes of No. 305 Squadron. It was used by the unit continuously from March 1944 until January 1945. It featured the pale band around the rear fuselage, seldom seen on fighter-bomber Mosquitoes. This was a regulation marking on day fighters finished in Ocean Grey/Dark Green camouflage on upper surfaces with Medium Sea Grey under surfaces. Few Mosquito FB.VIs were finished like this but this aircraft, transferred to the Polish unit from No. 613 Squadron RAF, as well as other examples from that unit displayed this colour scheme. Altogether the Poles took over 21 aircraft from No. 613 Sqn, finished in various colour schemes. The other photo shows the aircraft while still with No. 613 Squadron, with the upper surface camouflage clearly different from the under surface tone. At the time LR365 was coded SY-O and it seems the new code required only slight change, to turn the O into J, and the Y into M.

De Havilland Mosquito FB.VI NS927/SM-C, No. 305 Sqn, Lasham, late 1944. Overall Medium Sea Grey with Dark Green disruptive pattern. Standard British national markings. Black serial number. Code letters: Dull Red. Polish national markings on the nose. Invasion markings in form of white and black bands on the bottom of the fuselage and wings.

The most popular photo of a No. 305 Squadron Mosquito FB.VI, probably included in every publication that mentions the unit. NS927/SM-C, photographed in July 1944, displays the invasion striping applied rather hastily to its under surfaces, obscuring the bottom half of the code letters. Note also the invasion bands on wing under surface. No photograph has surfaced so far that shows a No. 305 Squadron machine with the invasion striping on both under and upper wing surfaces. On 8 January 1945 the British crew of F/O Eric Nuttall and Sgt William Wills were forced to land at Florennes. The aircraft was damaged and sent away for repairs.

De Havilland Mosquito FB.VI NS927/SM-C, No. 305 Sqn, Lasham, late 1944. Overall Medium Sea Grey with Dark Green disruptive pattern. Standard British national markings. Black serial number. Code letters: Dull Red. Polish national markings on the nose. Invasion markings in form of white and black bands on the bottom of the fuselage and wings.

This is one of two documented cases of personal names applied on the nose of a No. 305 Squadron Mosquito. The inscription 'Janka Kituś', which probably had sentimental meaning for F/O Julian Wielgosz and F/Sgt Mieczysław Perycz pictured here, was applied on NS927/SM-C that they flew most frequently in the second half of 1944

De Havilland Mosquito FB.VI NS927/SM-C, No. 305 Sqn, Lasham, late 1944.

De Havilland Mosquito FB VI NT227/SM-M, No. 305 Sqn, Lasham, late 1944. Overall Medium Sea Grey with Dark Green disruptive pattern. Standard British national markings, Black serial number. Code letters: Dull Red. Polish national markings on the nose. Invasion markings in form of white and black bands on the fuselage only.

Mosquito FB.VI NT227/SM-M from the Polish squadron seen from below. In late 1944 the stripes were reintroduced on the fuselage only. Note the external fuel tanks under the wings. The last operational sortie of this machine with No. 305 Squadron was recorded on 1 March 1945. At the time it was flown by the crew S/Ldr Philip H. C. Hanbury – F/Lt Jack P. Hart. Before that the aeroplane was usually flown by F/Sgt Antoni Mierzwa with navigator F/O Bogusław Panek.

De Havilland Mosquito FB.VI NT233/SM-X, No. 305 Sqn, Epinoy, March 1945. Silver Overall. Standard British national markings. Black serial number. Code letters: probably Black. Polish national markings on the nose.

The unique silver-coloured Mosquito FB.VI in tropicalised version (with the larger and longer air intakes under the engines) of No. 305 Squadron with the aircraft code letter X. Documents of the unit from the first quarter of 1945 show that NT233/SM-X was flown by G/Cpt Leslie William Clement Bower, commanding No. 138 Wing, and his navigator F/Lt Cairns. Most probably this was the personal aircraft of G/Cpt Bower and was maintained by the Polish squadron ground crew, hence the Polish marking on the nose. According to regulations, the aircraft should have black spinners, but it cannot be ruled out that their colour was in fact different, and the same applied to the code letters on the fuselage.

De Havilland Mosquito FB.VI PZ399/SM-G, No. 305 Sqn, Wahn, March 1946. Overall Medium Sea Grey with Dark Green disruptive pattern. Standard post-war British national markings. Black serial number. Code letters: Trainer Yellow. Polish national markings on the nose.

Mosquito FB.VI PZ399/SM-G was the assigned aircraft of the crew of F/Os Stefan Rose – Janusz Trojanowski. The earliest photo, taken in mid-1945 shows it still in the late-war scheme, with a black spinner and Sky codes. The next photos show it in late 1945. The photo right shows serial numbers applied in black on the wing under surfaces.

The air-to-air image allows comparison of the tone of the yellow roundel ring with that of the code letters.

De Havilland Mosquito FB.VI PZ399/SM-G, No. 305 Sqn, Wahn, March 1946.

The refuelling photo of PZ399 shows the spinners freshly repainted yellow and the code letter in the same tone applied on the nose

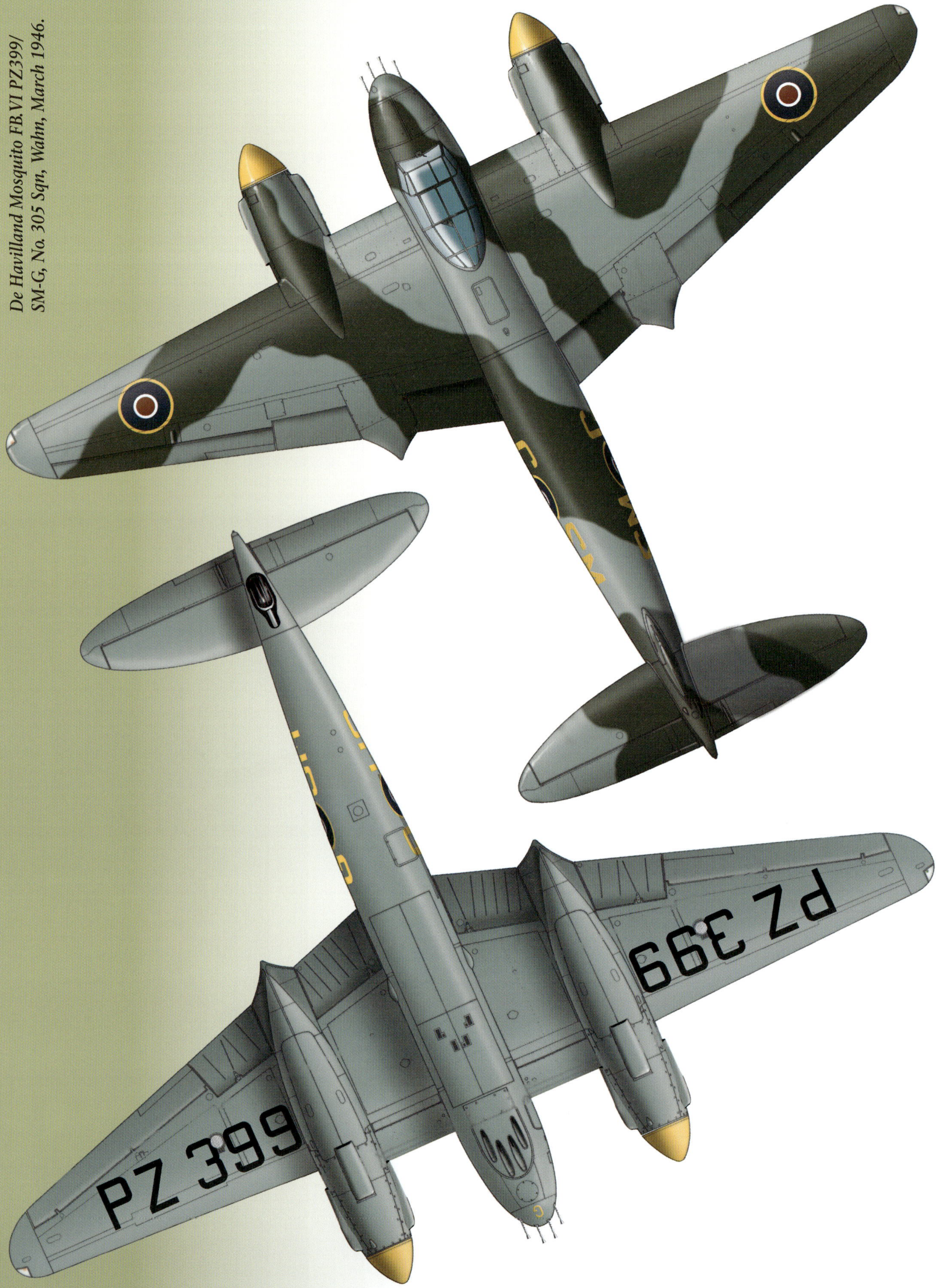

De Havilland Mosquito FB.VI PZ399/ SM-G, No. 305 Sqn, Wahn, March 1946.

De Havilland Mosquito FB.VI RF698 SNAKE, Egypt, March 1945. Silver Overall. Standard British national markings. Black serial number. No other markings.

A tropicalised Mosquito FB.VI built by Standard Motor Company at Coventry: RF698, was ferried by S/Ldr Edward Peterek and his navigator W/O Hewson (posing in the left photo) to the Far East in March 1945. This was the pilot's longest ferry flight: from Egypt via Habbaniyah in Iraq, and Karachi to Poona in India, and his last. The aircraft featured an additional marking: the word SNAKE next to the serial number, which clearly indicated that it was intended for use in the Far East and was not to be diverted from delivery while in transit through the Middle East. It was eventually delivered to No. 84 Squadron RAF at Yelahanka in India. Note the dark spinner, most probably red.

de Havilland Mosquito XII & XIII

No. 307 Squadron 'City of Lwów'

In January 1944 r No. 307 Squadron's Mosquito NF.IIs were about to be replaced by the improved Mosquito NF.XII and NF.XIII aircraft, fitted with the new AI Mk VIII centimetric radar with a rotating dish aerial. Covered by a fairing shaped like a thimble in the nose of the aircraft it was a significant progress compared to the earlier radar which used the arrow-shaped aerial. The new radar replaced the four machine guns in the nose, reducing the armament to just the four 20 mm cannon in the lower part of the forward fuselage.

Both versions had the same radar type, the AI Mk VIII, and the main design difference between the two was in the ability of the Mk XIII to carry external fuel tanks, which gave it an extended range and an endurance of up to 5 hours 45 minutes. Externally, the two Mosquito versions could also differ in the nose shape. The Mark XII had a smaller 'thimble' nose, while a large part of the Mk XIII production run featured the later standard 'bull' nose, typical for all subsequent Mosquito night fighters. Unfortunately, no photo of a No. 307 Sqn Mosquito XIII with the later nose has been found so far.

No. 307 Squadron took delivery of seven long-range Mosquito NF.XIIIs on 21 January 1944, followed by its first NF.XIIs on the 26th.

The Scramble patrols on the night of 11 February were the last for Mosquito NF.IIs (three sorties) and the first for the NF.XII (HK119/EW-D).

Three factory photos of Mosquito XIIs HK117 and HK129, from the same batch as the aircraft delivered to No. 307 Squadron. They are in standard night fighter camouflage, except for the dielectric radar radome, which was black, and the propeller spinners in a pale hue. All Mk XIIs had been built as Mk IIs by the de Havilland plant at Leavesden and were then converted by Marshalls of Cambridge.

A Mosquito XII with the Polish AF marking near the cockpit. Although several photographs of it are known, neither the serial number nor code letter is known.

The squadron moved from RAF Drem to RAF Coleby Grange near Lincoln on 2 March 1944. Its main role in the new place was to patrol the Humber Estuary, where the enemy activity had increased. The two-hour defence patrols, codenamed 'Patrington', were flown in rotation with two other squadrons. A the same time No. 307 Sqn crews learned to co-operated with searchlights and to overcome German jamming of the radar imaging.

Regardless of the training, operations of No. 307 Sqn also gained momentum. P/O Jerzy Brochocki and F/Lt Henryk Ziółkowski in Mosquito NF.XIII HK119/EW-D intercepted and downed an He 177 on 19 March.

On 8 April 1944 No. 307 Squadron transferred its seven Mosquito XIIIs to No. 29 Squadron at Drem, and two days later received seven NF.XIIs as a replacement, becoming equipped uniquely with the variant.

Starboard side of an unidentified Mosquito XII. The photo shows the code layout: on each side of the fuselage the squadron code was positioned to the left of the roundel.

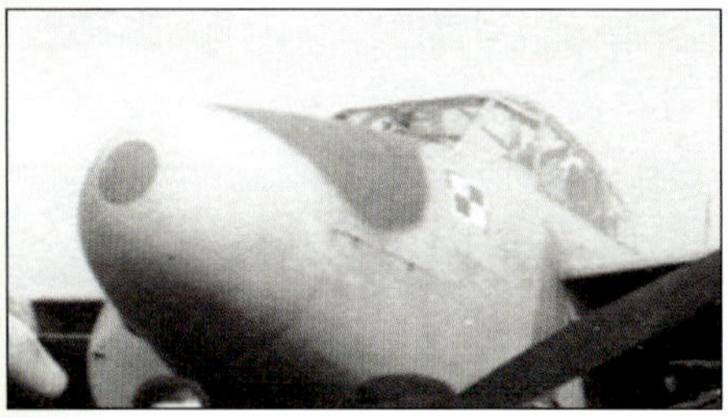
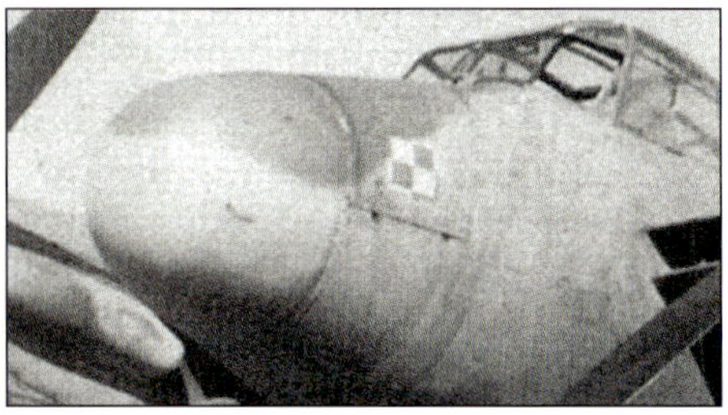

Variations of the colour schemes on Mosquito XII noses. Starboard view of a fully camouflaged nose and another where the radar 'thimble' was left in a dark colour. Four port views with various camouflage patterns and the Polish AF markings in different positions.

On 6 May 1944 No. 307 Squadron moved north, to RAF Church Fenton. 'Ranger' operations commenced on the night of 22 May and from that point on 'Ranger' or 'Intruder' operations were flown every night against targets in Denmark or France.

On the night of 5 June No. 307 Sqn flew a 'Flower' patrol over the Netherlands in indirect support for the invasion. Two nights later Sgt Kazimierz Oleszczuk and Sgt Jerzy Karais in Mosquito XII HK200/EW-G damaged a Ju 88 over the Netherlands, while Sgt Jan Górski and F/O Eric Thomason na HK129/EW-Z hit an ammunition train which blew up.

During July, in addition to the regular defensive missions from its home base, the squadron also flew defensive patrols over East Anglia from Coltishall, four Mosquitoes

De Havilland Mosquito XII Mosquito HK165/EW-A with the only documented case of a personal name applied on a Mosquito of the unit. However, this was not applied in the more usual place near the cockpit, but on an engine nacelle. The starboard engine was named 'Johnny II' applied on the bottom of the cowling. It is therefore possible that the port engine was called 'Johnny I'. Note the pale line applied mid-way down the propeller blade that was also seen on other machines. W/Cdr Maksymilian Lewandowski (at the time the squadron commander; left) and F/Lt Czesław Krawiecki pose with the aircraft. Above: Close-up of the name on the engine cowling. Standing, left to right: F/O Jerzy Brochocki, F/Lt Henryk Ziółkowski, W/O Stanisław Zendwalewicz and S/Ldr Ryszard Zwoliński. The photo was taken between February and August 1944.

being detached there. Thus the night defence of the entire area north of No. 11 Group was in the hands of No. 307 Sqn.

On 27 July the squadron carried out a very successful daylight attack against the radar and radio installations on Sylt.

Operations during August and September 1944 were much the same, with a growing number of 'Intruder' missions over Germany.

P/O Kazimierz Jaworski and F/O Zygmunt Szymilewicz were lost in HK223/EW-E on 17 September while on night patrol in protection of the airborne forces dropped at Arnhem. They were shot down off the coast and lost in the sea. 18 September saw the squadron's first ever mid-air collision, which took place during a non-operational daylight flying. F/Lt Stanisław Madej and F/O Józef Gąsecki were killed in HK194/EW-L, but F/Lt William John Griffiths and F/Lt George John Lane in HK228 escaped unhurt.

As the night attacks against Britain with V1s launched from He 111s began, No. 307 Squadron was deployed in September to intercept the carrier aircraft. First of these patrols was flown on the night of 26 September and these were flown every night between 28 September and 17 October. The mixed Czech-Polish crew of Sgt Vladimir Kepak – Sgt Franciszek Kot failed to return from one of such patrols. One hypothesis is that their aeroplane, DZ302/EW-E, was brought down by the explosion of a V1 they had hit with their fire. Then the operations were interrupted for six weeks in connection with the re-equipment with the Mosquito NF.XXX.

The last NF.XII sortie in No. 307 Sqn was flown by HK164/EW-C on the night of 17 December 1944.

Altogether, during ten months of 1944 No. 307 Squadron used 33 Mosquito Mk XIIs and seven Mk XIIIs. Fifteen Mk XIIs were written off, either on operations or in numerous accidents. Eight crew members were killed.

Other Units

F/Lt Piotr Ostaszewski-Ostoja and F/Sgt Józef Bachleda flew on operations with No. 85 Squadron RAF, equipped with Mosquito XIIs, from 8 February 1944. Between 10 and 13 February they flew three sorties in a Mosquito XII coded VY-E, but their subsequent operations were flown in the MosquitoNF.XVII. Polish ferry pilots flew these aircraft occasionally. For example, 1st/Off Anna Leska ferried five Mosquito XIIs.

Two Mosquito XIIs with interesting markings on propeller spinners: F/Lt Emil Chodacki in front of an unidentified aircraft with a small three-tone roundel, and LAC Józef Gliński by HK115/EW-F.

De Havilland Mosquito XII Mosquito HK111/EW-H, No. 307 Sqn, Coleby Grange, April 1944. Overall Medium Sea Grey with Dark Green disruptive pattern. Standard British national markings. Black serial number. Code letters: Dull Red. Polish national markings on the nose.

HK111/EW-H has the best photographic documentation of all the Mosquito XIIs of No. 307 Squadron. Note the pale colour of the propeller spinners and the radome. These items were most probably painted Sky. Two crews of No. 307 Squadron were photographed with Mosquito HK111: F/Sgt Ryszard Kiełczewski–P/O Jonathan Kirkbride and F/O Thomas Drinkwater–F/O Donald Miller. The aircraft was damaged on 12 April 1944 when it hit a 'pill box' while taxiing for take-off with the crew of F/Sgt Kiełczewski and P/O Kirkbride.

de Havilland Mosquito NF.XXX

No. 307 Squadron 'City of Lwów'

In the second half of October 1944 No. 307 Sqn crews commenced training in the use of the new AI Mk X radar and 'Gee' radio-navigation system of the Mosquito NF.XXX. The variant, powered with Merlin 72 or 76 engines, had much better performance than previous Mosquito variants. Deliveries of NF.XXXs to the squadron commenced on 24 October and five had been taken on charge by the 31st. The first three weeks of November were spent training and the first anti-diver patrol was flown on 23 November 1944 by the British crew of F/Lt William Griffiths and F/O Thomas Heatley in MV542/G coded EW-Y. Training on the NF.XXX was completed on 10 December. From the beginning of the month the number of aircraft at readiness was increased to six and all operations were flown by NF.XXXs.

After the last two anti-V1 patrols on the nights of 4 and 5 December, the Mosquitos were despatched individually on 'Intruder' operations over Germany. On the night of the 12th W/Os Sylwester Wieczorek and Henryk Ostrowski had to crash-land in MV542/G/EW-Y following a mid-air collision, probably with a V1. Both crew members were seriously injured.

Due to 'teething troubles' of the new radar and delays in delivery of under-wing fuel tank attachments only four 'Intruder' operations were flown in January. On the 5th W/O Albert William Martin and P/O Donald Frederick Prior were lost at sea in Mosquito NF.XXX MV545/G/EW-G due to icing. That was the last fatal loss of the squadron during the war. The same night another Mosquito was damaged.

On 25 January, No. 307 Sqn moved to RAF Castle Camps near Cambridge, in connection with the change in the role, as it would now fly 'Intruder' missions over the Continent to provide support to RAF night bombers. Enemy aircraft were seen but none were engaged. The under-wing fuel tank attachments were still not available but by the end of February 1945 all Mosquito NF.XXXs of No. 307 Squadron had been fitted with the AI Mk X radar and the 'Gee' system.

March saw a similar number of operations, a mix of bomber support and 'Ranger' sorties. The latter consisted in attacking targets of opportunity. On the night of 3 March F/Lt Czesław

Thanks to the relatively quiet service in the last months of the war 17 out of the total number of 27 Mosquito NF.XXXs used by No. 307 Squadron are known from photographs. The official photographic session at Church Fenton on 27 January 1945 captured most of these in winter scenery. This image shows five, of which four are fully identified, left to right: NT303/G / EW-Y, NT268/G / EW-Z, NT267/G / EW-J and NT547/G / EW-R. They all feature similar factory-applied camouflage pattern and red code letters. NT303/EW-Y, shown in the foreground, crashed into trees on the edge of the airfield at Horsham St Faith during an attempt to land on one engine on 14 January 1946, killing F/Sgt Roman Franciszek Skubik and Sgt Mieczysław Mróz. They were the last fatalities and the last aircraft loss of No. 307 Squadron.

Tarkowski and F/O Kenneth Taylor in Mosquito XXX MV544/G/EW-B were credited with a Ju 188 shot down west of Bonn. This was No. 307 Squadron's last aerial victory. A number of trains and transport vehicles were destroyed or damaged in the later part of the month. The drop tank attachments were finally received at the end of the month.

Operations in April were similar, ending on the night of the 25th. During the last but one, on the night of 24 April, the crews of W/Cdr Stanisław Andrzejewski–W/O Stanisław Kaliszewski and F/Sgt Kazimierz Leszkiewicz–Sgt Zbigniew Lewandowski successfully attacked German airfields near the Danish-German border. The former destroyed an Fw 190 and damaged another on the ground at Husum. The latter destroyed a Ju 88 there, but during the attack the starboard engine of their NF.XXX MV544/G/EW-B was hit and they had to ditch in the sea. They were picked up by the Germans and remained in custody until the end of the war, returning to Britain in early May 1945.

May 1945 saw just one mission, flown the day after VE-Day: Operation 'Nestegg' on the 9th. This was a show of force over the Channel Islands still occupied by the Germans, who had not yet surrendered. A strong Royal Navy formation sailed there, escorted by three aircraft each of the 'A' and 'B' Flights, led by W/Cdr Stanisław Andrzejewski and W/O Stanisław Kaliszewski in NT547/G/EW-R. Crews of the low flying aircraft saw white flags on German guns, masts and all sorts of other objects, so no combat action was necessary. The operation ended in a feast of colourful flares fired from the aeroplanes and the ships.

On 18 May 1945 the unit moved to Coltishall. This soon became a Polish Fighter Station with a number of Mustang squadrons, so No. 307 Squadron had to move again. On 7 August it transferred to Horsham St Faith, a few miles from Coltishall.

Training flying continued and on 14 January 1946 Mosquito NF.XXX NT303/EW-Y suffered an engine fire. The pilot attempted to land at the home base, but the aeroplane crashed in the trees surrounding the airfield, killing F/Sgt Roman Skubik and Sgt Mieczysław Mróz. This was the last fatal loss of No. 307 Squadron.

In 1945 and 1946 for a few weeks seven crews of No. 307 Sqn flew to Lubeck for training, including practice sorties in formation with bombers. On 14 September, to celebrate the Battle of Britain Day, No. 307 Squadron flew a flypast in perfect formation. In the British zone of occupation the Polish air crews were able to see the latest RAF aircraft and fly the latest jets. The unit was disbanded at the end of 1946.

Another exception in the colour scheme among the Mosquito XXXs of No. 307 Squadron: MV561/G / EW-V with spinner tips finished in a dark colour (red, navy blue, black?). This aircraft was flown by W/O Józef Radwański and F/O Bronisław Ferański on 'Intruder' sortie over Germany on 30 December 1944, one of the few flown in late 1944. Like most Mosquito XXXs, this example entered service with No. 307 Squadron in December 1944 and was used in it until the disbandment of the unit two years later.

De Havilland Mosquito XXX Mosquito NT259/G/EW-W, No. 307 Sqn, Church Fenton, 27 January 1945. Overall Medium Sea Grey with Dark Green disruptive pattern. Standard British national markings. Black serial number. Code letters: Dull Red. Polish national markings on the nose.

The similarly camouflaged Mosquito XXXs included few that differed from the standard pattern. Mosquito XXX NT259/G/EW-W was among such exceptions. It differed in having dark (black?) propeller spinners. On 5 January 1945 NT259/G/EW-W was damaged due to icing. The crew, W/Os Jan Pawlikowski and Ignacy Drewelus were unhurt. The different spinner colour may have resulted from the accident repair work.

Four views showing clearly the details of markings on Mosquito NF.XXX NT267/G/EW-J. The close-up view of the tail, on which F/O Jerzy Brochocki is seated, the '/G' suffix to the serial number is shown to advantage. This denoted aeroplanes that required to be specially guarded on the ground because of secret devices (radar in this case) fitted in them. During their initial service with No. 307 Squadron most Mosquito XXXs featured this marking. The head-on view shows clearly the aircraft letter J applied on the radar radome. Such marking was common in No. 307 in the late war period. Note also the four cannon ports in the bottom of the fuselage and the camera gun fairing beneath the Polish AF square on the side.

Other Allied Fighter Types

Squadrons of the exiled Polish AF used British and American fighter types described in the preceding parts of this work. Polish AF pilots on exchange postings also flew other fighter types operationally, also described earlier in this volume. However, Polish pilots in non-operational service flew nearly all other allied fighter types, including prototypes and experimental aircraft. This is a vast subject and to cover it thoroughly another whole volume of this work would be necessary. Only a brief overview is offered here. We have tried to collect examples of a variety of types in a variety of colour schemes.

The non-operational flying discussed here falls into a number of categories. Polish test pilots flew various fighter aircraft, both series-produced types/variants and purely experimental prototypes, in all sorts of trials at the Royal Aircraft Establishment (RAE) at Farnborough, the Aeroplane and Armament Experimental Establishment (AAEE) at Boscombe Down, the Air

The Gloster Gladiator was probably the first RAF fighter flown by pilots of the exiled Polish Air Force, when they made brief sorties in one with No. 6 OTU in July 1940. Notably, by the late 1930s biplane fighters were no longer in use even for training purposes in Poland, so it was a shock for the Poles that the mighty RAF still used such aircraft in this role! Subsequently, Gladiators were flown by Polish pilots during various tests at the RAE and AFDU, and also as hacks for high speed travel. Polish ferry pilots also flew the type. Shown here is K8042 during trials at the AAEE in August–September 1941. A year later, in September–October 1942, it was flown by S/Ldr Tadeusz Piotrowicz with No. 25 Group Communications Flight at Ternhill – the aircraft was officially allocated to No. 5 (Pilots) Advanced Flying Unit, also based at Ternhill. When flown by the Polish pilot K8042 probably looked similar, except for two items: the fin flash and roundel had by then been altered to the later style ('C'/'C1'), and the two guns removed from the upper wing. The absence of Sky band on the rear fuselage suggests that it was left in Temperate Land camouflage (Dark Earth/Dark Green/Light Earth/Light Green) with Sky undersides and standard RAF national markings. Notably, the AAEE reports that featured this photo referred to K8042 as a 'Sea Gladiator' but no other document seems to support this. K8042 survives to date and is on display at the RAF Museum.

Fighting Development Unit (AFDU) and at other units and establishments. Polish ferry pilots delivered a variety of operational types to and from operational and non-operational units. Obsolete types were flown in second-line units by Polish pilots under training or as high speed hacks by senior officers. Operational pilots sometimes used semi-official ways to fly a type new to them.

The types and variants discussed in this chapter can be categorised in various ways. They were day or night fighters, single – or twin-engined, single – or multi-seat, shore-based or carrier-borne, piston – or jet-engined. In terms of their age they ranged from obsolete ones, relegated to second-line duties, through those in current operational use, up to latest prototypes. The latter category included both one-off prototypes and experimental aircraft, and those subsequently manufactured in vast numbers and used operationally.

Their colour schemes were mostly the regulation RAF/FAA/USAAF/US Navy camouflage and markings for the type and/or operator, but some aircraft displayed non-standard finish.

Readers will notice that a disproportionate number of the prototype and experimental aircraft tested at the AAEE and shown here were flown by Janusz Żurakowski. This is because his flying log books are known to these authors, unlike those of many other Polish pilots flying at the AAEE in the same period. Unlike with the RAE, no general AAEE flying logs are known to survive, so without individual pilots' log books it is not possible to identify serial numbers of aircraft they flew (except for those in which they had accidents). Therefore, Żurakowski can be seen as a representative Polish AAEE pilot.

Wartime operational types

Blackburn Roc was another type flown by Polish pilots in 1940. The navy turret fighter was relegated to anti-aircraft co-operation and air sea rescue duties, and flown in these roles by No. 2 Anti-Aircraft Co-operation Unit (AACU), which had a number of Poles in late 1940 and 1941. Oddly, this was presumably the first British fighter type flown by P/O Eugeniusz Horbaczewski, a future ranking ace and truly legendary fighter leader! He flew with No. 2 AACU during March–May 1941. This particular Roc I, L3146/JQ-B (photographed with F/Lt Harold Wilson Wakefield), was flown by P/O Ignacy Olszewski in July 1941. In No. 2 AACU use the aircraft was finished in Temperate Land (Dark Earth/Dark Green) camouflage with yellow and black diagonal bands on under surfaces standard on target-towing aircraft. The serial number was in small characters in a box of Sky on the tail section, presumably masked off when the aircraft was resprayed from its original FAA colour scheme. The engine cowling was clearly in paler colours, perhaps a replacement item in FAA camouflage.

The Westland Whirlwind was not flown officially by Polish AF pilots with any RAF unit. However, several were ferried by Jerzy Drzewiecki who was flying with the Air Transport Auxiliary (ATA). P7110 was one of these, ferried by him on 26 September 1941 from the factory airfield at Yeovil to No. 39 MU at Colerne. It was in standard Day Fighter colour scheme (Ocean Grey/ Dark Green) on upper surfaces with Medium Sea Grey under surfaces, with a full set of markings, including the Sky spinners and fuselage band of Fighter Command aircraft.

Westland Whirlwind P7055 SF-S, No. 137 Squadron, Charmy Down, July 1942. Upper surface camouflage: Ocean Grey and Dark Green ('A' pattern); under surface colour: Medium Sea Grey. Standard British national markings.

P7055 was another Whirlwind ferried by Jerzy Drzewiecki. On 1 November 1941 he flew it from Colerne to No. 137 Squadron at Charmy Down. It was still used by the unit, coded SF-S, on 4 July 1942, when P/O Antoni Głowacki, a No. 303 Squadron pilot, flew a 35 minute sortie in it at Matlaske (entered in his flying log book as 'landings/aerobatics'). The photo shows the aircraft at the time. It was in standard Day Fighter colour scheme and markings.

Another type not officially flown by Polish AF pilots was the Bell Airacobra. Several were ferried by Polish pilots with the ATA, including at least one 'Spitfire girl', 1st/Off Anna Leska. This example, AH589, was ferried by Jerzy Drzewiecki on 15 June 1942 from the AAEE at Boscombe Down to Colerne. It is shown here in No. 601 Sqn service as UF-L. It was from that unit that it went to the AAEE, so it is likely it still looked the same when ferried by the Polish pilot. The colour scheme was typical for all Fighter Command aircraft at the time.

The Lockheed P-38 Lightning was the first American-made fighter type flown by USAAF units from Britain. In the summer of 1942 No. 303 Sqn shared RAF Kirton-in-Lindsey with the 94th Fighter Squadron of the 1st Fighter Group USAAF. A number of Polish pilots made informal flights on the type, although no serial numbers seem to have been recorded. This is P-38F-1-LO s/n 41-7634, ferried across the Atlantic during Operation 'Bolero' by Maj. John O. Zahn, Commanding Officer of the 1st FG, and subsequently used by the 94th FS until written off on 15 October 1942 at Ibsley when flown by Lt. Jack S. Longseth. This particular image was included in No. 303 Sqn diary, so it is likely this was the aeroplane flown by S/Ldr Jan Zumbach and other Polish pilots at Kirton. It was in standard USAAF colour scheme of the time, with upper surfaces in Olive Drab and lower surfaces in Neutral Gray, serial number (less the initial '4') in yellow on the fins and rudders, and the US insignia (at the time just the star-on-disc, without the side bars) on outer sides of both tail booms, on top of the port wing and underneath the starboard one.

The Fairey Fulmar was the first carrier-borne fighter type flown by Polish test and ferry pilots. Fulmars were ferried by several Polish ATA pilots, both male and female. The type was also flown at the RAE Farnborough by P/O Zbigniew Oleński and F/Lt Roland Kalpas. This particular machine, N4079, was flown by Oleński on 17 May 1941. The colour scheme was standard for FAA fighters at the time: Temperate Sea camouflage (Dark Slate Grey/Extra Dark Sea Grey) with Sky undersides.

Fairey Firefly I Z1828, Aeroplane and Armament Experimental Establishment, Boscombe Down, December 1942. Upper surface camouflage: Extra Dark Sea Grey and Dark Slate Grey; under surface colour: probably yellow. Standard British national markings. Prototype marking (capital P in a ring, in yellow) on both sides of the fuselage.

Several dozen Fairey Fireflies were ferried by Polish pilots, boys and girls. The type was also flight tested by Poles (although not aboard aircraft carriers as far as is known). This prototype Firefly I, Z1828, was test flown at the AAEE by F/O Stanisław Kulczycki. On 7 December 1942 he belly landed it at Boscombe Down following an undercarriage failure. He was unhurt, as was Sgt Trevor Rees Benbow who accompanied him during the flight. The aircraft was in standard Temperate Sea colour scheme on upper surfaces and sides, with under surfaces probably in yellow (although Sky cannot be ruled out).The serial number was applied in black in standard FAA fashion with 'ROYAL NAVY' above it. The 'P in ring' in yellow was applied on both sides of aircraft.

Grumman Wildcat VI (FM-2 BuNo. 55320) JV752, Aeroplane and Armament Experimental Establishment, Boscombe Down, February 1945. Upper surface camouflage: Extra Dark Sea Grey and Dark Slate Grey; under surface colour: Sky. Standard British national markings.

A number of Grumman Martlet/Wildcat fighters were ferried by Polish pilots and at least two were tested by Poles at the RAE and the AAEE. Wildcat VI JV752 was test flown at the AAEE by S/Ldr Janusz Żurakowski on 14 February 1945. The aircraft was in standard FAA Temperate Sea scheme with Sky undersides. The number '320' on the side of the engine cowling was presumably the ending of the aircraft's US Navy Bureau Number, 55320. The significance of the digit 9 on the front cowling ring is not clear.

Grumman Hellcat F.II (F6F-5 BuNo. 71645) JX822, Aeroplane and Armament Experimental Establishment, Boscombe Down, January 1945. Glossy Sea Blue overall. Standard British national markings. Serial number and 'ROYAL NAVY' titling: white.

Several dozen Grumman Hellcats were ferried by Polish pilots, both with the ATA and with service ferry units. A number of these aircraft were also flight tested by Janusz Żurakowski at the AAEE in 1945. Hellcat F.II JX822 was one of the latter. It was finished in the US Navy camouflage of Glossy Sea Blue overall. The 'ROYAL NAVY' titling and the serial number were white, as was the US variant designation on the rudder (F6F-5) and the diagonal line that marked the foot rests in the fuselage side. The British roundels were applied in all six positions (both sides of the fuselage and each wing). Traces of the large digits 822 were quite prominent on the engine cowling. These three-digit serial endings were applied at the factory as a temporary measure for delivery.

The Grumman Hellcat I in the foreground of this photo, of which only the tail section is shown, is believed to be Mk I JV156, ferried by 1st/Off Ludwik Tokarczyk with the ATA on 24 March 1944. This is the deck of HMS Emperor *in the summer of 1944, presumably in Malta, with No. 800 Sqn FAA aircraft. All the Hellcat Is shown here are finished in the FAA scheme of Temperate Sea on top and Sky underneath (at least three also display full D-Day bands). When ferried by the Polish pilot, JV156 must have looked this way, albeit with no code markings of any kind. Note the US variant designation, F6F-3, marked in black on the rudder. It also is noteworthy how the camouflage tones and patterns on the ailerons do not match those of the wings in which they are fitted, both on the upper and under surfaces.*

The Chance Vought Corsair was another American wartime carrier-borne fighter ferried in significant numbers by Polish ferry pilots. S/Ldr Janusz Żurakowski flight tested several of these aircraft at the AAEE in early 1945, including Corsair II, III and IV variants. Corsair II JT562, shown here, was one of these, finished in the FAA Temperate Sea scheme with Sky undersides.

Types that Failed to Reach Operational Status

The lightweight Miles M20 'panic fighter' was test flown by F/O Zbigniew Oleński at Farnborough on 1 November 1941. By that time it had received the RAF serial number DR616 in place of the temporary number U-0228 as shown here. Otherwise it probably looked the same, finished in Temperate Land scheme (Dark Earth/Dark Green) on upper surfaces with yellow undersides. The British national markings were applied in the usual positions, but the fin flash was tapered to match the shape of the fin.

Another unexpected fighter prototype flown by F/O Zbigniew Oleński at Farnborough was the Hawker Hotspur turret fighter. By the time he flew K8309 on 10 February 1942 the turret had been removed and replaced by a streamlined rear cockpit. It, too, was finished in Temperate Land scheme on upper surfaces with yellow under sides. RAF national markings were applied in the usual positions, and the yellow 'P in ring' prototype marking was applied on the rear fuselage.

The second prototype Supermarine Spiteful NN664 was flown by Janusz Żurakowski at the AAEE repeatedly between 29 June and 10 July 1945, and then a few more times in August 1945 ad March 1946. By the time of his first flight in it the aeroplane had been fitted with the enlarged fin and rudder, as shown here. Most of the airframe in the photo is in natural metal finish, but the fin seems to be finished in a primer and the rudder in standard Day Fighter camouflage. The yellow 'P in ring' marking can be seen on the fuselage. The serial number was, unusually, applied in the FAA style: in small size characters with 'ROYAL NAVY' stencilled above it.

Supermarine Spiteful NN667, Aeroplane and Armament Experimental Establishment, Boscombe Down, April–July 1946. Upper surface camouflage: Ocean Grey and Dark Green ('A' pattern); under surface colour: Medium Sea Grey. Standard British national markings.

The third prototype Supermarine Spiteful NN667 was test flown by S/Ldr Janusz Żurakowski in April 1946. It was finished in standard Day Fighter scheme on upper surfaces and Medium Sea Grey under surfaces. The national markings and the serial number were also applied in standard RAF fashion.

Westland Welkin I DX290, Westland Aircraft factory, Yeovil, May 1944. Upper surface colour: Medium Sea Grey overall; under surface colour: PRU Blue. Two-tone British national markings.

The Westland Welkin was test flown by Polish pilots at Boscombe Down, but a few production aircraft were also ferried by Poles. Welkin DX290 shown in the foreground here was flown by 1st/Off Jerzy Drzewiecki, ATA, on 8 May 1944 from the factory airfield at Yeovil directly into storage at No. 18 Maintenance Unit at Dumfries. In line with other production aircraft of the type it was finished in the High Altitude Fighter colour scheme.

Martin-Baker MB-5 R2496, Aeroplane and Armament Experimental Establishment, Boscombe Down, April–July 1946. Upper surface camouflage: probably unspecified dark green and dark grey hues (non-standard pattern); under surface colour: probably yellow. Standard British national markings. Prototype marking (capital P in a ring, in yellow) on both sides of the fuselage.

The sole prototype Martin-Baker MB-5 R2496 was flown by Żurakowski in testing at the AAEE between April and July 1946, and he also displayed it during air shows. The colour scheme of the aeroplane is not certain. The under sides were certainly yellow but the tones of the upper surface camouflage in black and white photos do not conform with either Temperate Land or Day Fighter schemes. In those photos where the MB-5 can be seen alongside operational RAF types the tones of its camouflage colours are clearly darker than those of either Dark Green/Ocean Grey or Dark Green/Dark Earth. It seems that it was painted in a scheme similar in concept to the Day Fighter one, but using markedly darker hues of grey and green. Note how the yellow areas look nearly black or very pale in ortho – or panchromatic photographs, respectively.

When S/Ldr Janusz Żurakowski test flew DK373, the prototype Blackburn Firebrand III, in March 1945, it was finished in Temperate Sea (Extra Dark Sea Grey/ Dark Slate Grey) on upper surfaces with yellow under sides. The 'P in ring' was applied in yellow on the rear fuselage. There were also additional test markings in yellow about mid-way up the fin and rudder.

Probably the most exotic type flown by Żurakowski at the AAEE: one of two Grumman Tigercats delivered to Britain. Żurakowski flew TT349 in February 1945. Since the type was only intended for testing by the British, it was left in standard US Navy colour scheme and markings. It was Glossy Sea Blue overall and featured US star-and-bar markings on both sides of the rear fuselage, on top of the port wing and underneath the starboard one.

Hawker Sea Fury SR661, Aeroplane & Armament Experimental Establishment, Boscombe Down, April 1946. Upper surface camouflage: Dark Earth and Dark Green ('A' pattern); under surface colour: yellow. Standard British national markings. Prototype marking (capital P in a ring, in yellow) on both sides of the fuselage.

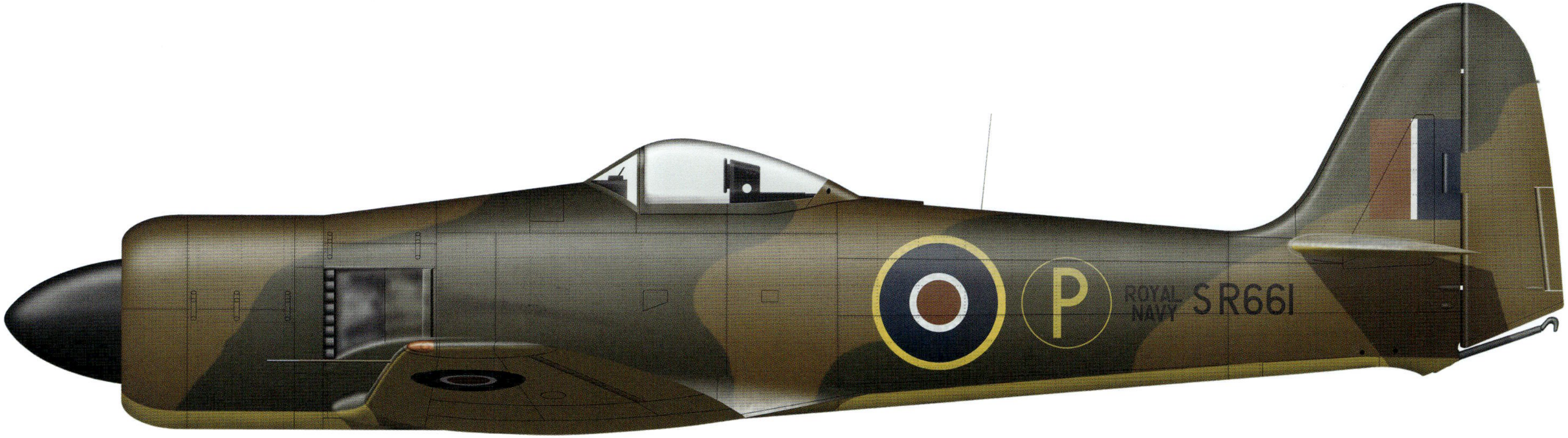

The land-based Fury was never used by the RAF, but was sold abroad (such aircraft were flown by ex-Polish AF pilots in Pakistan during the early 1950s). The prototype Hawker Fury NX798 was among many types of prospective post-war fighters flown by S/Ldr Janusz Żurakowski at the AAEE. He tested it in May 1945. It seems to have been finished in Temperate Land scheme of Dark Green/Dark Earth with yellow under sides at the time. The yellow 'P in ring' was applied on the rear fuselage.

The navalised prototype Sea Fury SR661 was tested by Żurakowski at the AAEE in April 1946. It seems that at the time, even though intended for naval use, the aircraft was finished in a similar colour scheme to that of NX798: Temperate Land scheme on upper surfaces with yellow under sides.

De Havilland Hornet F.I PX210, Aeroplane and Armament Experimental Establishment, Boscombe Down, April 1945. Upper surface colour: Medium Sea Grey; under surface colour: PRU Blue. Two-tone British national markings.

PX210, an initial production de Havilland Hornet F.I was test flown by S/Ldr Janusz Żurakowski at the AAEE in April 1945.

PX210 was one of a number of Hornets flown by this pilot, who has contributed significantly to the development of the type. In line with all initial production aircraft of the type it was finished in the High Altitude Fighter scheme of Medium Sea Grey upper surfaces and PRU Blue under sides. Standard high altitude fighter national markings were applied in typical positions.

Gloster Meteor F.I EE214/G, Aeroplane and Armament Experimental Establishment, Boscombe Down, March–June 1945. Upper surface camouflage: Ocean Grey and Dark Green ('A' pattern); under surface colour: Medium Sea Grey. Standard British national markings.

Although the Gloster Meteor did enter operational service during the war, its principal career with the RAF was over the next 20 years. S/Ldr Żurakowski flew a number of these aircraft at Boscombe Down, and did it so well that he was subsequently employed by Gloster. EE214/G, an early production Meteor I used for trials at the AAEE, was the first jet of any type flown by Żurakowski, when he tested it on 21 March 1945. At the time the aircraft was in the Day Fighter scheme on upper surfaces with Medium Sea Grey undersides and the Sky fuselage band. It wore standard British national markings.

Gloster Meteor F.III EE317 XL-Y, No. 1335 Conversion Unit, Colerne, July 1945. Upper surface camouflage: Ocean Grey and Dark Green ('A' pattern); under surface colour: Medium Sea Grey. Standard British national markings.

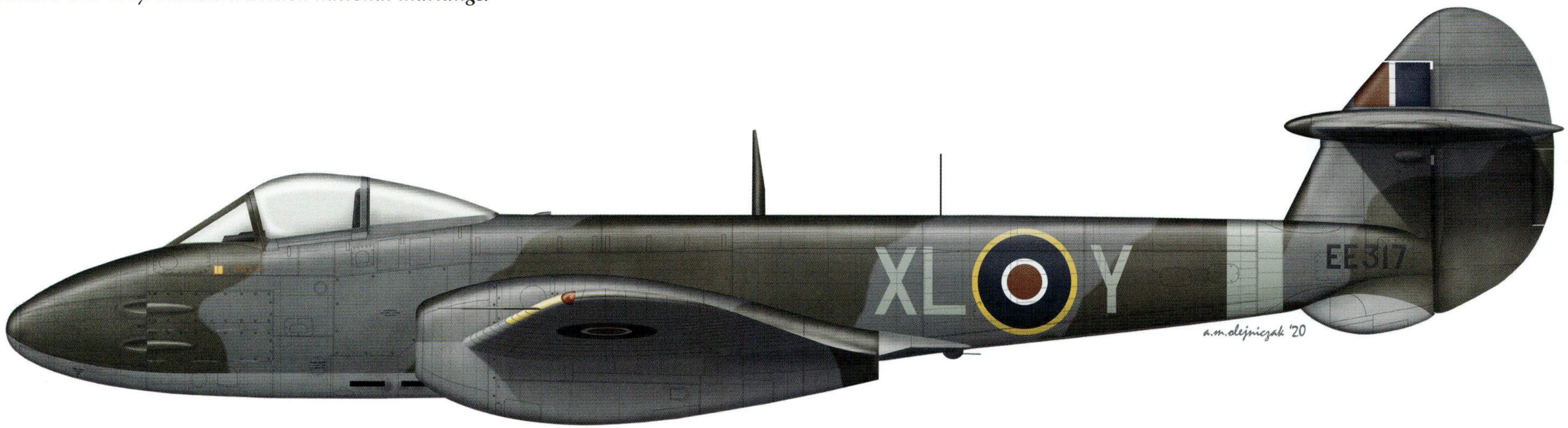

The Meteor III was the only jet fighter flown by exiled Polish AF members other than test pilots. A number of regular Polish fighter pilots trained on the type with No. 1335 Conversion Unit at RAF Colerne. S/Ldr Antoni Głowacki and F/Lt Maciej Kirste both flew a Meteor III coded XL-Y in July 1945, believed to be this machine, EE317. It was finished in standard Day Fighter Scheme with a standard set of markings.

On 12 July 1945 1st/Off Jerzy Drzewiecki of No. 2 Ferry Pool ATA delivered Meteor III EE343 to RAF Colerne, where it became 4D-X with No. 74 Sqn. The camouflage and markings were, again, in conformance with the standard Day Fighter Scheme.

Meteor III EE455 was converted for the World Air Speed Record attempts in late 1945 and finished in the striking scheme: most of the airframe was bright yellow, with the outer wing panels and the empennage from the tailplane up in natural metal finish (inevitably, it was dubbed the Yellow Peril). A large Union Jack was painted on both sides of the nose with accompanying description of the aircraft and engine type. After the new record was set in November 1945 (by the similarly modified but camouflaged EE454!), EE455 was allocated to the AAEE for new wing tests. It is not known if the flag and titling on the nose was still retained when it was repeatedly flown by Żurakowski in July and August 1946 with the new wing, as shown in the lower image (it is an orthochromatic photo, which renders the yellow scheme unnaturally dark).

De Havilland Vampire I TG386, Aeroplane and Armament Experimental Establishment, Boscombe Down, April 1947. Upper surface colour: Medium Sea Grey; under surface colour: PRU Blue. Two-tone British national markings.

On 25 April 1947 Żurakowski flew 'handling trials' in Vampire I TG386 at the AAEE. The machine was in the High Altitude Fighter scheme of Medium Sea Grey on upper surfaces and PRU Blue on under surfaces, with two-tone fuselage roundels and fin flashes. The tail boom serial number with a slash between the letters and digits was typical for the factory finish on early Vampires.

De Havilland Vampire I TG274/G, Aeroplane and Armament Experimental Establishment, Boscombe Down, June–December 1945. Upper surface camouflage: Ocean Grey and Dark Green ('A' pattern); under surface colour: Medium Sea Grey. Standard British national markings.

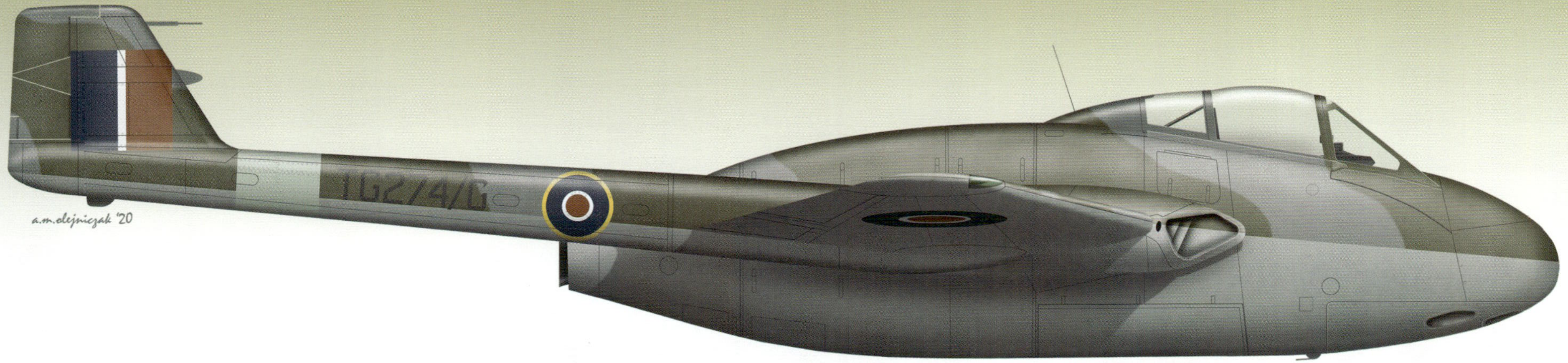

Vampire I TG274 was flown by S/Ldr Żurakowski over thirty times at Boscombe Down between June and December 1945. During an air display on 3 December he inadvertently stalled and crashed it. The aircraft was damaged severely, but the pilot escaped unhurt.

TG274 was in the standard Fighter Command camouflage and markings. The '/G' suffix added to the serial number was the only designation of its special nature. It was obliterated at some point while TG274 was at Boscombe Down. Note the fin flash applied on the inner surface also – this was standard on RAF Vampires.

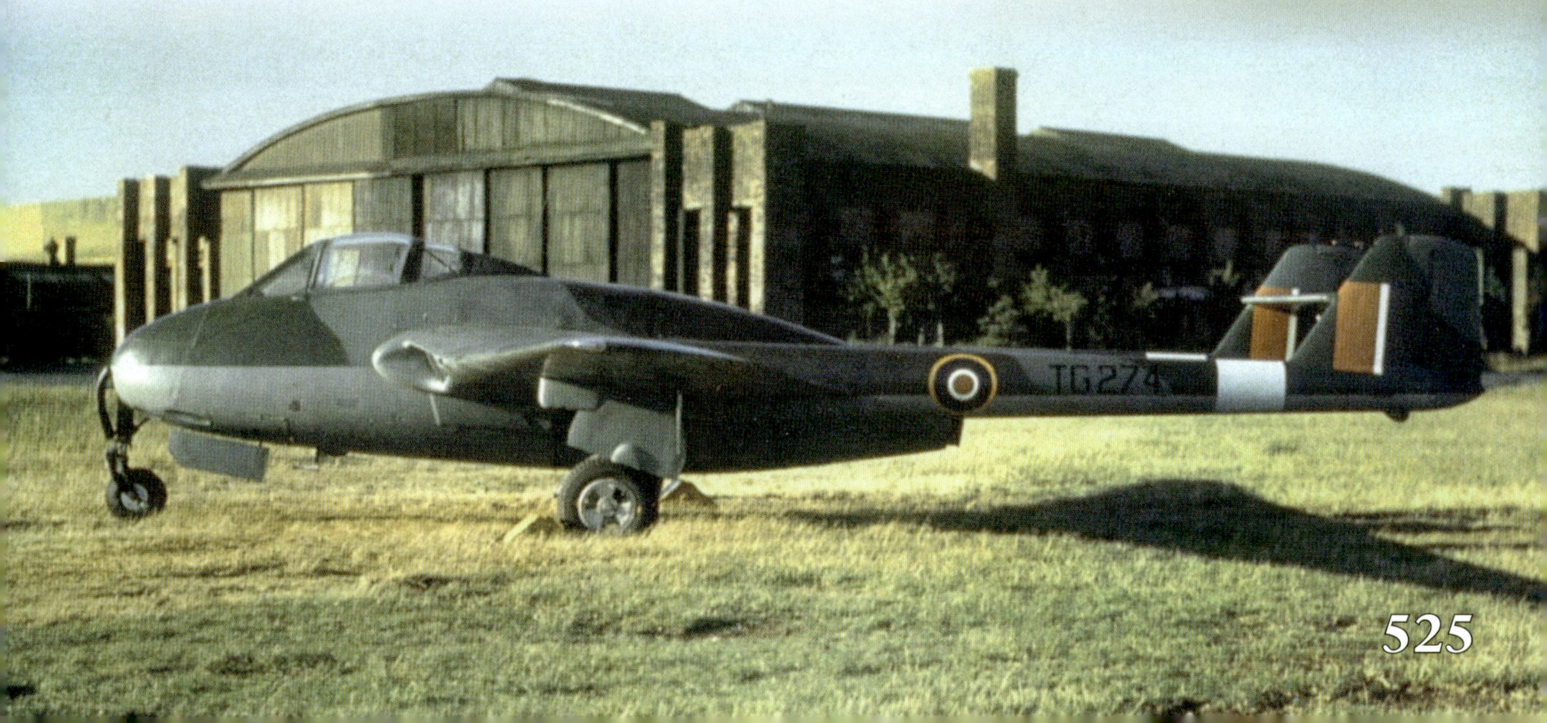

Arguably the most unusual markings seen on a fighter flown by a pilot of the exiled Polish AF in Britain: Swiss AF Vampire I no. J1004 tested at the AAEE. S/Ldr Żurakowski flew it in on dive bombing trials on 26 February 1947. The aircraft seems to be in the High Altitude Fighter scheme similar to that on TG386. Note that the Swiss markings were only applied on the outer surfaces of the fin and rudder.

Vampire I TG330, flown by Żurakowski several times in April 1946 at the AAEE, was in natural metal finish, with standard RAF markings. Note the tail boom serial number with a slash between the letters and the digits and the under-wing serial with a gap between the first and second digits to make room for the underwing pylon there.

TG276 was modified as a Vampire II prototype. It was flown by S/Ldr Żurakowski at Boscombe Down nearly thirty times between November 1946 and May 1947. By the time this photo was taken in early 1947 it had been fitted with the 'elephant ear' dorsal air intakes and was in NMF. Note the entirely different style of the serial number on the tail boom compared to that on TG330.

The prototype Supermarine Attacker TS409 as test flown by Żurakowski on 9 June 1947. At the time it did not have the cannon fitted in the wings. The aircraft was in overall natural metal finish, with standard British national markings. Apart from the serial number in all the standard positions (and without any non-standard breaks or slashes), it was also adorned with the yellow 'P in ring' on both sides of the rear fuselage.

Captured Axis Types

Pilots of the exiled Polish Air Force flew numerous captured enemy aircraft.

Polish pilots took part in flying trials of German and Italian fighters with the Air Fighting Development Unit (AFDU) and the Royal Aircraft Establishment.

In 1943 a group of Polish Air Force members who volunteered for clandestine service in the German-occupied Poland were given brief training in handling of a few types of German twin-engined aeroplanes, which included the Messerschmitt 110.

Finally, one captured Messerschmitt 109 was also acquired informally and used briefly by No. 318 Squadron in Italy.

As regards the colour schemes, most of the aircraft were in standard allied colour schemes for experimental aircraft, with the 'prototype yellow' under sides. However, there were also cases where Polish pilots flew ex-Axis aircraft left partly or wholly in their original camouflage and markings.

Shown here are examples of various types of Axis fighters known to have been flown by pilots of the exiled Polish Air Force. Similarly to the Allied types shown in the previous pages, this is not a complete list. Without access to individual pilots' flying log books it is not possible to identify all of the machines they flew.

Junkers 88R-1 W.Nr. 360043 D5+EV was flown to RAF Dyce by German defectors on 9 May 1943. Five days later S/Ldr Roland Kalpas ferried it from Dyce to Farnborough. At the time the aircraft was still in its original Luftwaffe *colour scheme, with just the German national markings obliterated and replaced by RAF roundels and fin flash. The photo was probably taken at RAF Hartford Bridge/Blackbushe (with Airspeed Horsas of the Airborne Forces Experimental Establishment in the background). The original negative was dated 18 May 1943, soon after the Junkers was delivered to Farnborough. Note the absence of the radar aerials, as at the time the entire radar system was removed from the airframe and subjected to ground testing.*

FIAT CR.42 BT474, Air Fighting Development Unit, Duxford, September 1941. Upper surface camouflage: Giallo Mimetico 3 *base, pattern* Verde Mimetico 3 *and* Marrone Mimetico 2, *retouched with British paints where Italian markings have been obliterated; under surface colour: yellow. Standard British national markings*

The FIAT CR.42 was captured during an Italian raid on Britain on 11 November 1940. It was flight-tested by F/O Marian Skalski (not to be confused with the famous ace, Stanisław Skalski!) at the AFDU in early September 1941. He found it to be a very pleasant, if obsolescent, flying machine. The peculiar Italian disruptive camouflage on upper surfaces and sides was retained, with just the RAF markings applied on top of the Italian ones. The under surfaces were repainted yellow, as was typical with captured aircraft, with RAF roundels applied on the wings.

Messerschmitt 109E AE479, Air Fighting Development Unit, Duxford, October 1941. Upper surface camouflage: Dark Earth and Dark Green ('A' pattern); under surface colour: yellow. Standard British national markings.

The Messerschmitt 109E AE479 was flown by F/O Marian Skalski at the AFDU on 6 October 1941. He was scheduled to ferry it from Duxford to Ibsley for use in the filming of 'The First of the Few' there. To his chagrin, the starboard main wheel leg collapsed on landing, and the wing was damaged. The aeroplane was in RAF Temperate Land camouflage on upper surfaces with yellow under surfaces. It displayed standard British national markings and RAF-style serial on both sides of the rear fuselage.

Messerschmitt 109F ES906, Air Fighting Development Unit, Duxford, October 1941. Upper surface camouflage: Dark Earth and Dark Green ('B' pattern); under surface colour: yellow. Standard British national markings.

F/O Marian Skalski first flew the Messerschmitt 109F ES906 on 19 October 1941. Tragically, during his next sortie the following day he was killed when it crashed at Fowlmere. It is believed he was overcome by carbon monoxide poisoning. The Messerschmitt was in the Temperate Land scheme on upper surfaces with yellow under surfaces, standard British national markings and the serial on both sides of the rear fuselage.

Messerschmitt 109G-14/AS LW, No. 318 Squadron, Italy, September 1945. Upper surface camouflage: Ocean Grey and Dark Green or similar hues (non-standard pattern); under surface colour: unspecified grey, possibly Ocean Grey. The informal squadron badge near the windscreen on the port side only. Polish national marking on both sides of forward fuselage.

The sole WW2 Luftwaffe *fighter type ever operated by a Polish AF unit: Messerschmitt 109G acquired by No. 318 Squadron in Italy in September 1945. When it was ferried by P/O Bolesław Stramik from Iesi to Lavariano it still displayed its wartime camouflage and markings. The cross stylised to look like a maple leaf and the white-and-red chequered shield on the fin and rudder instead of the swastika identified it as an aeroplane of the Axis-allied Croat Air Force.*

Once delivered to No. 318 Sqn, the Messerschmitt was duly repainted in the camouflage and markings similar to those on the squadron's Spitfires that can be seen far in the background. The upper surface colour scheme was probably Day Fighter. The Polish AF marking was applied on the engine cowling in the unit's standard size. The code letters LW identified No. 318 Sqn, as did the informal emblem near the cockpit: 3 of hearts, ace of spades and 8 of diamonds referred to the squadron number.

Focke-Wulf 190A-4 PE882, Royal Aircraft Establishment, Farnborough, June 1943. Upper surface camouflage: Dark Earth and Dark Green ('A' pattern); under surface colour: yellow. Standard British national markings. Experimental marking (capital P in a ring, in yellow) on both sides of the fuselage

Fw 190A PE882 was flown by F/Lt Zbigniew Oleński at Farnborough on 26 June 1943. These photos were taken the same day with another pilot at the controls. The aircraft is in Temperate Land scheme of Dark Earth and Dark Green, with yellow undersides. The yellow 'P in ring' on both sides of the fuselage was a standard marking on experimental aircraft. Two months later, on 27 August, PE882 was flown by F/Lt Tadeusz Ciastuła at the same establishment.

S/Ldr Roland Kalpas flew Focke-Wulf 190A PM679 in handling trials at the RAE Farnborough on 13 July 1943. This photo was taken in 1944 after it went to No. 1426 Flight RAF ('Enemy Aircraft Circus'). It was in the Temperate Land scheme on upper surfaces with yellow under surfaces and standard British national markings. While at Farnborough it had probably displayed the yellow 'P in ring' on the fuselage (note the irregular patch near the cockpit where that marking has been obliterated). The spinner was half white/half black, this probably dating back to its Luftwaffe *service.*

Fw 190A no. PN999 in late April 1944 during No. 1426 Flight's visit at RAF Martlesham Heath. Again, a patch of different colour near the cockpit is where yellow 'P in ring' was probably obliterated. The colour scheme was similar to that on the other Fw 190s. S/Ldr Kalpas flew PN999 repeatedly at the RAE Farnborough in September 1943 during trials of its FuG 16Z radio system. The nose section of this Focke-Wulf (the annular oil tank and cooler) was in original German camouflage colours, presumably a replacement item from another machine.

Messerschmitt 110C AX772, No. 1426 Flight RAF, Collyweston, September–October 1943. Upper surface camouflage: probably Ocean Grey and Dark Green ('A' pattern); under surface colour: yellow. Standard British national markings.

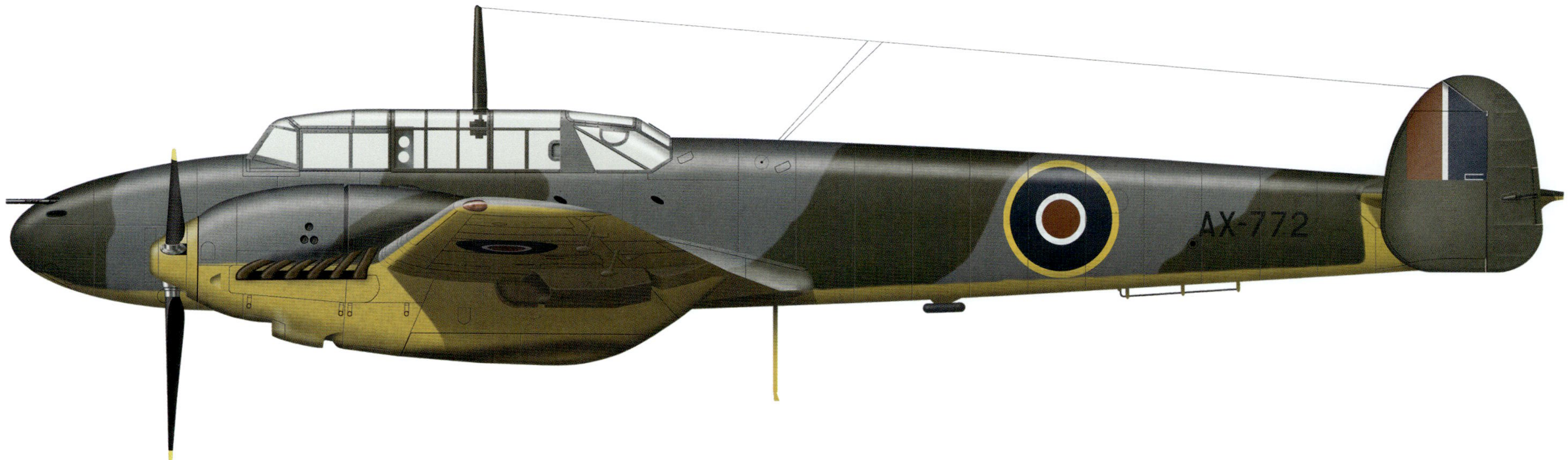

Messerschmitt 110 was flown by S/Ldrs Jan Biały and Jerzy Iszkowski with No. 1426 in September and October 1943. They were members of a group of Polish Air Force flyers who volunteered for work with the underground resistance network in the German-occupied Poland. Before they were parachuted into Poland they underwent comprehensive training, and part of it was to learn to fly some Luftwaffe *aircraft types, including the Bf 110. At the time the aircraft seems to have been in RAF-style Day Fighter camouflage on upper surfaces with yellow undersides.*

Organisation of Soviet-controlled Polish Fighter Units

Before describing the fighter aircraft of the 'People's' Polish Forces, we need to explain the 'Polish' label of the forces.

These forces were established originally in 1943 in the USSR by the Stalin-sponsored communists, and had no connection with the Polish Forces in the West (the latter being subordinated to the exiled Polish Government based in London, which was recognised until the summer of 1945 as the political representation of the Polish nation). Originally, the 'People's' Polish Forces were made up of Poles resident in the USSR (who were, in their majority, victims of mass forced deportations of 1940–1941 in the wake of joint Soviet-German invasion of Poland in 1939) and of Soviet citizens with some Polish ancestry. As German forces were expelled from Polish territory during 1944–1945, Polish citizens were conscripted into these forces. The army expanded at an increasing rate, but the time necessary to train an infantryman or a gunner was much shorter than that of a pilot. To provide the army with a proportionally appropriate air support, a number of purely Soviet units were transferred in the autumn of 1944 to the, nominally, Polish Forces.

Until the summer of 1945 the 'People's' Polish Forces were not legally recognised internationally as the armed forces of Poland[1], so their 'Polish' nature can only be regarded in terms of the nationality of the servicemen. During WWII the only fighter unit with a large proportion (about half) of Polish staff was the 1 *Pułk Lotnictwa Myśliwskiego 'Warszawa'* (1 PLM; 1st Fighter Regiment 'City of Warsaw'), formed in July 1943. The content of this chapter of the book will focus on this unit's aircraft.

Two other units of the 'People's' Polish Forces equipped with fighter aircraft had a proportion of Polish personnel: the 15 *Samodzielny Zapasowy Pułk Lotniczy* (15th Independent Replacement Air Regiment), renamed the 15 *Szkolny Pułk Lotniczy* (15th Air Training Regiment) in March 1945, the 15 *Mieszany Szkolno-Treningowy Pułk Lotniczy* (15th Mixed Air Training Regiment) on 15 July

1 On 6 July 1945 the USA and UK withdrew their recognition of the exiled Polish Government in London and recognised the Provisional Government of National Unity (Tymczasowy Rząd Jedności Narodowej) in Poland, which controlled the 'People's' Polish Forces.

Standard finish of a Yak-1b of the 1 Pułk Lotnictwa Myśliwskiego 'Warszawa', *with a Soviet star and a Polish white-red square, camouflaged in blue-grey (AMT-11), dark grey (AMT-12) and light blue (AMT-7). Gostomel, June-August 1944.*

1945 and the 1 *Samodzielny Szkolno-Treningowy Mieszany Pułk Lotniczy* (1st Independent Mixed Air Training Mixed Regiment) on 13 September 1945; and the *Wojskowa Szkoła Pilotów* (Military Pilots' School), renamed the *Oficerska Szkoła Lotnicza* (Air Force Officers School) in May 1946.

Other units had negligible numbers of Polish personnel, or none at all. These included the three fighter regiments of the *Voyenno-Vozdushniye Sily* (the Soviet Air Force) transferred to the 'People's' Polish Forces on 20 September 1944 and renamed the 9th, 10th and 11th Fighter Regiments (9, 10 and 11 PLM) that formed the 3 *Dywizja Lotnictwa Myśliwskiego* (3 DLM; 3rd Fighter Division). These had originally been, respectively, the 248, 246 and 832 *Istrebitelniy Aviatsionniy Polk* that had been withdrawn from front line operations and replenished with freshly trained Soviet pilots.

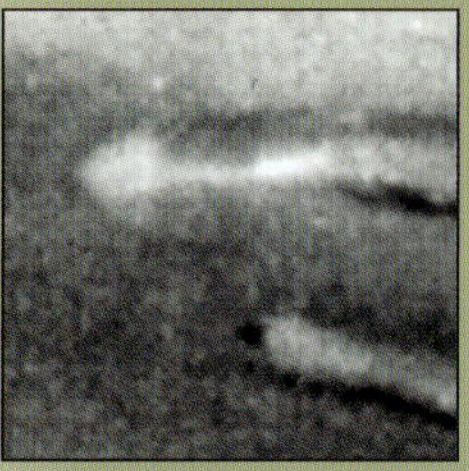

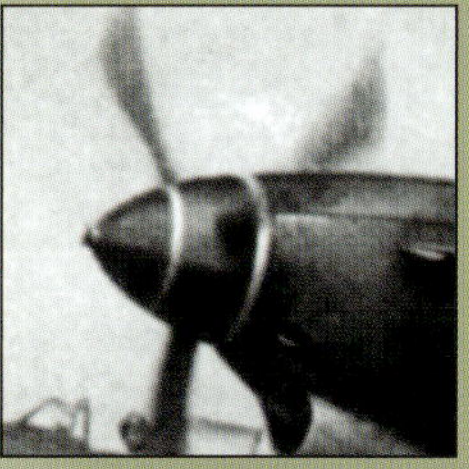

Propeller spinners of 1 PLM aircraft: 1 eskadra *(yellow)*, 3 eskadra *(blue)*, *3 eskadra – later version (blue with a white stripe) and the regiment HQ (two-tone).*

Camouflage and Markings

During 1943–1945 the Yak-1b, Yak-3, Yak-7, Yak-9D, Yak-9M and Yak-9T aircraft of the 'People's' Polish Forces were camouflaged in accordance with the fighter scheme as defined by the VVS orders no. 389/0133 of 3 July 1943. Upper surfaces were painted in a disruptive scheme of blue-grey (AMT-11) and dark grey (AMT-12), while the lower surfaces were light blue (AMT-7). The AMT symbol defined nitrocellulose lacquer for painting mixed-construction aircraft. AMT paints were semi-matt upon application and turned matt when ageing.

Soviet red stars in double outlines (broad silver and narrow red) were applied on both sides of the fuselage and vertical tail, while those on the wing under surfaces had either no outline or the double outlines (broad silver and narrow red).

As virtually no photographs of aircraft from other fighter units of the 'People's' Polish Forces could be accessed, the following description applies solely to the 1 PLM.

Yak-1b aircraft displayed single or two-digit code numbers applied between the fuselage star and the tail. These were sprayed on at the factory, using stencils, and consisted on the first two digits of the construction number or just the second digit if the first one was a zero (for example: aircraft with the construction number 48184 was coded 48, while that with the construction number 01189 was coded 1).

Most Yak-1bs used by the regiment after May 1944 known from photos featured white-red squares. These were painted at the regiment on both sides of the fuselage level with the exhausts,

A 1 PLM Yak-1b, code number unknown, during 1943–1944 with a tiny white-red square of the Polish Air Force applied on the propeller blade. The machine has standard camouflage and a Soviet star on the tail, but no Polish square on the engine cowling.

Kpt. *Nikolay Buyevich (Soviet) in the cockpit of a Yak-1b, probably code no. 40, with the presentation inscription:* 'ot Putyevogo obkhodchika / Yelizarova' ('от Путевого обходчика / Елизарова'; *'from rail track inspector Yelizarov') applied in red under the cockpit. Apparently this aircraft was funded by one rail track inspector (a railway technician performing inspections and minor repairs on railway tracks) named Yelizarov. The aircraft was delivered to the 1 PLM at the end of 1943.*

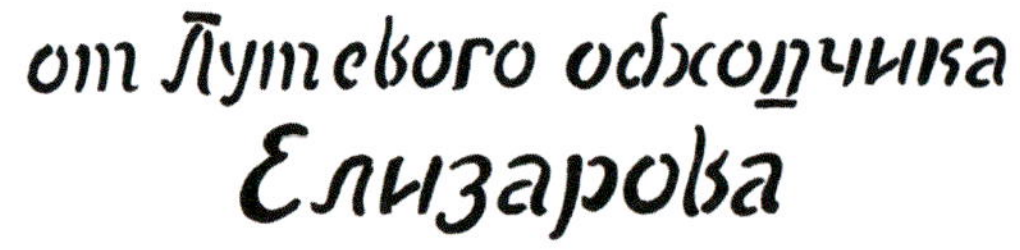

Reconstruction of the presentation inscription based on the sole known photo and the knowledge of the full phrase. Artwork: Wojciech Sankowski

below the windscreen. The squares were in accordance with the pattern used in the Polish Air Force during 1921–1939 (upper left and lower right fields were red, and the other two white; the width of the outline in reverse colour was 1/5 of the square side). No known photo from the 1 PLM shows reverse colours of the square. The red in the squares was not necessarily the same as that of the Soviet stars applied on the fuselage at the factory.

Since some codes were duplicated within the regiment (for example, each of the three flights had a Yak-1b coded 4) an additional quick recognition marking was introduced: propeller spinner tips in various colours. The spinner tips in the *1 eskadra* had yellow, in the *2 eskadra* white, and in the *3 eskadra* blue (later blue with a white stripe). Probably the aircraft of the regiment HQ had special two-colour spinner markings. Some aircraft had grey, factory finished, spinners and these were probably the machines that were not used operationally. The spinner colours were introduced about August 1944, after the 1 PLM had arrived at Zadybie Stare.

Yak-9D, Yak-9M and Yak-9T aircraft featured code numbers applied between the fuselage star and the cockpit, in silver or white. These were much larger than those on Yak-1bs. It is not certain if these were applied at the factory or at the regiment. They consisted of the last two digits of the construction number or just the last digit if the preceding one was a zero (for example, the aircraft with construction number 3215386 was coded 86, and the aircraft with construction number 4115304 was coded 4).

A Yak-9M of the 3 eskadra *of the 1 PLM photographed in 1945. The aircraft features the Polish square, but it is not known if there were also Soviet stars on the fuselage. There are many similar photos but neither of these answers the question whether Yak-9s were marked with the squares alongside the stars during the war.*

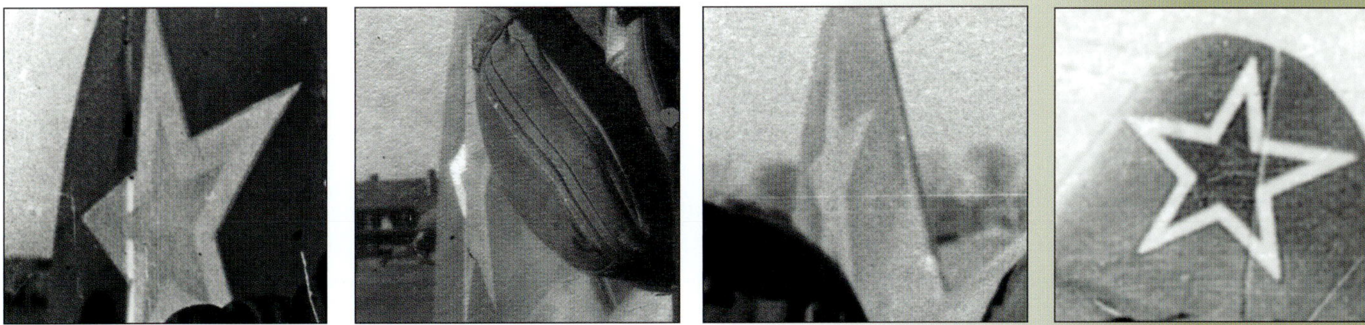

Examples of regulation and non-regulation (partial outline, no outline, oversize) Soviet stars on the tails of 1 PLM aircraft.

Examples of regulation and non-regulation (no outline) Soviet stars on the fuselages of 1 PLM aircraft.

Many post-war photos show Yak-9s with smaller Polish squares on the engine cowling or between the cockpit and the exhausts, and with full size ones on the fuselage and tail. This seems to indicate that during the war the small squares were applied in addition to the stars, similar to those on Yak-1bs. However, this cannot be confirmed positively, because none of the known photos of 1 PLM Yak-9s with the Soviet stars shows those Polish squares.

Photos show that 1 PLM Yak-9s also featured the spinner tip markings, similar to those on the Yak-1bs: yellow in the *1 eskadra*, white in the *2 eskadra*, and blue in the *3 eskadra*, outlined with a white stripe.

Yak-7 aircraft used by the 1 PLM known from photos featured no code numbers. One of the Yak-3s displays a silver code number between the fuselage star and the tail.

No personal emblems on 1 PLM aircraft during 1943–1945 are known. The most interesting motif known from photographs is a small Polish white-red square applied on the front surface of a propeller blade of a Yak-1b.

No victory markings are known, either, even though 1 PLM had a number of pilots with *Luftwaffe* aircraft shot down to their credit. The only reference to such markings is known from a verbal account by ppor. Viktor Kalinovskiy (or plut. Jan Okulicz, the fitter of his personal mount), who had his victories marked on a Yak-9 no. 87 as twelve white eagle insignia motifs. However, no photographic corroboration for that has been found so far.

At least three aircraft of the 1 PLM featured presentation inscriptions. Yak-1b no. 48 (constr. no. 48184) was adorned with the inscription in Russian 'A gift from Professor Wolf Messing to Polish pilots in the USSR' (according to an account of a pilot of the machine; no photographs of the inscription are known). Yak-1b no. 13 (constr. no. 13163) featured the inscription in Russian '*Ot pol'skogo patriota / prof. Wolf-Messinga / pol'skomu letchiku*' ('От польского патриота / проф. Вольф-Мессинга / польскому летчику.'; 'From a Polish patriot / Prof. Wolf-Messing / to a Polish pilot') and the Polish equivalent added later: '*Od polskiego patrioty / prof. Wolf Messinga / polskiemu lotnikowi*'. Another Yak-1b (probably no. 40) the inscription: '*ot Putyevogo obkhodchika / Yelizarova*' ('от Путевого обходчика / Елизарова'; 'from rail track inspector Yelizarov'). The port side of Yak-9 no. 93 or 94, aft of the cockpit, displayed a white inscription that commenced *'ZA TA…'*. This may have read *'ZA TAŁDYKINA'* ('FOR TALDIKIN'), to commemorate *ppłk* Ivan Taldikin (Soviet), the regiment commander killed in an aircraft crash. After the war, between 11 and 20 July 1945, Soviet stars were overpainted and replaced with the Polish squares. The stars were in most cases overpainted with paints of different tone than the factory ones, which makes them conspicuous in black & white photos.

Some aircraft differed from the general guidelines described above as regards the camouflage or the application of Soviet stars or code numbers.

Yak-1

A photo depicting the most typical camouflage and markings of 1 PLM Yak-1b's. 3 eskadra *aircraft with their engines running, preparing for take-off, guided while taxiing by the take-off officer. All aircraft are in standard camouflage of blue-grey (AMT-11), dark grey (AMT-12) and light blue (AMT-7), with Soviet stars in double outlines (broad silver and narrow red) and Polish squares. The second and third aircraft from the right are nos. 35 and 22 respectively. The code numbers have also been applied with the silver paint at the factory, using the same stencil.*

The first Yak-1b aircraft were delivered to the 1 PLM, which was being formed since July 1943 at Grigoryevskoye, about 160 km south-east of Moscow. For the first year the unit was in fact a pilots' school, providing both elementary and fighter flying training. Three Yak-1bs, second-hand aircraft previously used by the VVS, were delivered to the regiment in September 1943. By the end of October 1943 the regiment had 15 fighter aircraft. Then factory-fresh examples built by No. 292 Plant (Завод № 292 / *Zavod No. 292*) at Saratov were delivered to the unit in two batches: ten on 27 February 1944 and nineteen on 29 March 1944 plus, separately, one aircraft with a presentation inscription, donated to the regiment by a Polish Jew named Wolf Messing, who lived in the USSR at the time. On 1 April 1944 the regiment had 45 aircraft, and on 3 June 1944 it had 43. On the latter date the unit commenced its move from Grigoryevskoye to Gostomel near Kiev. There, on 7 June 1944 the regiment took delivery of its last 15 brand new Yak-1bs as replacement for its older machines. Some 60 aircraft of the type were used by the 1 PLM in total.

The first tragic crash of a 1 PLM Yak-1b took place on 17 May 1944. *Starshiy leytenant* Andrei Gavrilov, a Soviet pilot attached to the 1 PLM as an instructor, took off in Yak-1b no. 40 (constr. no. 40155) performed unauthorised aerobatics at low level. The aircraft stalled and crashed about 20 km west of Grigoryevskoye, killing the pilot.

Another pilot, *chor.* Jan Grabarz, was killed before the unit was deployed to the front line. On 25 July 1944 he took off from Gostomel for a training sortie. Having completed his flight, he approached on a wrong path and hit a hangar at the airfield. The aircraft somersaulted, landed upside down and burst into flames, the ammunition exploding in the fire.

A group of pilots pose with Yak-1b no. 42, assigned for the personal use of the 1 PLM commander, ppłk *Ivan Taldikin (Soviet, standing third right), at Grigoryevskoye in early 1944. Note the absence of the square on forward fuselage and the tip of the Soviet star partly overlapping the code number. The camouflage pattern on the aircraft cannot be seen in the photo, but without a doubt it was composed of three colours (AMT-11, AMT-12 and AMT-7).*

When the regiment left for the front line in August 1944, it had 41 machines. The older aircraft were left at Gostomel, and the newer ones were ferried to Dys near Lublin, and then to Zadybie Stare (about 90 km south east of Warsaw). It was from there that the pilots commenced operations on 23 August 1944. By the end of the war they had participated in operations in Warsaw area (capturing bridgeheads across Vistula river, the part of the city on the eastern bank of Vistula in 1944 and then the western part of Warsaw in January 1945), fighting in Pomerania and the battle of Kolberg (now Kołobrzeg) in March 1945, operations along the Baltic coast in late March/early April 1945, and finally in the battle of Berlin in April and May 1945.

1 PLM pilots scored no aerial victories during combat operations on the Yak-1b. On the other hand, they claimed numerous targets destroyed on the ground, including vehicles, trains or columns of troops. Five aircraft were lost, all during operations in the Warsaw area during autumn 1944 and when capturing the western part of the city in mid-January 1945.

On 24 September 1944 the aircraft of *mjr* Tadeusz Wicherkiewicz, commanding the 3 *eskadra*, was shot down by light AA fire during a patrol over Warsaw. The pilot baled out from his Yak-1b no. 4 (constr. no. 04173) and survived. He came down in enemy held territory between Vistula and the Bielański Wood north of Warsaw, becoming a Prisoner of War.

Yak-1b no. 20 (constr. no. 20170) of *ppor.* Aleksandr Verbitskiy (Soviet) was lost on 24 November 1944 during a reconnaissance sortie north west of Warsaw (no details are known).

Yak-1b no. 35 (constr. no. 35175) of *chor.* Roman Wierzchnicki suffered a mechanical failure on 17 January 1945 during a reconnaissance sortie west of Warsaw. The pilot made a forced landing at Wieliszew, north of Warsaw on the east bank of Vistula. The following day Yak-1b no. 15 (constr. no. 15175) of *chor.* Vladimir

Another photo of a 1 PLM Yak-1b with winter camouflage applied also on the propeller spinner, propeller blades and the engine cowling. The photo shows well the low durability of the paint, already worn off near the cockpit (by the entering pilots). Pilot chor. *Dymitr Kotek is standing in the middle, accompanied by two ground crews. Grigoryevskoye, winter 1943–1944.*

Two photos of chor. *Viktor Poruchnichak (Soviet, in one he is accompanied by a mechanic,* kpr. *Naftali Fajersztajn) with Yak-1b no. 2. The code number of the aircraft is much larger than on all other known Yak-1s of the 1 PLM and located in a different place. Numerous signs of chipped paint indicate the aircraft had been used heavily, so perhaps it was not delivered to the 1 PLM from the factory (like most aircraft used it at the front line), but from a Soviet unit. The photos were probably taken at Märkisch Friedland (now Mirosławiec) in March 1945.*

Sushek (Soviet) was damaged by AA fire during a patrol over Warsaw, and it made a forced landing at Mińsk Mazowiecki. On 19 January 1945 *chor.* Czesław Bogusiewicz suffered a similar mishap, landing his shot-up Yak-1b no. 33 (constr. no. 33173) at Ząbki. All these pilots survived their forced landings unhurt and soon returned to the unit.

From 19 January 1945 until the end of the war, the 1 PLM flew both the preferred Yak-9 and Yak-1b (the latter accounting for one third of sorties during that period). The last Yak-1b combat sorties were flown on 3 May 1945.

Soon after the war ended the 1 PLM received a substantial delivery of Yak-9s, and the times of Yak-1s came to an end. Most were sent back in late June 1945 for an overhaul at the workshops in Dęblin, only a handful then returning to the regiment. On 1 October 1945 the 1 PLM had six machines of the type, and all were struck off charge by the end of February 1946.

Pilot chor. *Czesław Bogusiewicz and mechanic* kpr. *Naftali Fajersztajn working on the 12.7 mm (0.5 in.) UBS machine gun of a 1 PLM Yak-1b. The acronym UBS stood for Universalniy Byeryezina Sinkhronniy (*Универсальный Березина Синхронный*), meaning Byeryezin's Universal Synchronised (gun). The Polish square looks relatively even in shape, though it was probably applied by hand, and matches the official prewar colour layout. Note the conifer branches used as camouflage, visible on the left. Zadybie Stare, autumn 1944.*

Yak-1b no. 4 (constr. no. unknown), 1 PLM, Grigoryevskoye, May 1944. Upper surface camouflage colours: blue-grey (AMT-11) and dark grey (AMT-12); under surface colour: light blue (AMT-7).

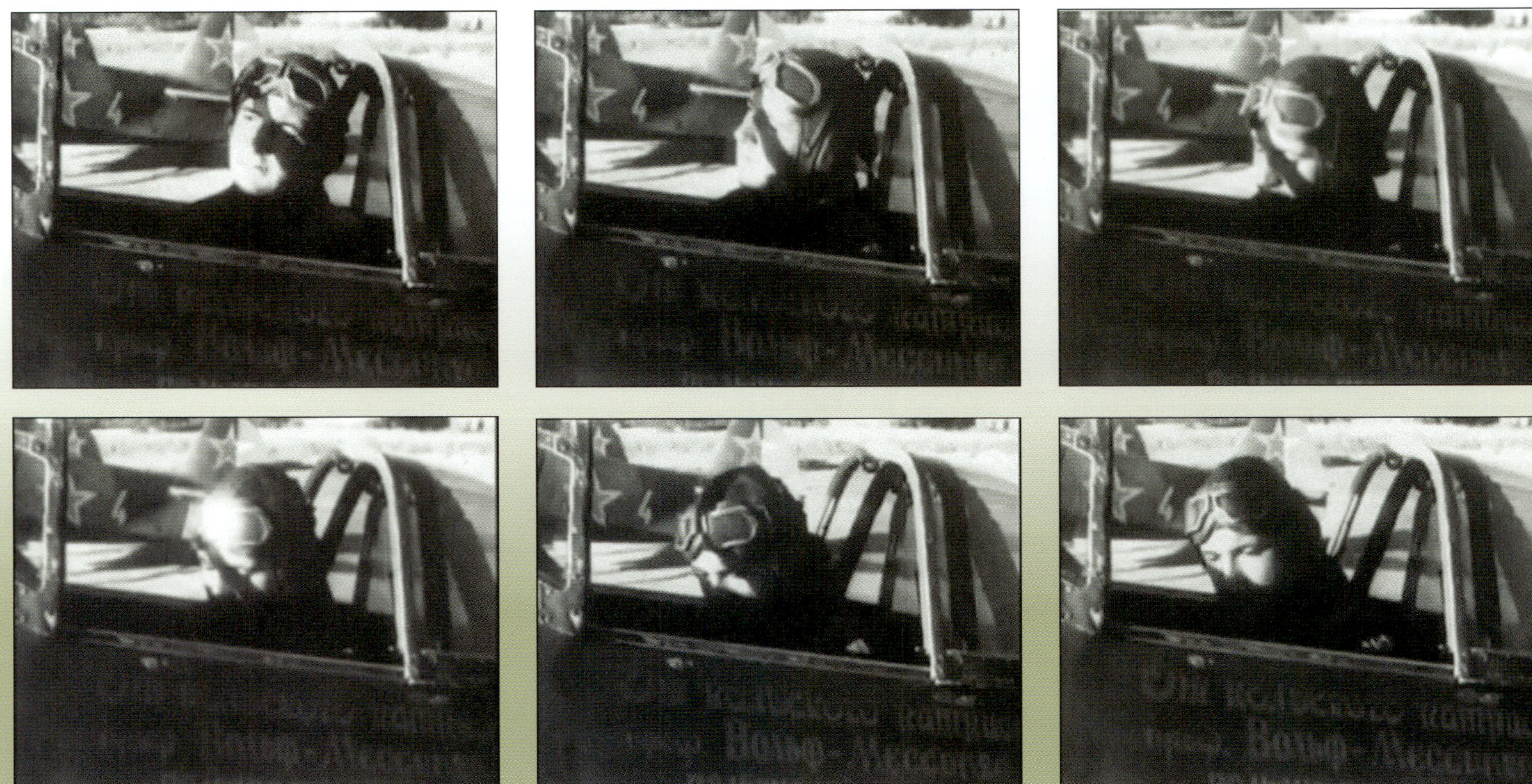

Frames from a wartime newsreel showing chor. Jerzy Czownicki in the cockpit of Yak-1b no. 13 and with Yak-1b no. 4 in the background. Grigoryevskoye, 28 May 1944. Although the nose of the aircraft cannot be seen, most known photos of 1 PLM Yak-1b's from the period show grey propeller spinners and Polish squares applied. The aircraft in the photo is one of three Yak-1b's of the 1 PLM marked with no. 4 at the time, assigned to chor. Edward Chromy (1 eskadra), ppor. Iosif Gostiuminskiy (Soviet, 2 eskadra) and mjr Tadeusz Wicherkiewicz (commanding 3 eskadra).

Yak-1b no. 38 (constr. no. probably 38161), 1 PLM, Grigoryevskoye, January 1944. Upper surface camouflage colours: blue-grey (AMT-11) and dark grey (AMT-12); under surface colour: light blue (AMT-7). Additional coat of washable white paint (MK-7) on upper surfaces.

Four members of the 1 PLM – three ground crews and a pilot standing second right (probably ppor. *Iosif Gostiuminskiy) – photographed during the winter 1943–1944 at Grigoryevskoye, during training. This is one of few photos depicting a Yak-1b of the Polish unit with the winter camouflage. The aircraft was repainted this way even though the 1 PLM airfield at the time was located several hundred kilometres from the front line. This was probably done with the paint used in the Soviet Air Force, designated the MK-7, which was made up of chalk or gypsum, water, alcohol, casein (protein used in production of adhesives) and ultramarine (to correct the yellow hue of the chalk). Not all upper surfaces of the aircraft were covered with it. Standard camouflage colours (blue-grey and dark grey) were retained on metal parts of the windscreen, aerial mast, propeller spinner, propeller blades and the engine cowling, seen here partly removed. The white paint surrounding the Soviet star was applied quite neatly, while that around the code number looks rather careless and obscures it partly. Hand brush strokes are quite clearly visible (airbrushing was also used in the VVS). The tail of the aircraft, not shown here…*

…was included in another photo (the code number on the starboard side is barely visible). It was repainted completely (the darker colour under the tailplane is a shadow of the horizontal tail). The photograph was taken on 1 January 1944 at Grigoryevskoye during a ceremony in which the unit received its colours. Yak-1b no. 38 was not used in combat.

Yak-1b no. 38 (constr. no. probably 38161), 1 PLM, Grigoryevskoye, January 1944.

Yak-1b no. 13 (constr. no. 13163), 1 PLM, Grigoryevskoye, May 1944. Upper surface camouflage colours: blue-grey (AMT-11) and dark grey (AMT-12); under surface colour: light blue (AMT-7).

Three photos of chor. Jerzy Czownicki in the cockpit of Yak-1b no. 13 during a ceremony of concluding training of the second group of 1 PLM pilots. Grigoryevskoye, 28 May 1944. In the third photo mjr Nikolay Buyevich is standing at left. Unfortunately, no photo is known of the entire machine, with the code number and Soviet star on the tail visible. The profile here is based on the assumption that the code number was applied with a stencil similar to that used on all Yak-1bs delivered directly from the No. 292 Plant (Завод № 292) at Saratov.

Yak-1b no. 13 (constr. no. 13163) was one of at least three aircraft in the 1 PLM adorned with a presentation inscription on the fuselage. This aircraft was funded by a Polish communist Wanda Wasilewska and presented to the Polish unit on behalf of the so-called Union of Polish Patriots. For unclear reasons it displayed an inscription copied from Yak-1b no. 48 of kpt. Medard Konieczny, which read: 'Ot pol'skogo patriota / prof. Wolf-Messinga / pol'skomu letchiku' ('От польского патриота / проф. Вольф-Мессинга / польскому летчику.'; 'From a Polish patriot / Prof. Wolf-Messing / to a Polish pilot'). It was assigned as the personal machine of chor. *Jerzy Czownicki (the unofficial best student of the second officers' commission in the 1 PLM) during a ceremony held on 28 May 1944 at Grigoryevskoye. Jerzy Czownicki used the aircraft during training only. Later, at the front line, he never flew it on operations. Most combat sorties were flown in Yak-1b no. 13 by* chor. *Stefan Łazar,* chor. *Ryszard Ber,* chor. *Kazimierz Rutenberg and* st. sierż. pchor. *Hugo O'Brien de Lacy, while* por. *Vitold Gabis (Soviet) and* st. sierż. pchor. *Sergey Danovskiy (Soviet) each flew a single sortie in the aircraft. The photo shows* kpt. *Oleg Matveyev (Soviet, left) and* ppor. *Vitold Gabis.*

After a while Polish translation was added, with slightly paler paint, below the Russian text on Yak-1b no. 13: „Od polskiego patrioty / prof. Wolf Messinga / polskiemu lotnikowi.". Wolf Messing was a Polish Jew, who found himself in the USSR during WWII and had a successful career there as a person with supernatural abilities, while having no real scientific title. His good financial standing and warm feelings towards Poland made him fund an aircraft for Polish flyers, Yak-1b no. 48 mentioned earlier (its presentation inscription then transferred onto no. 13). The aircraft went to the 1 PLM between December 1943 and February 1944. Initially it was flown by mjr Tadeusz Wicherkiewicz, and then by kpt. Medard Konieczny. Unfortunately, no photo is known of the inscription on that aircraft.

Yak-1b no. 15 (constr. no. 15175), 1 eskadra 1 PLM, Zadybie Stare, autumn 1944. Upper surface camouflage colours: blue-grey (AMT-11) and dark grey (AMT-12); under surface colour: light blue (AMT-7).

Yak-1b no. 15, photographed during take-off from Zadybie Stare airfield in the autumn of 1944, was the personal aircraft of chor. Ryszard Horodecki. It was lost on 18 January 1945 when flown, unusually, by chor. Vladimir Sushek (Soviet). During a patrol over Warsaw to protect own troops, the aircraft was damaged by German AA fire and forced to land near Mińsk Mazowiecki. The machine was struck off charge by the regiment. The aircraft displays standard Yak-1b style of insignia: the Polish square and the Soviet stars with double outlines (broad silver and narrow red). The yellow propeller spinner tip identifies the 1 eskadra.

Yak-1b no. 12 (constr. no. 12181), 1 PLM, Zadybie Stare, autumn 1944. Upper surface camouflage colours: blue-grey (AMT-11) and dark grey (AMT-12); under surface colour: light blue (AMT-7).

Two pictures of the former personal aircraft of kpt. *Oleg Matveyev, the regiment's chief air gunnery instructor (killed on 14 February 1945 in a Yak-9), taken in May 1945 at Bydgoszcz. Typical colour division lines near the fuselage star had been changed (most probably during fuselage repairs carried out some time after the aircraft left the factory). The original Soviet star was probably overpainted on that occasion and applied anew with a white outline. Propeller spinner shows three colours: blue-grey at the base, with the tip in a pale colour outlined in a dark one (possibly yellow and red, as shown in the profile). Matveyev flew 33 combat sorties in no. 12, while* por. *Michał Jakubik and* mjr *Nikolay Buyevich flew one sortie each in the machine.*

Left: From August 1944 Yak-1bs of the 1 PLM's 3 eskadra *were identified by painting the propeller spinner tips blue, as on the aircraft in the photo.* Chor. *Roman Wierzchnicki is posing.*

Right: After a while the manner of painting the spinners in the 3 eskadra *of the 1 PLM was altered by adding a white stripe that separated the grey based from the blue tip of the spinner.* Chor. *Mieczysław Podgórski is standing on the right. A Yak-9 with the Polish Air Force square can be seen in the background.*

One of these, Yak-1b no. 107 (constr. no. 01189) was handed over to the Polish Military Museum in Warsaw in January 1946. This was probably the machine that had the code no. 1 during the war, initially flown regularly by *mjr* Nikolay Buyevich (Soviet) from the regiment HQ, and then by various pilots of 1 *eskadra*. It had completed 41 combat sorties with the 1 PLM. Sadly, the aircraft did not survive. After two-three years of outdoor display, the structure of wood, plywood and fabric started to fall apart. It was decided to scrap it and replace with an all-metal Yak-9P (handed over to the museum on 10 August 1950) which, however, lacked an operational record. The latter aircraft is still on display at the Museum.

Ppłk *Ivan Taldikin commanding the 1 PLM poses with a Yak-1b, presumably his personal machine no. 42. The aircraft has an unusual three-tone spinner, similar to the spinner of Yak-1b no. 12 shown earlier. It can be guessed that this was the marking on Yak-1bs of the regiment HQ. These machines were flown by the commander, two deputy commanders (for operations and for political-educational duties), chief air gunnery instructor and chief navigator of the regiment, and in the 1 PLM also by the chief flying technique inspector of the* 4 Mieszana Dywizja Lotnicza.

The 1 PLM was not the only unit equipped with the Yak-1b. Two regiments of the 3 DLM, the 9 and 10 PLM, initially flew the Yak-1b, but these aircraft were replaced entirely with Yak-9s in the first half of October 1944.

Several other units had individual examples of the Yak-1. During late 1944/early 1945 one aircraft was on charge of the HQ of the 1 *Mieszany Korpus Lotniczy* (1 MKL; 1st Mixed Air Corps), which included the 3 DLM and the 2 *Dywizja Lotnictwa Szturmowego* (2 DLSz; 2nd Attack Division). In May 1945 six aircraft were used by the 15 *Szkolny Pułk Lotniczy*, and in October 1945 ten were with the *Wojskowa Szkoła Pilotów* at Dęblin. Additionally, from October 1945 until February 1946 one Yak-1 was used by the 1 *Samodzielny Szkolno-Treningowy Mieszany Pułk Lotniczy*. All the machines were struck off charge by the end of March 1946.

Yak-9

Yak-9s formed the principal equipment of the 'People's' Polish Forces fighter units. Three variants were used during the war: the Yak-9D (1 PLM only), – 9M and – 9T. According to uncorroborated data, the 1 PLM received its first (first two?) machines of the type in April 1944, still during training. These were used by the regiment probably until August 1944, when they were handed back in connection with the move from Gostomel to the front line. These aircraft had earlier been used by Soviet units.

The first four Yak-9Ds for combat use were delivered to the 1 PLM in December 1944. The maiden combat sortie was flown by *kpt.* Oleg Matveyev (Soviet) on 28 December 1944 (no code number was entered in the records for this aircraft).

On 18 January 1945 the regiment received another delivery of Yak-9s, followed by more on 26 January 1945. These aircraft came from No. 153 Plant (Завод № 153 / *Zavod No. 153*) at Novosibirsk. Altogether, the 1 PLM used 25 Yak-9s on operations, flying them regularly from 19 January 1945 until the end of the war. They were used to carry out two thirds of all combat sorties.

All aerial victories of the 1 PLM were scored in Yak-9s, but also some pilots were killed in these aircraft. *Ppor.* Iosif Gostiuminskiy (Soviet; his name was rendered in some Polish publications as Józef Gościumiński) was the first of these fatalities. He was shot down on 13 February 1945 by Messerschmitt Bf 109s over Ogorzeliny village near Chojnice in Yak-9 no. 53 (construction no. 3715353).

The first success recorded in documents was a Junkers 52 parked at an airfield at Schneidemühl (now Piła), credited as destroyed on 14 February 1945 to *kpt.* Oleg Matveyev in Yak-9 no. 86 (constr. no. 3215386) and *ppor.* Vitold Gabis (Soviet) in Yak-9 no. 68. According to recent research the aircraft was in fact an unserviceable machine abandoned by the Germans. However, Matveyev failed to return from the sortie, killed when his aircraft crashed in the suburbs of the town[2].

Chor. Aleksander Broch was killed on 15 March 1945 during a patrol over Kolberg (now Kołobrzeg). His leader lost sight of him in bad weather and he could not be found despite a search.

2 Documents recorded that he was shot down by a German tank, but this seems doubtful, as the Germans had left the town before Matveyev flew that sortie.

A Yak-9D from the 15 Szkolny Pułk Lotniczy (15th Air Training Regiment) at Radom-Sadków airfield, showing clearly the contrasting areas of AMT-11 and AMT-12 camouflage colours on its upper surfaces. Unfortunately, the photograph has been cropped in such way that no markings are visible. Considering the timeframe of the photo (summer 1945) these may have been either the Soviet stars or the Polish squares. Soviet and Polish airmen are posing with the aircraft. Three of them were veterans of the 1939 campaign: lying on the wing is ppor. *Władysław Ryżko (who had flown PZL 37 Łoś twin-engined bombers), leaning on the engine cowling is* por. *Alfons Kabat (PZL P.11 fighter pilot), and standing by the wing is* por. *Wiktor Pełka (RWD-8 liaison pilot).*

Yak-9M or Yak-9T no. 32 of the 1 PLM with unusually applied code numbers, presumably a trace of the machine's former service with a Soviet unit. It is possible that this is one of the aircraft allocated to the regiment in 1944 to introduce the type to the unit. Code number 32 was applied on the rudder in ornamental style in black. A white digit 2 can be seen to the right (the same stencil was used to apply the code number on a Yak-1b described earlier). A large white digit 3 applied in the same style is obscured by the posing men (this is confirmed by another photo of the same aircraft). The large code number was probably applied in the 1 PLM. Members of ground personnel pose with aircraft: por. *Eduard Shafranskiy (Soviet, third left),* ppor. *Ludvig Gorbachevskiy i (Soviet, fourth left) and* chor. *Jan Kurażyński (fifth left).*

His body was later found and buried, but details of his last sortie and his death are still unknown. That day Broch flew Yak-9 no. 81 (constr. no. 3315381).

Ppłk Ivan Taldikin, commanding the 1 PLM, was killed on 16 March at Bad Polzin (now Połczyn-Zdrój) while escorting Il-2s. This was a flying accident due to pilot error: he descended too low in bad visibility and hit the ground. The machine he flew was no. 15 (constr. no. 3415315).

Following these losses, 19 April 1945 was the day of the regiment's great success. During several missions over Brandenburg throughout the day no fewer than five pilots were credited with Fw 190s destroyed: *ppor.* Viktor Kalinovskiy (machine no. 87), *ppor.* Vsevolod Bobrovskiy (Soviet, known in the regiment under the Polish first name of Wiesław; Yak no. 68), *kpt.* Vladimir Bayov (Soviet; no. 32), *ppor.* Yuliy Kozak (Soviet; no. 93) and *por.* Anatoliy Shirokun (Soviet; Yak no. 4). Bobrovskiy's victim was a Fw 190F-8 from the II./SG 3, shot down over Finow (Finowfurt) airfield.

The following day, on 20 April, another Focke-Wulf was damaged by *chor.* Stefan Łazar, flying Yak-9 no. 58.

Chor. Roman Wierzchnicki was killed the same day while taking off for a combat sortie from Berneuchen (now Barnówko) airfield. His Yak-9 no. 80 (constr. no. 3915380) hit a tree near the runway when the pilot turned too soon.

Also on 20 April *por.* Valeryan Shtakhauz (Soviet) flying Yak-9 no. 74 (constr. no. 4115374) on a reconnaissance sortie was attacked by two groups of Focke-Wulf 190s and narrowly escaped them in a badly shot-up aircraft (with bullet holes in the wings and the fuel tank). He made a forced landing in a field between Mantel (now Mętno) and Altenkirchen (now Łukowice) east of Königsberg in der Neumark (now Chojna) and returned to the 1 PLM the following day.

Three days later another tragedy struck at Berneuchen. *Por.* Anatoliy Shirokun was killed in Yak-9D no. 4 (constr. no. 4115304) while returning from a reconnaissance sortie. His aircraft half-rolled at 400 metres above the airfield and dived into the ground, burst into flames and burned out completely. This was seen as an accident due to broken control cables, but some pilots believed that Shirokun was killed while attempting a victory roll.

25 April was another successful day. Three Focke-Wulf 190s were claimed destroyed, one each by *ppor.* Nikolay Khaustovich (Soviet), *ppor.* Viktor Kalinovskiy and *chor.* Juliusz Szwarc (Szwarc and Łazar were the only Polish citizens credited with air-to-air victories in the 'People's' Polish Forces air units).

On 30 April, while flying cover to own troops, Yak-9 no. 93 (constr. no. 3215393) flown by *kpt.* Stanislav Lisyetskiy (Soviet) suffered a mechanical failure. The pilot made a forced landing suffering minor facial injuries, but the machine was written off.

Por. Aleksandr Verbitskiy was the last 1 PLM pilot credited with an aerial victory, claiming a Messerschmitt 109 on 1 May 1945 (flying Yak-9 no. 68 – which made the aircraft the top-scoring machine of the 'People's' Polish Air Force, with two air-to-air kills and a shared destroyed on the ground).

In July 1945 the 1 PLM received more Yak-9s, allowing the first unit of the 'People's' Polish Air Force to finally convert fully to the variant.

The 3 DLM eventually arrived at the front line on 24 April 1945, and the next day flew its first combat missions. Its main role was to escort Il-2s of the 2 DLSz (composed of the 6, 7 and 8 *Pułk Lotnictwa Szturmowego* / 6th, 7th and 8th Attack Regiment) and to provide air support (air cover for the troops and reconnaissance) for the 1st Army of the 'People's' Polish Forces. Already on 25 April three pilots scored their first victories, when 10 PLM's Yaks[3] engaged twelve Focke-Wulf 190s escorting six Junkers 88s. *Kpt.* Aleksandr Kuznetsov (Soviet) and *por.* Nikolay Vanikovskiy (Soviet) were each credited with an Fw 190 destroyed. *Kpt.* Vasiliy Bistrov (Soviet) failed to return from the sortie and was initially believed shot down, since a parachute was seen to open over Bötzow. However, Bistrov returned to base in his aircraft the following day, claiming a third Fw 190 shot down (this was credited as probably destroyed).

3 In most cases the author was not able to ascertain if the victories were scored while flying Yak-9s or the less numerous Yak-3s, hence the general term of 'Yaks'.

Two Yak-9Ms of the 1 PLM and chor. *Juliusz Szwarc at Modlin airfield after the war, presumably during the summer of 1945. The photos confirm that various spinner markings to identify the* eskadra *were used on Yak-9s as well:* 2 eskadra *had spinners with white tips, and* 3 eskadra *spinners with a white stripe and blue tip. The Polish AF square on the engine cowling in one of the photos is interesting. Although this suggests that Yak-9s of the 1 PLM were adorned with both Soviet stars and Polish squares during the war, no photos have been unearthed so far to confirm it positively.*

Left: *The Polish Air Force Commander's orders of 11 July 1945 (a few days after the Western allies withdrew recognition of the exiled Polish Government in London and recognised the one in Soviet-controlled Poland) required obliteration of Soviet stars and application of the Polish squares in their place, to be completed by 20 July.* Chor. *Kazimierz Rutenberg of the 1 PLM is seated on a Yak-9 with such changed markings. Modlin, summer 1945.*

Above: Ppor. *Vladislav Zhuravskiy (Soviet) posing during the summer of 1945 by the tail of a Yak-9 at Modlin airfield. The photo documents the careless manner of overspraying the stars, and the appearance of the Polish squares on the tail, with the outline too broad compared to the size of the square.*

Mjr *Nikolay Buyevich, the deputy commander of the 1 PLM, about to enter the cockpit of Yak-9 no. 44 at Modlin airfield during the summer of 1945. This photo shows clearly the form of the code number digits and the fact that the aircraft has no Polish AF square beneath the exhausts (and no trace of obliterating such square there). The colour division line between the blue-grey (AMT-11) and dark grey (AMT-12) is clearly visible, as is paint chipping on the metal framing of the cockpit and on the propeller blade.*

On 25 April three Yak-9s failed to return from sorties over Brandenburg, having gotten lost in smoke from the fires. These were flown by *chor.* Mikhail Baychikov (Soviet) and *chor.* R. Bratskiy (Soviet) of the 10 PLM and by *chor.* Skibin[4] (Soviet) of the 11 PLM. In subsequent days Bratskiy returned to his unit, and news were received that Baychikov was heavily wounded (available documents make no mention of the fate of their aircraft). The wreck of Skibin's machine and his body were found two days later near his home airfield at Belgen (now Białęgi): at Fürstenfelde (now Boleszkowice), 10 km west of Neudamm (now Dębno).

On 26 April 1945 the 9 PLM lost two aircraft that crashed at Berneuchen upon return from an Il-2 escort mission. First, the Yak-9 of *chor.* Sokolov overturned at that difficult airfield, and soon afterwards, due to limited visibility (clouds of dust were raised from the airfield) *chor.* Burachevskiy collided with it. Both pilots survived, although the former's Yak was completely destroyed, while the latter's had its propeller bent and the starboard wing broken. The same day *chor.* V. Krapukhin of the 10 PLM was shot down by AA fire in the area of Fehrbellin. The pilot made a forced landing near Großer Zechliner See lake and soon returned to his unit. Another pilot of the unit, *chor.* Dmovskiy (Soviet), managed to return to base despite damage from AA fire.

Kpt. Shota Grdzelishvili (Soviet) of the 11 PLM (who will be mentioned in the Yak-3 chapter) was killed on 27 April 1945.

Two pilots of the 10 PLM, *ppor.* N. Smirnov (Soviet) and *chor.* Yu. Panov (Soviet), were each credited with a Focke-Wulf 190 destroyed on 29 April. That day another accident took place in the 10 PLM at the new airfield at Grüntal. While taking off for a combat sortie *chor.* A. Yelizarov's (Soviet) aircraft swung off the runway. In order to avoid hitting a parked aircraft, he turned 45° to starboard and lifted his Yak-9 off, but due to insufficient speed he hit the ground with a wing. The machine was completely destroyed, but the pilot survived with no major injury. *Chor.* Panov failed to return from a sortie, overturning his damaged aircraft during an emergency landing at Vehlefanz airfield, and returning to the 10 PLM the following day.

Chor. Boris Tsarev's (Soviet) Yak-9 was shot down by AA fire and crashed about 16 km north west of Nauen on 30 April 1945, killing the pilot.

4 Some publications quote him with Polish first names Sławomir or Jan, but no documents to verify this are available.

Yak-9M no. 44 (constr. no. unknown), 1 eskadra *1 PLM, Märkisch Friedland (now Mirosławiec), March 1945. Upper surface camouflage colours: blue-grey (AMT-11) and dark grey (AMT-12); under surface colour: light blue (AMT-7).*

1 PLM pilots look on as ground crew work at Märkisch Friedland in March 1945. Yak-9M no. 35 with yellow propeller spinner tip, identifying the 1 eskadra*, can be seen in the foreground. The Yak-9s in the background on the left show code numbers 4 and 8… (one digit is obscured; no machine of the 1 PLM had no. 8, but there were nos. 80, 81, 86 and 87). The aircraft no. 4 is most probably the Yak-9D of* por. *Anatoliy Shirokun (Soviet, Yak constr. no. 4115304), in which on 19 April 1945 he shot down a Focke-Wulf 190 and in which he was killed four days later in a crash at Berneuchen (now Barnówko). Yak-9 no. 44, visible at right in the background, participated in 27 combat sorties: fifteen of these were flown by* ppor. *Yuliy Kozak (Soviet), nine by* kpt. *Stanislav Lisyetskiy (Soviet), two by* chor. *Ryszard Horodecki and one by* chor. *Ivan Golubitskiy (Soviet).*

Yak-9M no. 43 (constr. no. unknown), 3 DLM (?), Dęblin, 21 June 1945. Upper surface camouflage colours: blue-grey (AMT-11) and dark grey (AMT-12); under surface colour: light blue (AMT-7).

A photograph depicting the first post-war commissioning at the Wojskowa Szkoła Pilotów *at Dęblin, which took place in front of the school HQ building on 21 June 1945 and was given particularly ceremonial character, despite the eerie ruins of hangars and other facilities of the pre-war Polish AF College in the background. Two Yak-9s (9M or 9T) can be seen at the airfield. One displays code no. 43, and an indistinct (presentation?) inscription can be seen on the fuselage. The other machine has an illegible two-digit code number on the tail. It is hard to judge whether the Polish squares on the fuselages of both aircraft were applied in their regiment, or were added in Dęblin to match those of UT-2 trainer aircraft used there (visible in the foreground on the left). It seems that the combat aircraft (Il-2s and Pe-2s as well as the Yaks) had flown to Dęblin from airfields in Łódź area, coming from the units of the* 1 Mieszany Korpus Lotniczy: *the* 1 Dywizja Lotnictwa Bombowego, 2 Dywizja Lotnictwa Szturmowego *and* 3 Dywizja Lotnictwa Myśliwskiego.

Yak-9M no. 100 (constr. no. unknown), 1 PLM, Modlin, 1945. Upper surface camouflage colours: blue-grey (AMT-11) and dark grey (AMT-12); under surface colour: light blue (AMT-7).

A post-war photo of Yak-9M no. 100, with clear traces of Soviet stars obliterated with paint in a different hue. Note the maintenance stencilling in Russian near the exhausts. The aircraft, probably of the 1 eskadra (code number beginning with 1) presumably has a yellow propeller spinner tip.

On 2 May two more enemy aircraft were added to the scoreboard of the 3 DLM by 11 PLM pilots on reconnaissance sorties. At Wüsterhausen *chor.* Mikhail Ponomaryev (Soviet) shot down a low flying Fieseler 156, and moments later his wingman, *chor.* Aleksandr Krasutskiy (Soviet) destroyed a reconnaissance Henschel 126.

Another accident took place on 3 May in the 10 PLM. While taking from Eichstädt for a combat mission *chor.* P. Zaytsev (Soviet) swung to starboard and hit a Yak-9 of the 11 PLM readiness section. Both machines were damaged, with bent propellers and broken wings, but the pilots escaped unhurt.

Apart from front line units Yak-9s were used during wartime by the *Wojskowa Szkoła Pilotów* (which in April 1945 had 22 of these aircraft), the 15 *Szkolny Pułk Lotniczy*, the 2 *Samodzielna Sztabowa Eskadra Lotnicza* (2nd Independent Staff Air Flight), and the 14 *Pułk Rozpoznania Lotniczego i Korygowania Ognia Artylerii* (14th Air Reconnaissance and Artillery Spotting Regiment). These units also suffered some accidents involving Yak-9s. The most tragic of those cost the life of *por.* Robert Janota (a veteran of the Polish campaign of 1939 and the French campaign of 1940), who was killed in an accident on 27 April 1945 at the 15 SzPL in Radom in unknown circumstances.

At the end of the war (according to a census of 24 April 1945) there were 130 machines of the type in Polish service, while according to another, of 1 October 1945, there were already 182.

Above: *Wartime camouflage survived on Polish Yak-9s for a few years after the war, although the two-tone camouflage on upper surfaces gradually merged into one (at least in black & white photos), and various areas of the airframe were retouched with paint in hues different from the factory-applied ones. Yak-9T no. 84 shows barely visible remains of the AMT-11/AMT-12 camouflage on the fuselage and wings. Traces of obliterating the Soviet star can be seen on the tail, with the Polish square applied on top. Its uneven fields show that it was applied by hand. The absence of the Polish AF square on the fuselage is interesting (the next Yak in the line-up does not have it, either). The machines in the photo presumably belonged to the 1 PLM and were photographed in Modlin in 1946–1947.*

Below: *Yak-9M no. 34 of the 2 PLM at the Cracow airfield in 1946. This might be one of the aeroplanes dating back to the times of war, when the unit (at the time known as the 10 PLM) participated in the Berlin fighting. Despite the good quality of the photo it is difficult to ascertain the colour scheme. This could be badly faded factory-applied disruptive camouflage (AMT-11/ AMT-12/AMT-7) or a single-tone olive green scheme on upper surfaces and light blue underneath (as applied in overhaul workshops after the war). The airframe has been repainted between the cockpit and the tail (including a segment of the red outline of the Polish AF square), probably during minor repairs.*

Yak-7

In July 1947 the Polish Air Force took delivery of the first Yak-9Ps, of all-metal construction. This variant became the primary fighter type in Polish service until replaced by jets in the 1950s.

The Yak-7 was the third most numerous fighter type of the 'People's' Polish Forces during 1943–1945. However, none were used in combat.

The first machines, two Yak-7Vs and a Yak-7B, were delivered to the 1 PLM in September 1943. During that period the regiment was in fact a school, providing ab initio flying training followed by fighter training. The Yak-7s were used for conversion training between the UT-2 and Yak-1b. In December 1943 the 1 PLM had no less than five Yak-7s (including four -7Vs), and in April 1944 – three (including a single -7V). After the regiment completed its training in the summer of 1944 two-seat training aircraft were no longer needed and, from August 1944, when the 1 PLM moved to the front line, until the end of the war, the unit had just one Yak-7V, which was used by the divisional flying inspector to check regiment pilots' skills. Oddly, photos show that at least one Yak-7B of the 1 PLM was in fact a two-seat conversion of a single-seater. After the war ended, at the end

A group of pupil-pilots of the 1 PLM 'Warszawa' posing with an interesting Yak-7 variant at Volosovo (a satellite airfield of Grigoryevskoye) in April 1944. The aircraft shown is a late version of the Yak-7B, converted to two-seat configuration, and lacking a radio. This is revealed by the presence of armament, retractable undercarriage, engine cowling design and the cut-down rear fuselage. The machine is most probably in AMT-11, AMT-12 and AMT-7 camouflage, although it is difficult to discern any colour division lines in this image. The large Soviet star has double outlines (broad silver and narrow red), and there is no Polish square, this being typical for all known wartime photographs featuring Yak-7s of the 'People's' Polish Air Force.

of the summer of 1945, 1 PLM took delivery of some more Yak-7B's and -7V's, but eventually all the machines had been struck off charge by 23 September 1946

The sole fatal (and particularly tragic) accident of a Yak-7 in the 'People's' Polish Forces took place on 5 May 1944 at Zhytov, a satellite airfield of Grigoryevskoye. It happened during a last check flight before *st. szer. pchor.* Jerzy Czerny was allowed to fly solo. Soviet officer *st. leyt.* Vsevolod Anikin flew with Czerny as the instructor. During the landing approach the aircraft caught fire due to a broken fuel pipe that fed the carburettor. When at a few metres above the ground, the aircraft was already completely engulfed in flames. Nevertheless, the pilots made a correct landing. The instructor managed to jump out of the rear cockpit, saving his life. Czerny stayed in the cockpit until the aircraft came to a halt and it took him a while to get out. He was thrashing around in his burning clothes on the runway when witnesses ran to help him. Pupil-pilot *chor.* Ivan Golubitskiy (Soviet) got to him first, pulled out Czerny's parachute from its cover and used it to extinguish the flames. A military ambulance took the badly burnt Czerny to a military hospital at Ryazan, where he died on 7 May 1944. The Yak-7, constr. no. 0479, was destroyed by fire.

Apart from the 1 PLM the Yak-7B and – 7V aircraft were used mostly by the 15 *Samodzielny Zapasowy Pułk Lotniczy* (15th Independent Replacement Air Regiment) / 15 *Szkolny Pułk Lotniczy* (which, among others, provided training to pre-war Polish pilots liberated from captivity, even before the end of the war), and by the *Wojskowa Szkoła Pilotów.*

Above: *A later production single-seat Yak-7B of the 15 SzPL at Radom-Sadków in the spring of 1945. The machine has its main undercarriage covers removed (though the inboard covers are still in place). All camouflage colour division lines are sharp, and the camouflage is of a splinter form. A small fragment of the Soviet star on the fuselage (red with double outlines, broad white or silver and narrow red) can be seen at the right edge of the photo, as can a similar star on the bottom of the wing. A late Yak-7B, probably converted to a two-seater, is visible in the background, showing a similar camouflage scheme and no code number on the fuselage. The spinner is pale but evidently not white.* Ppor. *Władysław Ryżko is seated on the wing of the machine in the foreground.*

Below: *Yak-7V of the 1 PLM in a photo taken in 1943 at Grigoryevskoye. The aircraft wears the standard painting scheme of AMT-11, AMT-12 and AMT-7. The photograph shows Soviet stars on the fin (with double outlines, broad white or silver and narrow red) and on the under surface of the wing (red with no outline). The curved exhaust staining under the cockpit is shown to advantage. Wheel chocks can be seen in the grass.*

Yak-7V (constr. no. unknown), 1 PLM, Grigoryevskoye, winter 1943–1944. Upper surface camouflage colours: green (AMT-4) and black (AMT-6); under surface colour: light blue (AMT-7).

A poor quality photograph depicting ppor. Michał Jakubik *at Grigoryevskoye during the winter of 1943–1944. The aircraft displays the old-style 1941-standard camouflage, as shown both by the characteristic pattern, and the absence of AMT-7 light blue paint under the tailplane, which was normally applied in that location on aircraft camouflaged with AMT-11 and AMT-12. This scheme included green (AMT-4) and black (AMT-6). The lower surfaces of the machine must have been painted in regulation light blue (AMT-7), even though it is not apparent in this photograph.*

Yak-3

Individual examples of Yak-7Vs (used for courier flying and pilot checks) were also allocated to the three regiments of the 3 DLM (the 9, 10 and 11 PLM).

Although the Yak-1b and the Yak-9 were the primary types used by the 'People's' Polish Forces, Yak-3s were also used in combat. They were the least numerous fighter type in Polish units at the Eastern front. This was largely due to the role of the regiments, supposed to perform tactical duties and mostly fly attack aircraft escort, reconnaissance, long range patrol and ground attack missions. The Yak-9s, more heavily armed and with greater fuel capacity, but less manoeuvrable, were better suited for this kind of operations than the Yak-3s. The latter were typical air-to-air fighters.

The first 'Polish' Yak-3 was delivered to the 1 PLM in the autumn of 1944. Until 1 May 1945 the regiment had just one aircraft of the type, then only a few more. The regiment's last four machines of the type were struck off charge on 4 September 1946.

The regiment flight log and the log books of individual pilots of the unit show that the machine was not used in combat at all, while training sorties were rare and the privilege was only granted to pilots at command posts, with long flying experience (most pilots of the unit had been hurriedly trained during 1943–1944). The Yak-3 was flown, among others, by *kpt.* (later *mjr*) Vasiliy Gashin (Soviet), the flying technique inspector of the 4 *Mieszana Dywizja Lotnicza* (4th Mixed Air Division) who flew regularly with the 1 PLM and subsequently took command of the regiment, and by *por.* Vitold Gabis (commanding the *2 eskadra* of the 1 PLM), who were both considered excellent pilots. Such use was without a doubt due to the aircraft's excellent manoeuvrability and flying characteristics, useful in performing advanced aerobatics during training.

Other examples of the type were allocated to the remaining air units of the 'People's' Polish Forces. Most of these were delivered to the regiments of the 3 DLM: the 9, 10 and 11 PLM. These three regiments were initially equipped with Yak-1bs (9 and 10 PLM) and Yak-9s (9 and 11 PLM) and in October 1944 they started the full conversion to Yak-9s. The 10 PLM and 11 PLM each received a single Yak-3. Soon before the units were deployed to the front line, on 8 April 1945 the 3 DLM took delivery of 10 Yak-3s. Several more were delivered to the 3 DLM already at the front

Two frames from newsreel footage depicting an aerobatic display by two Yak-3s from the 10 PLM over Pole Mokotowskie airfield, Warsaw on 2 September 1945, to mark Polish Aviation Day. The aircraft featured Polish Air Force squares on wing undersurfaces, nose, fuselage and fin.

Yak-3, no code number (constr. no. unknown), 1 PLM, Modlin, summer 1945. Upper surface camouflage colours: blue-grey (AMT-11) and dark grey (AMT-12); under surface colour: light blue (AMT-7).

Mjr *Vasiliy Gashin (Soviet), commanding the 1 PLM, poses with a Yak-3 during the summer of 1945 at Modlin airfield. Although he obscures a large portion of the aircraft, the camouflage pattern, the Polish squares on the fuselage and the tail (applied on top of overpainted Soviet stars) and black propeller blade tip (not painted in any other colour as a warning) can all be seen clearly. Another known photo of the aircraft shows that it had no code number.*

line, in the last week of April 1945. According to the census of 1 May 1945 each regiment had four of these aircraft, while the 3 DLM HQ had two.

Individual examples were also used as 'hacks' by the HQs of the Polish Air Force and the 1st Mixed Air Corps. Altogether, the Polish Air Force never had more than 20 Yak-3s at any one time during 1945–1946.

While there are several photographs of the Yak-3 in the 1 PLM, the aircraft of the 3 DLM are only known from documentary records that confirm their presence in the inventory. This is due to the fact that at the time of their front line service those were in fact Soviet units. Therefore, both the air and ground crews were nearly entirely Soviet and virtually all memorabilia, such as photos, went back to the USSR with them both inaccessible and uninteresting for Polish aviation historians.

Little is known about front line operations of the Yak-3s. The machines of the 3 DLM took part in the short episode of the battle of Berlin (from 24 April 1945 until the end of the war). Their pilots scored some victories and suffered some losses, but it is not always known whether these involved Yak-3s or the more numerous Yak-9s. It is certain that one Soviet pilot serving in a Polish unit was killed in a Yak-3. While returning from a combat mission on 27 April 1945, some 30–40 km east of Berlin *kpt.* Shota Grdzelishvili, commanding officer of 11 PLM's *1 eskadra* and an ace of the VVS left the formation of his unit. He failed to return to base and was listed as missing, presumed killed.

Two Yak-3s of the 10 PLM were shown to the public on 2 September 1945 during the Polish Aviation Day air show over Pole Mokotowskie airfield in Warsaw.

After the war ended, during the process of unifying aircraft types in fighter regiments, Yak-3s were transferred for brief periods to rear-line units, such as the 1 *Samodzielny Szkolno-Treningowy Mieszany Pułk Lotniczy*, the 2 *Samodzielna Sztabowa Eskadra Lotnicza*, the *Oficerska Szkoła Lotnicza* and, as an instructional airframe, to the *Techniczna Szkoła Lotnicza* (Air Technical Training School) at Warsaw-Boernerowo.

Two photos, taken late in the war or soon after it ended, showing chor. *Ivan Golubitskiy (by the tail) and* kpt. *Vladimir Bayov with a Yak-3. The aircraft has code number 4 (or beginning with a 4), a part of which can be seen in the photo. Soviet stars (with double outlines, broad silver and narrow red) can be seen on the tail and the fuselage, as can the camouflage of blue-grey (AMT-11) and dark grey (AMT-12).*

Bell P-39Q Airacobra

The aircraft described in this section was not part of standard equipment of the 'People's' Polish Forces. As a matter of fact only one example of the US-built Bell P-39Q Airacobra, among the 4,719 aircraft of the type delivered to the USSR, was used in Polish markings. It is worth mentioning here, however, due to its unusual story.

The 'People's' Polish Air Force was formed from scratch, starting in July 1943. Initially it included just one flight, then a regiment, then several regiments, later divisions, and eventually a corps. In the autumn 1944 *general leytenant* Fyodor Polynin was transferred from the Soviet Air Force and appointed to command the new air force. He was Russian and had previously commanded the 6th Air Army of the VVS. When he arrived at Chyża airfield near Zamość in Poland on 31 October 1944 to take up the new appointment, he flew his assigned personal aircraft that he had used at his previous VVS post. The aircraft was an Airacobra (in the USSR the name was altered to Аэрокобра/Aerokobra). Even though Polynin's operational career had been on bombers, he had himself converted onto fighters at his higher command posts in order to (as he then wrote in his memoirs) 'have positive influence of authority onto his men'.

The general's machine had been built as a P-39Q-20BE, one of 1,000 of the variant (serial nos. 44-3001 to 44-4000). Its serial number was 44-3658 (abbreviated to '43658' on the vertical tail). The aircraft was powered by a Allison V-1710-85 engine. The standard armament of a 37 mm cannon and two 0.5 in. (12.7 mm) machine guns had been removed. When transferred to the Polish Air Force inventory, the Airacobra was accompanied by a stock of spares, including three engines, which were still on record in September 1949. Polynin used his aircraft on service trips, when visiting his units at various airfields.

The aircraft was officially on charge of the 2 *Samodzielna Sztabowa Eskadra Lotnicza*. In the autumn of 1944 the Airacobra was based at Chyża and Mokre airfields. At the end of January 1945 it moved to Parzniew near Pruszków (on western outskirts of Warsaw). It was later based at other airfields, moving further and further west with the front line. After the end of the war it was based at Parzniew and at several different airfields in Warsaw (eventually at Okęcie). Its official allocation was also changing: from July 1945 it belonged to the *2 eskadra* of the 17 *Mieszany Pułk Lotniczy* (17th Mixed Air Regiment), renamed in mid-September 1945 as the 2 *Mieszany Specjalny Pułk Lotniczy* (2nd Mixed Special Air Regiment). When Polynin left the Polish Air Force in March 1947, the Airacobra was left behind in Poland as a 'hack' of the Polish AF HQ. From 25 February 1947 until 21 January 1948 the aircraft belonged to the *Specjalny Pułk Lotniczy* (Special Air Regiment). It was then struck off charge and transferred as an instructional airframe to the *Techniczna Szkoła Lotnicza* at Warsaw-Boernerowo. The aircraft was stored there, its condition gradually deteriorating. After the school moved to Zamość in February 1950 the Airacobra was declared non-standard equipment surplus to requirement. It was earmarked for scrapping and no material component of it survives.

There was another Airacobra in the history of Polish aviation, not of the air force but its civilian scientific background. The aircraft of the Soviet Air Force, left in a railway car near Radom (according to other sources near Warsaw) was found by Polish railwaymen in the autumn of 1945. With no interest on the part of military authorities, it went to the *Szkoła Inżynierska im. Wawelberga i Rotwanda* (Wawelberg & Rotwand Engineer School) in Warsaw as an instructional airframe. After the school was merged with the Warsaw Institute of Technology, it was moved to another facility and continued to be used in the same role. As time went by and aircraft technology developed, it lost its value due to obsolescence. Today only the starboard wing and parts of the tail survive, transferred in June 1999 to the Polish Aviation Museum in Cracow.

Bell P-39Q-20-BE Airacobra s/n 44-3658/01, 17 Mieszany Pułk Lotniczy/2 Mieszany Specjalny Pułk Lotniczy/Specjalny Pułk Lotniczy, Warsaw, 1945–1948. Upper surface camouflage colour: Olive Drab; under surface colour: Neutral Gray. Fin: an unspecified yellowish colour. Rudder: red.

All known photos of the Airacobra of general leytenant Fyodor Polynin show it in post-war markings, with Polish squares in place of Soviet stars. The machine was finished like most aircraft of the type in Soviet service, in the Bell factory-applied scheme: uniform green hue known as Olive Drab on upper surfaces and Neutral Gray underneath. Before application of the Soviet stars the US-applied markings were obliterated with a Soviet paint. It seems that the tail surfaces were repainted completely. While the rudder may have been repainted in a uniform dark colour (red, for example) as a special marking, the fin was probably repainted (following repairs, for example) to obtain a large area of uniform finish in a colour similar to the factory-applied Olive Drab. This may have been the yellowish primer that was used both in the USAAF (Zinc Chromate) and the Soviet AF (ALG-1). The background of the photo shows a Li-2 (on the right), the nose of a Po-2 under a canvas cover, and the tail of a Yak fighter. Warsaw, 1947.

The other photo shows the same Airacobra in a similar scheme, but with the fin and rudder in a grey tone similar to that of the forward portion of the airframe. The puzzle of the apparently different scheme can be explained by a matt hue used to paint the fin (which, depending on the lighting conditions, can appear paler or as dark as a glossy finish of the same colour). It cannot be ruled out, either, that the photo was taken using a filter (or photographic material) that enhanced the warm hues (yellow tones) and weakened the cold ones (blue hues). This made the speculative yellow fin look as dark as the rest of the airframe. The code number colour (apparently paler than in other known photos) may result from the deflection of the rudder in opposite directions in various photos. The tail of a Pe-2 bomber is shown on the left. Warsaw-Mokotów, 1945.

Kpr. pchor. *Adam Borowczyk in the cockpit of the Airacobra when it was an instructional airframe at the* Techniczna Szkoła Lotnicza. *The inscription below the cockpit: 'U.S. ARMY AIR FORCES / P-39-Q-21-BE SERIAL NO. AAF. S/n 44-3658' proves that the aircraft has never been repainted overall. Warsaw-Boernerowo, 1949–1950.*

Bell P-39Q-20-BE Airacobra s/n 44-3658/20, Techniczna Szkoła Lotnicza, Warsaw-Boernerowo, *1948–1950. Upper surface camouflage colour: Olive Drab; under surface colour: Neutral Gray. Rudder: red.*

An Airacobra with Polish markings. Its condition suggests that it had not been airworthy for a long time. Since there is no information about any other machine of the type in the Polish Air Force, it is reasonable to assume this is the former aircraft of general leytenant *Fyodor Polynin towards the end of its existence at the* Techniczna Szkoła Lotnicza *at Warsaw-Boernerowo. The worn finish has revealed the sequence of application of the national markings: US and Soviet stars, on top of which the Polish marking was re-applied. The aircraft featured a dark rudder with the code number 20 applied in white. The fin shows no trace of repainting the Olive Drab finish with a different colour (well visible on the photos of the port side of the aircraft). Notably, a small patch that obliterated the US serial number can be seen clearly. There is an account of a student of the* Techniczna Szkoła Lotnicza *at Warsaw-Boernerowo, who recalled that the forward part of the Airacobra was in the factory-applied colour scheme, the rudder was red, the fin was yellow, and the code number 01 was white or yellow. In comparison with the photo the description seems only partly correct, and it must have been influenced by the well known photos of the Airacobra shown on page 566. (Daniel Buszyński coll.)*

The Airacobra fuselage in the hall of the Szkoła Inżynierska im. Wawelberga i Rotwanda *in Warsaw during student classes between 1946 and 1951. The aircraft is presumably finished in the factory applied Olive Drab on upper surfaces. Note the Soviet star with white outline, presumably applied in place of the US white star on dark blue background. It is not known if this had been overpainted, or is it simply not discernible in the black & white photo. The wing of the aircraft, preserved at the Polish Aviation Museum in Cracow features a US star on the bottom surface. The Willys Jeep visible in upper left corner of the photo, another evidence of the US aid for the USSR, has an inscription on the bottom of the windscreen which reads: 'AIRCRAFT GROUP OF STUD.[ENTS] OF THE ENGINEER SCHOOL'.*

Students of the 4th year of the Airframe Section of the Aircraft Department of the Szkoła Inżynierska im. Wawelberga i Rotwanda *in Warsaw during a class with the Allison V-1710 engine. The Airacobra fuselage, without its skin, can be seen in the background.*

The Airacobra fuselage at the Warsaw college photographed at a later date, with even more components missing.

Polikarpov I-16 & UTI-4

The Polikarpov I-16 could equally well be described in a publication on enemy types engaged by Polish fighters. When during 1939–1941 the Soviet Union was an enemy of Poland and an occupant of large parts of Poland, I-16 fighters were the main equipment of VVS fighter regiments. From 17 September 1939 onwards, when Soviet forces invaded Poland, I-16s were seen by Polish servicemen, including air force personnel. For example, *kpt.* Adam Kowalczyk, commanding the *IV/1 Dyon Myśliwski*, described in his report nine such aircraft overflying the airfield at Petlikowce. The fact that no air combats between Soviet and Polish fighters were recorded was only due to the fact that the Poles did not have enough serviceable aircraft, fuel and armament to engage enemy aircraft. On the day of the Soviet invasion Polish air units were ordered to evacuate to neighbouring neutral countries.[5]

Polish fighters then narrowly missed fighting against the I-16 in 1940 in the so-called Finland Squadron, planned to be deployed to the front of the Winter War[6]. This never happened, however, as armistice was signed between Finland and the USSR in March 1940.

The outbreak of the Soviet-German war in 1941 reversed the entire situation. After the Polish-Soviet treaty signed that summer, I-16 fighters and their pilots suddenly changed from enemies to allies.

When the 'People's' Polish Forces air arm started to be formed in 1943, the I-16s were already obsolete, mostly used in training and replacement units. They were phased out from front line units in favour of Yakovlev and Lavochkin designs, as well as of British and US fighters. The one and only I-16 of the Polish Air Force was allocated to the 1 PLM in March 1944. This was an early version I-16 type 5, construction number 521560, powered by the Wright Cyclone R-1820F-3 (licence-built in the USSR as the M-25) and armed with two 0.3 in. (7.62 mm) machine guns. The aircraft was on charge of the regiment at Grigoryevskoye until June 1944, when the unit moved to Gostomel.

It is difficult to ascertain why the unit received the 'Ishak' (as the aircraft was known in the regiment; the word, Russian for 'donkey', was pun on the official designation and became an informal nickname of the type in Soviet service during WWII). Some publications mention that the aircraft was used for courier sorties. If that was really the case, it was only incidental. According to accounts of 1 PLM veterans known to the author, the I-16 was virtually never used, and this is confirmed by available flying log books. One of the pilots, *chor.* Andrzej Jaworski, recalled that 'nobody wanted to fly the I-16' and the only pilot brave enough to do it was a Soviet instructor, a VVS officer. This was due to the I-16's flying characteristics, advantageous for dog-fighting, but making low speed flying difficult. The out-of-proportion engine size seriously reduced forward visibility,

Ceremony of commissioning the cadet officers of the second training group of the 1 PLM at Grigoryevskoye, 28 May 1944. Just visible in the background is the sole I-16 of the Polish unit, and this is the sole known photo of the aircraft. Because of the poor quality of the photo and of the fact that what little of the aircraft can be seen is in shadow, nothing certain can be said about the camouflage and markings of the aircraft.

5 See vol. 1, pp. 34 and 53.

6 See vol. 1, pp. 100 and 142.

which was particularly important for take-offs and landings. The machine was simply impractical in the 1 PLM, and courier flying was performed in the available UT-2 and Po-2 aircraft that could carry a passenger as well as a pilot.

However, many pilots of the 1 PLM had had some experience on the type. Most Soviet officers who first trained before 1941 had flown it at training establishments or in front line units of the VVS. At least two of them had been shot down on the I-16 (*mjr* Nikolay Buyevich and *ppłk* Ivan Taldikin), and the latter one had scored in it. Also the chief instructor of the Polish pilots, *st. leyt.* Pavel Yasinskiy had been shot down in the I-16 and wounded. His face bore a characteristic scar of his burns. *Chor.* Jan Kurażyński, a Polish mechanic who had been a civilian employee of the aircraft park of the *5 Pułk Lotniczy* in Lida, worked in late 1939/early 1940 at the workshops there, now overtaken by the Soviets and overhauling I-15 and I-16 fighters.

Apart from the single-seat I-16, two examples of the UTI-4 dual-control trainer were also used by the Polish Air Force. The first of these was allocated in November 1944 to the 15 *Samodzielny Zapasowy Pułk Lotniczy* (15 SZPL), and the other in January 1945 to the HQ of the 4 *Mieszana Dywizja Lotnicza*. In the former unit it was used for blind flying training (the pupil's cockpit was covered with tarpaulin). The 15 SZPL machine was displayed for general public during the Polish Aviation Day air show over Pole Mokotowskie airfield in Warsaw on 2 September 1945. The aircraft was used by the unit (which had by then changed its name to 15 *Mieszany Szkolno-Treningowy Pułk Lotniczy*) until it disbanded in February 1946

One of the above UTI-4s later went to the *Techniczna Szkoła Lotnicza* at Warsaw-Boernerowo, where it was placed as a gate-guardian. Judging by the surviving photos, this was probably the aircraft previously used at the 15 SZPL. Even though it no longer flew, it had a serviceable engine, which was overhauled and regularly ran. The aircraft remained there most probably until the school moved to Zamość in February 1950: the last information about it dates from the second half of 1949.

Polish pilots also encountered UTI-4 aircraft during training at the *Kachinskaya Krasnoznamiennaya Voyennaya Avyatsyonnaya Shkola Pilotov* (*Качинская Краснознаменная военная авиационная школа*; Kachinskaya 'Red Banner' Air Force Pilots' School) at Krasniy Kut. 58 Polish fighter pilots were trained there during 1944–1945.

Newsreel frames showing a low flying UTI-4 of the 15 Mieszany Szkolno-Treningowy Pułk Lotniczy *during a display over Pole Mokotowskie in Warsaw on 2 September 1945. The machine was finished in a single colour overall, with exception of the black engine cowling, and had no Polish AF squares on wing upper surfaces. The aircraft had retractable undercarriage that was fitted to some UTI-4 aircraft only (most had fixed undercarriage).*

UTI-4, 15 Mieszany Szkolno-Treningowy Pułk Lotniczy / Techniczna Szkoła Lotnicza, *Radom/Warsaw-Boernerowo, 1945–1949. Upper and under surface colour: grey. Engine cowling: black.*

The 'gate guardian' at the Techniczna Szkoła Lotnicza *at Warsaw-Boernerowo featured in many souvenir photos. Thanks to a few images that we have it is clear that its upper and under surfaces were finished in a single tone, probably grey (one of the theories mentions captured German RLM 02), except for the black engine cowling. The photo at right (Muzeum Sił Powietrznych Dęblin coll.) shows st. szer. pil. Jerzy Lisowski.*

Lavochkin La-5FN & La-7

During the last year of the war the fighters designed by the Lavochkin design office, the La-5FN and La-7, were the main types in use with the *Voyenno-Vozdushniye Sily*, alongside the Yak-1b, Yak-3 and Yak-9. Despite that, they were never introduced into service as combat aircraft with the 'People's' Polish Air Force. Only a few of these aircraft had any connection with Polish aviation.

During WWII it was planned to equip the *14 Pułk Rozpoznania Lotniczego i Korygowania Ognia Artylerii* (14th Air Reconnaissance and Artillery Spotting Regiment) with the La-5FN. That decision had been altered towards the end of 1944 and when it was eventually formed in February 1945, it was equipped with Po-2s and Il-2s. The plans to use the Lavochkins, though, had led to one La-5FN being put on charge of the *817 Ruchome Warsztaty Lotnicze* (817th Mobile Aircraft Workshops) at Podlodów near Dęblin from November 1944, the unit probably being scheduled to provide maintenance of the type. The non-establishment aircraft was at the disposal of the unit commander.

In February 1945, when the 817th Workshops moved from Podlodów to Bydgoszcz, the aircraft was handed over to the *Wojskowa Szkoła Lotnicza Wojska Polskiego* (Military Air Training School of the Polish Forces) at Dęblin and then, no earlier than April 1945, to the *Wojskowa Techniczna Szkoła Lotnicza* (Military Air Technical Training School) at Zamość. In mid-1945 the aircraft was struck off charge and its further fate is not known.

No photo of the sole documented La-5FN of the Polish AF has surfaced so far. Oddly, photos of no fewer than two Polish La-7s are known, but rather than aircraft on charge of the 'People's' Polish Air Force, these machines had only incidental connection with Polish aviation.

Ła-7 in the standard scheme of the Voyenno-Vozdushniye Sily *(AMT-11, AMT-12, and AMT-7, with the Soviet star on the wing under surface) photographed somewhere in Poland soon after the war. The couple posing in front of the aircraft wear LOT Polish Airlines uniforms. It is not clear if this is the aeroplane from Dęblin or from Mielec, or yet another example. (Daniel Buszyński coll.)*

The first of these had been abandoned by the Soviets at the Dęblin airfield. Initially it was stored in hangar no. 5, used by the *Lotnicze Warsztaty Remontowe nr 3* (No. 3 Aircraft Overhaul Workshops). It deteriorated in non-airworthy condition, and in 1947 it was moved outdoors, to a scrapyard near the battery charging station. The aircraft's rear fuselage was damaged, and it gradually lost some components, including the cockpit canopy and the engine cowling.

The other aircraft must have also originated from the VVS (or, less likely, from the Czechoslovak unit that also used the type and was based in Poland for a while). At some point, probably during the late 1940s, it was displayed in the Rynek Square in Mielec, parked in a lawn as a memorial. Unlike the one at Dęblin, it featured a complete airframe, with newly-applied camouflage and Polish national markings on the fuselage. Its location suggests that it had been overhauled by the *Państwowe Zakłady Lotnicze nr 1* (from 1949 *Wytwórnia Sprzętu Komunikacyjnego*) aircraft factory at Mielec. Its earlier and subsequent fate is unknown.

Students and staff members of the Oficerska Szkoła Lotnicza *with the vandalised La-7 at the Dęblin airfield during the late 1940s. The finish of the aircraft was in the factory-applied (although badly worn) scheme: the AMT-11 blue-grey and the AMT-12 dark grey (the under surfaces of La-7s were in the AMT-7 light blue). A small pale triangle can be seen below the remains of the rear cockpit glazing: this is the forward tip of the Soviet star.*

La-7 (constr. no. unknown), Państwowe Zakłady Lotnicze nr 1 (Wytwórnia Sprzętu Komunikacyjnego)*, Mielec, late 1940s. Upper surface colour: olive green overal. Under surface colour: light blue. Polish national markings on the fuselage.*

The La-7 displayed in the Rynek Square in Mielec. The aircraft has Polish national markings and a single-tone camouflage (probably olive green, standard on the 'People's' Polish Air Force fighters repainted by overhaul workshops in the late 1940s). The aircraft had a complete radio aerial and there was a canvas cover over its cockpit.